Accession no.
36169104

WITHDRAWN

KU-364-349

Gendered Discourses

Gendered Discourses

Jane Sunderland
Department of Linguistics and Modern English Language
Lancaster University

LIS - LIBRARY

Date	Fund
13/02/13	l-che

Order No.

2375710

University of Chester

© Jane Sunderland 2004

All rights reserved. No reproduction, copy or transmission of this
publication may be made without written permission.

No paragraph of this publication may be reproduced, copied or transmitted
save with written permission or in accordance with the provisions of the
Copyright, Designs and Patents Act 1988, or under the terms of any licence
permitting limited copying issued by the Copyright Licensing Agency, 90
Tottenham Court Road, London W1T 4LP.

Any person who does any unauthorised act in relation to this publication
may be liable to criminal prosecution and civil claims for damages.

The author has asserted her right to be identified
as the author of this work in accordance with the Copyright,
Designs and Patents Act 1988.

First published 2004 by
PALGRAVE MACMILLAN
Houndmills, Basingstoke, Hampshire RG21 6XS and
175 Fifth Avenue, New York, N.Y. 10010
Companies and representatives throughout the world

PALGRAVE MACMILLAN is the global academic imprint of the Palgrave
Macmillan division of St. Martin's Press, LLC and of Palgrave Macmillan Ltd.
Macmillan® is a registered trademark in the United States, United Kingdom
and other countries. Palgrave is a registered trademark in the
European Union and other countries.

ISBN 1–4039–1344–7 hardback
ISBN 1–4039–1345–5 paperback

This book is printed on paper suitable for recycling and made from fully
managed and sustained forest sources.

A catalogue record for this book is available from the British Library.

Library of Congress Cataloging-in-Publication Data
Sunderland, Jane.
    Gendered discourses / Jane Sunderland.
        p. cm.
    Includes bibliographical references and index.
    ISBN 1–4039–1344–7 – ISBN 1–4039–1345–5 (pbk.)
        1. Language and languages – Sex differences. 2. Discourse analysis.
    I. Title.
P120.S48S86 2004
306.44—dc22   2003066802

10 9 8 7 6 5 4 3 2
13 12 11 10 09 08 07 06 05 04

Transferred to digital printing 2005

To Emily and Graham

Contents

Acknowledgements

Thanks are due to many people for help in the writing of this book. The 'Gender and Language Research Group' at Lancaster University have read and discussed several draft chapters, and questions such as 'what exactly do we mean by construction?' and 'can we talk about *damaging discourses?*' have been regular topics for the group in recent years. In particular, I would like to thank Juliane Schwarz and Stephanie Suhr for constantly 'being there' and being continually enthusiastic about gender and discourse. For use of their data, I would like to thank Catherine Kitetu, Sarah Ogbay and Kay Wheeler. For providing me with time and space to write, as well as ideas, I would like to thank all the staff of the English Language Institute, University of Michigan, particularly Diane Larsen-Freeman, Joan Morley, John Swales and Amy Yamashiro. The Academic and Humanities Research Board also enabled me to take a one-term 'Leave award'. For constructive comments on the book I would also like to thank readers Judith Baxter, Sara Mills and Joan Swann. Thanks are also due to Jill Lake of Palgrave Macmillan, for so calmly helping me through the writing and publishing process. And, lastly, I need to acknowledge the whole 'gender and discourse' academic discourse community, and all the interesting work produced which I simply have no space to refer to in this book.

Permission is gratefully acknowledged for use of the following copyright materials:
In Chapter 2: Extracts from *The Times*, 12 January 2002, 'Why Women are First Class', and from the *Lancaster Guardian*, 11 January 2002, 'A Dream Wedding'.
In Chapter 9: The photograph 'If this lady was a car...' © Jill Posener 1979.

Every effort has been made to trace copyright holders. In the event that any have been inadvertently overlooked, the author and publisher will be pleased to make amends at the earliest opportunity.

Part I
Discourse and Gender

Introduction

This book looks at what gendered discourses are, and what gendered discourses do, from theoretical and empirical perspectives. (This use of 'discourses', in a countable and specific sense, goes beyond 'language use' and will be explored in Chapter 1.) The main focus is the identification of gendered discourses produced in written and spoken texts. Discourse identification is important for (or at least of interest to) anyone working within discourse analysis, but is particularly relevant to those working within critical discourse analysis, post-structuralism and/or much discursive psychology. Discourse identification is, however, not only the province of the 'professional discourse analyst', but also of the graduate or postgraduate researcher, and this book illustrates how discourse identification can be done.

Identifying gendered discourses is not a new intellectual endeavour, either inside or out of gender and language studies, but I believe that this is the first time that documented gendered discourses have been brought together and new ones explored. This book then is also a selective 'part-survey' of gendered discourses that have already been identified and named. 'Survey' is misleading, however, suggesting that a finite and existing set of bounded discourses has been identified and that another existing set is out there, waiting for the linguist, like a bird-watcher, to identify and name them. There is no finite set of discourses; discourses are not bounded and not even visible; they are historical and transient; they are continually produced and reproduced. Individuals and different social groups will see the same discoursal 'cues' or 'traces' (again see Chapter 1) and will recognize (or better, 'co-construct') different discourses. Discourse identification is thus always *interpretive*. Other individuals and social groups may see the same discourse in different sets of discoursal cues or traces. The activity is, however, still a little like 'birding': just as the birdwatcher may first spot the bird, and verify its species through such cues as movement and song, the discourse analyst focusing on gender may first 'spot' what looks like a gendered discourse, which will then need to be verified through linguistic and other traces and relations. Alternatively, like the birdwatcher who notices just a movement or rustle or flash of colour, the discourse analyst might notice recurrent linguistic features, or a set of phrases which echo those in another text or genre, which suggest a particular discourse. An identified discourse might thus be familiar and instantly recognizable, or redolent of another, perhaps obscure one (a relative newcomer, perhaps a 'migrant' from an unfamiliar order of discourse, or even a hybrid).

But just as the birdwatcher may need to satisfy her or his friends that she or he really did see a particular bird, by providing details of its plumage, coloration, flight pattern or song, the discourse analyst should, I claim, be able to identify what it was about a particular spoken or written text that suggested the presence and workings of a particular discourse.

Having interpretively identified a discourse, it is important to look at its social and political significance. Is it a dominant discourse, or a marginal one? How does it 'subject position' women and men, boys and girls? Discourse, from several theoretical perspectives, is not just a concept or entity, but also a *social and constitutive process*. In aiming to explore what discourse *does* and discourses *do*, this book also looks at how they work, or can be theorized to work, in the construction and performance of gender.

Part I of *Gendered Discourses* examines the notions of discourse, discourse analysis and gender, which are fundamental to making use of the book. In Chapter 2, I provide two examples of newspaper texts in which a range of discourses (both 'general' and 'gendered') is interpretively identified, with the help of linguistic 'traces', and named. This process is intended to be broadly replicable by readers in their own discourse analyses. In Chapter 3, I look at several studies – well known and 'classic', and less well known but interesting – in which the identification of discourses is paramount.

Part II has an empirical focus. It takes different 'epistemological sites' – the classroom, parenting magazines, newspaper texts and award-winning children's books – and looks at the different gendered discourses which appear to 'flow through' particular texts in these sites. Part III addresses theoretical concerns such work raises – in particular, what is meant by the *construction* of gender in relation to discourse, whether and in what senses gendered discourses can be described as *damaging*, and the role of linguistic intervention here.

1
Discourse, Discourse Analysis and Gender

This chapter discusses the two key concepts of the book: *discourse* and *gender*. This is not an easy task, partly because different approaches theorize these concepts, and the relationship between them, differently; partly because of the rapid development in and increasing sophistication of these fields. Because I find it difficult to talk about gender without talking about discourse, I start by looking at discourse and discourse analysis, move on to gender, then look at these together ('Gender and discourse/Gendered discourse/Gendering discourse'). I conclude the chapter by looking briefly at four other concepts: *construction* and *performance*, *representation* and *indexing*. Relevant to the study of gender and discourse, these are used in and outside this book, and will hopefully be useful analytical concepts for those embarking on their own analyses of gendered discourses.

Discourse and discourse analysis

Discourse is omnipresent and enduringly fluid, and there is no shortage of discourse to analyse. This is especially true as modes of communications expand, exponentially more texts are published year on year, more information of different sorts becomes available, and discourses take on characteristics of each other, combine and recombine (see below; see also Chapter 2). In particular, as Cameron notes, 'Men and women ... are members of cultures in which a large amount of discourse about gender is constantly circulating' (1997a: 60). The number and diversity of discursively gendered sites and topics is equally vast.[1] *Discourse analysis* is also a broad *concept* encompassing, *inter alia*, classroom discourse analysis, critical discourse analysis (CDA), critical classroom discourse analysis (Kumaravadivelu, 1999), (feminist) post-structuralist discourse analysis ((F)PDA) (Baxter, 2002a,b, 2003) and conversation analysis (CA).

Discourse has a variety of meanings, these varying not only with discipline but also with intellectual persuasion. 'Linguistic' meanings include, first, the broad *stretch of written or spoken language* and, second, the more specific 'linguistic, and accompanying paralinguistic, interaction between people in a specific context' (from Talbot, 1995a: 43), for example, 'Classroom discourse'. I refer to these as 'descriptive discourses'. Though at times I also use *discourse* in these two, descriptive senses, in this book the primary meaning of *discourses* is equivalent to *broad constitutive systems of meaning* (from post-structuralism) and to 'knowledge and practices generally associated with a particular institution or group of institutions' (Talbot, 1995a: 43) or 'different ways of structuring areas of knowledge and social practice' (Fairclough, 1992: 3) (from critical social theory). I refer to these as 'interpretive discourses'. *Discourse(s)* in this third sense is (are) at times used indistinguishably from *ideology* – Eckert and McConnell-Ginet gloss this 'shared' use as 'projections of the interests of people in a particular social location', a useful reminder that we are not simply talking about 'perspectives' (2003: 412). *Ideology* can, in fact, be seen as the cultural materialist antecedent of the post-structuralist use of *discourse*, and, for both post-structuralism and CDA, discourse can be seen as *carrying* ideology (see also Mills, 1997; van Dijk, 1998). Foucault's major contribution to post-structuralism has been crucial here (though see e.g. Fairclough, 1992).

Discourse is, however, sometimes used 'in an unreflecting way' (Wodak, 1997: 4; see also Mills, 1997; Weiss and Wodak, 2003), which can verge on vagueness. To quote from Popper:

> We are always conscious that our terms are a little vague (since we have learned to use them only in practical applications) and we reach precision not by reducing their penumbra of vagueness, but rather by keeping well within it, by carefully phrasing our sentences in such a way that the possible shades of meaning of our terms do not matter. This is how we avoid quarreling about words. (1966: 19)

Whereas this can, I think, apply to *discourse* (in the descriptive sense) it applies less satisfactorily to interpretive *discourses*.

A useful and provisional starting point in the study of discourse in the interpretive sense is to see discourses as *ways of seeing the world*, often with reference to relations of power and domination (Fairclough, 2003). Language users however also *use* discourses, 'drawing on', 'invoking', 'producing', 'reproducing' and even 'inserting themselves' within discourses (this last from Foucault, 1981). Although in this book I largely use the verb *produce* to cover all these possibilities, the different verbs imply particular degrees of speaker/writer agency. I am not, however, suggesting that discourses are produced ahistorically, from nothing. Rather, discourses almost always *pre-exist* individual speakers (it seems reasonable to assume that discourses have been around as long as there have been human, social practices), and speakers through their language and social actions constantly revise and re-produce these.

Discourses are not themselves visible. However, as a 'way of seeing the world' a given discourse may be recognizable to analysts and other language users through its manifestation in characteristic linguistic 'traces' in talk or written text, i.e. speakers' and writers' own words. A distinction can thus be made between *discourse* and *text* – though they are sometimes used synonymously (Halliday and Hasan, 1989) – and both can refer to written and spoken language. Here I use *text* to mean spoken or (usually) written 'output'. In this sense, *text* is narrower than *discourse*; it is 'the fabric in which discourse is manifested' (Talbot, 1995a: 24). As this 'fabric', it contains in its formal features the linguistic 'traces' of how it was produced and the 'cues' for how it can be understood (Talbot, 1998: 154) – the actual words spoken or written. It is possible to see a given *discourse* as relatively permanent and continuous (though invisible and 'floating'), and at the same time as undergoing local (and visible) transformations in *texts* (Fairclough, 2001), i.e. through the produced entextualization of one set of discoursally-related linguistic 'traces' after another.

Discourses are often verbally *qualified*. Cammack and Kalmbach Phillips (2002), for example, refer to *powerful discourses, gender discourses* and *power-knowledge discourses*; Weedon (1987) cites *dominant discourses*.[2] A *discourse* benefits, I believe, from the addition of a descriptor. This may be a 'general' descriptor like *powerful*, or a specific and *substantial* one – 'a something discourse' (e.g. *an equality discourse*) or 'discourse of something' (*a discourse of sexual equality*). If a writer refers to 'different discourses', it is helpful to the reader if these are differentiated, and generally or substantially named. Nigel Edley (2001) similarly refers to *interpretative repertoires* (which overlap considerably with *discourses*), which can also be identified and named.

Discourses are not ubiquitous, but the fact that they are relatively unbounded means that the same discourse may be produced all over the place, in different linguistic guises. First, it can appear in both a written and a spoken text. It is not hard to envisage this – there is no mode or genre restriction on either a discourse of feminism or a discourse of sexism, for example. Both can be encountered in print media, political speeches (spoken but often scripted) and naturally occurring talk. Importantly, the same discourse can also be produced by men and by women: Wetherell et al. (1987) demonstrated that both drew on a discourse of 'equal opportunities' in interviews about employment and gender *and* on a limiting 'practical considerations' discourse (see also Chapter 3). Women can also produce sexist (anti-women) discourses, and men feminist discourses. For some people this is counterintuitive: I have several times encountered assumptions that women writers of foreign language textbooks will represent women in their textbooks better than their male colleagues will, and that female researchers of gender and language will represent their findings in a way that casts men and boys in a poor light. I do not think either is true. Women cannot be *assumed* to support women, that is, to articulate feminist discourses. Walsh, for example, has documented how complaints by 'New Labour' women MPs of sexual harassment by their male colleagues were dismissed by Tory women MPs – with the riposte, for example, that they should not have a 'sense of humour bypass' (2002: 99). Walsh also observes, sadly, that 'strategic misunderstanding' can be exploited by women 'to distance themselves from the charge of "political correctness" and the related charge of lacking a sense of humour'. That discourses are not sex-exclusive is, of course, a reason to look at *what* is said (and written), as well as how and by whom.

This initial sketch indicates what discourse is and how it is produced, rather than what it does (see Fairclough, 2001). I suggest that both recognition and production of familiar (and sometimes less familiar) discourses help the language user and her interlocutors maintain a sense of control and *make sense of the world*. More importantly, as regards what discourses *themselves do*, for both critical social theory and post-structuralism, discourses are *potentially constitutive* – in the famous Foucault definition, 'practices that systematically form the objects of which they speak' (1972: 49), and 'abstract vehicle[s] for social and political processes' (Jaworski and Coupland, 1999: 498). For Foucault (e.g. 1984), discourses are inherently ideological 'flows of information' which construct the world through language and texts, and 'subject position' individuals. This 'subject positioning' is sometimes gendered, for example, when women are positioned as carers by default. It is also potentially powerful, both in large-scale political processes and small, everyday exchanges (Jaworski and Coupland, 1999), powerful in the sense of enabling as well as hindering (Mills, 1997). Power for post-structuralism is an *effect of discourse* (not an entity that can be possessed), and power relations between women and men are accordingly seen as effects of gendered discourses (Weedon, 1987; Halperin, 1995; Weatherall, 2002; see also Thornborrow, 2002; and Chapter 9).

Constitution can be seen not just as symbolic, semiotic and discoursal, but also as potentially cognitive, material and social. Francis (1999) talks of a discourse *constituting subject and objects*. Cammack and Kalmbach Phillips refer ideologically to the possibility of discourses 'binding' people 'so that they cannot see connections or construct meaning outside the set of definitions given them' (2002: 126). Such claims are, however, often theoretical and rhetorical. Accepting that a given discourse is constitutive, i.e. is constructing language users in some way, often requires an intellectual act of faith. While accepting in principle rhetorical claims about what a discourse *does* (or can do), we can then also interrogate such claims – 'constitute' in what sense? As evidenced in or by what? (Issues surrounding the actual workings of discourse are looked at briefly below and more fully in Chapters 8 and 9.)

Different theoretical approaches conceptualize discourse and its workings in different, though overlapping, ways. In this book I refer chiefly to the approaches associated with post-structuralism, critical discourse analysis (CDA) and conversation analysis (CA). I also refer to discursive psychology (one branch of social psychology), which draws variously on post-structuralism and CA.

Post-structuralist approaches to discourse analysis

Post-structuralist approaches to discourse analysis are concerned relatively broadly with linguistic analysis and with the notion of constraining and enabling *power*. Judith Baxter's (2002b) *post-structuralist discourse analysis* (and its later development, *feminist post-structuralist discourse analysis* (2002a), FPDA), for example, addresses questions of power by stressing the possibility of its different forms for an individual at different times. (F)PDA has not (yet) become a prevalent tradition in the field of discourse analysis more widely; however, since Baxter is centrally concerned with discourse and gender, I will be referring to her work in later chapters (see also Baxter, 2003).

Post-structuralism has played a major role in shaping understandings of the 'strength' of the constitutive potential of discourse. For Judith Butler, discourse is radically constitutive: she sees 'performativity' (which as is related to, but not synonymous with, the performatives of speech act theory) as 'that aspect of discourse that has the capacity to produce what it names' (1993; see also 1990, 1994, 1999). Baxter's FPFA, which draws heavily on Foucauldian understandings of social 'realities' as always discursively produced, claims that 'identities and therefore subject positions as speakers are being continually reconstructed and open to redefinition *through* discourse, not outside it' (2002b: 830; emphasis in original). And, from Potter, writing from the perspective of discursive psychology:

> The strongest version of the [construction yard] metaphor would have the world literally springing into existence as it is talked or written about. Ridiculous, surely! Perhaps, but I want to opt for something nearly as strong. Reality enters into human practices by way of the categories and descriptions that are part of those practices. The world is not ready categorized by God or nature in ways that we are all forced to accept. It is constituted in one way or another as people talk it, write it and argue it. (1996: 98)

Post-structuralism and much discursive psychology have been critiqued for their apparent relativism and accused of ignoring material and biological constraints (e.g. Crawford, 1995; Gill, 1995; Walsh, 2002; see also Chapter 9). Citing the example of rape, for example, Crawford writes, 'If speakers create their social worlds in interaction, and meanings are multiple and context-specific, how can we argue for the validity of one interpretation [e.g. the rapist's, the victim's] over another?' (1995: 175). Neither post-structuralism nor discursive psychology *has* to stick to a relativist, value-free path, however (Gill, 1995; Baxter, 2002a,b).

Critical discourse analysis

Critical Discourse Analysis (CDA) 'aims to show non-obvious ways in which language is involved in social relations of power and domination' (Fairclough, 2001: 229; see also Fairclough, 2003). Fairclough goes on:

> The starting point for CDA is social issues and problems ... it does not begin with texts and interactions. ... The dramatic problems in economy and society ... lie, I would argue, at the root of the problems, insecurities of contemporary social life. If CDA wants to address the latter, it has to have a picture of how language and semiosis figure in the former. (2001: 229, 232)

The social issue and dramatic problem here is *gender* – an issue and often a problem for women and girls; in different ways, for men and boys; and accordingly for gender *relations*. CDA is thus theoretically well placed to seek and identify gendered discourses of a 'damaging' kind (see Chapter 9). CDA refers to textual 'traces of differing discourses and ideologies contending and struggling for dominance' (Weiss and Wodak, 2003: 15), making an important distinction between the notions of power and the more institutionalized *dominance*.

Crucial to CDA are *dialectical* relations – in particular between discourse and other social practices, including processes of power and economic production. Analysis must, therefore, include consideration of the extra-discursive, including the material. CDA *entails* the extra-discursive: that there is a 'real world' where reality does not depend on what is known about it. Chouliaraki and Fairclough accordingly claim that 'the question of power in social class, gender and race relations is *partly* a question of discourse' (1999: vii; emphasis added). In CDA, in addition to being potentially constitutive, discourse is *itself* socially conditioned, shaped by material and by social structures. At the CDA end of the theoretical spectrum is therefore a view of new discursive forms for women, and the potential of discourse to improve women's lives, being seriously circumscribed.

CDA also foregrounds the importance of human values, interests and understandings (eschewing the conventional 'sociological neutrality' of CA), and sees extra-textual, subjective insights as *valuable* in analysis. The analyst can, indeed must, rely not only on available discursive 'traces' in the data, but also on her own informed insights about wider discursive and social practices – though always with reflexivity and always documenting her stance. Here CDA shows similarities with feminist research. CDA remains, however, fairly marginal in gender and language research (see Cameron, 1998a).

For both post-structuralism and CDA, the analysis of discourses is never straightforward in that it cannot, in contrast to the analysis of more formal or more purely linguistic features, deal with 'bounded' units. Although we may unintentionally *imply* that discourse (*a* discourse) has boundaries (fuzzy-edged), as Wodak observes, a discourse has no objective beginning and no clearly defined end (1997: 6). This is not only in terms of the 'length' of a unit of analysis of talk or written text, but also because of its *intertextuality*. A given discourse is always related to others – diachronically and synchronically. Diachronically, 'With each word spoken, the meanings within particular discourses are carried through time' (Peterson, 2002: 352); synchronically, similar *and* different discourses exist in contemporary relation to each other. There is, for example, a related *diversity* of discourses of sexism (from misogyny to *Vive la différence!*).

Intertextuality may refer to 'manifest intertextuality' – for example, the use of extracts from *Taming of the Shrew* in Cole Porter's musical *Kiss Me Kate*, and direct reported speech as we shall see in Chapter 6 in 'celebrity fatherhood' media reports. Alternatively, it may refer to 'inter-discursivity', the 'mixing together of different discourses and genres' (Fairclough, 1992).

As an example of inter-discursivity, the following text will be familiar in nature to many. With the overall title of 'Project Planet', and featuring a picture of three horses on a hill in the mist or perhaps at dawn, this card was found in a city hotel bathroom in North America:

PLEASE REUSE THE TOWELS
We invite you to join with us to conserve water by using your towels more than once. In addition to decreasing water and energy consumption, you help us reduce the amount of detergent waste water that must be recycled within our community.

Please hang towels up if you wish to participate in this program – if not, simply leave them on the floor.

The card is 'Printed on recycled paper' and 'Laminated to reduce waste'. An 'Environmental discourse' is very much in evidence here, in terms of advocating the conservation of water and energy and limitation of (presumably) polluting detergent, and note the term 'our community'. But the 'invitation' to 'participate in this program' has been issued by a major hotel chain, whose bottom line is to succeed financially in a competitive leisure industry. So while individual promoters of the 'program' may be sincere in their concern for the environment, it is very hard to read this text and not consider that the *main* intention for the hotel chain is to save on laundry costs and perhaps accrue economically useful 'green' values, and that the promoters are textually 'appropriating' this familiar environmental discourse to accomplish these. Behind the traces of the environmental discourse we can recognize a hard-headed commercial one.

When several discourses are produced simultaneously (by one individual, or more, in interaction), as they characteristically are, discourses can be seen as jostling together, but also as *competing* and often as contradictory. *Contradictions*, together with gaps and incompletions (e.g. how far does an 'Equal opportunities discourse' extend?), are of interest to both CDA and post-structuralism, including FPDA. As an example, there is a contradiction in the two parenthood discourses of 'Father as line manager' and 'Mother as manager of the father's role in childcare'

(Sunderland, 2002). Contradictions may signal discoursal instability and hence act as pointers to struggle and avenues of social change (Pecheux, 1982), perhaps playing a 'disturbing' role themselves. In particular, they can create room for contestation in the form of an explicit challenge to a speaker, or commentary on the contradictions in one's own talk. *Agency* is an important concept here. Though there are always structural inequalities and constraints on agency (Bucholtz, 1999), within these a given individual can select a given discourse, and *with volition* can produce linguistic traces aimed at contesting a particular, dominant discourse (for more on *contradictions*, including their potentially *conservative* function, see Chapters 3, 8 and 9).

Conversation analysis approaches to discourse

In contrast to the theoretical approaches of post-structuralism and CDA, the conventional focus of conversation analysis (CA) is a close study of what is achieved *in words spoken* – the micro-analysis of conversational details – and speakers' apparent *orientations* to these. Conventional CA is thus problematic for feminist analyses of language, since for these it is precisely social structures *external* to talk which have important explanatory potential. Anne Weatherall (2002) argues that CA is valuable but insufficient for a complete analysis of gender. However, both CA and discursive psychology (which sometimes draws on CA) currently seem to be in the ascendance in gender and language study, and benefiting from a debate about their value for feminist analysis (see Kitzinger, 2000; Stokoe and Smithson, 2001; *Discourse and Society*, 2002, 17/3; Weatherall, 2002). CA's focus on talk itself enables consideration of *construction* of gender in that talk. In *this* sense, and in its concerns with *orientations*, CA dovetails well with language and gender study's shift away from searches for fixed 'gender differences' (see below; see also Kitzinger, 2000),[3] towards the study of ongoing gender construction in *discourse*.

* * *

Discourse analysis varies in the extent to which it takes account of the understandings of the speakers and writers who are (co-)producers of the discourse (see, e.g. John Swales' forthcoming work with writers of academic books and articles), and of listeners'/readers' (consumers') interpretations of spoken and written texts. CDA has been in the firing line here, accused of privileging the text and the analyst's perspective, and of being heavily dependent on a non-cooperative approach to text interpretation, and on *perceived* speaker/writer intentions (Schegloff, 1998;

Widdowson, e.g. 2000; see also Potter, 1996). CDA may, however, be taking the perspectives of producers and consumers more seriously than
hitherto, with Chouliaraki and Fairclough, for example, advocating the
combination of discourse analysis and ethnography, in order to explore
'the beliefs, values and desires of…participants' (1999: 62; see also
Christie, 1994). Conversation analysis, in contrast, is characteristically
solely and explicitly concerned with participants' own 'orientations' in
talk (e.g. Schegloff, 1998), but, as indicated, has been critiqued for its over-
circumscription (e.g. Wetherell, 1998).

Gender

While one use of *gender* indicates particular grammatical properties of a
language, the use of *gender* with which we are concerned here concerns
humans and entails any differences between women and men being
socially or culturally *learned, mediated* or *constructed. Gender* thus contrasts with the biological essentialism of the term *sex*, and was an important concept for feminism as *learning* entails tendencies and variation
rather than absolutes. More importantly, it shifted the focus from a grim
determinism to the possibilities of unlearning and relearning, resistance
to the existing order, and change, on both an individual and social level.
Gender thus meant new opportunities. Women did not have to stay at
home, did not have to earn less than men, did not have to wait for men
to propose marriage, to invite them out, to make sexual advances, did
not have to attach themselves to men at all, and did not have to have
babies, or more babies than they wanted.

This was all to the good and, drawing on the more familiar 'nature or
nurture' debate, the related notion of 'socialization' also proved useful
to the second wave of the Women's Movement in the 1970s and 1980s
(the phrase 'socialized into' was, I recall, critically and frequently used).
However, though it may have been something of an antidote to biological determinism, *gender* was – as it sometimes still is – nevertheless often
seen and used in a *socially* deterministic, even explanatory way. One
meaning of *gender* thus became, especially in popular discourse, gender
differences ('a question of gender').

Because of the inevitable overlap in any apparent boy/girl or
man/woman contrast, 'differences' are, of course, more likely to be 'tendencies'. And, though gender differentiation as expressed in discourse
may be a global or near-global phenomenon, *specific* behavioural (including linguistic) differences are likely to be *situated*, or *local*, related to a particular speech community or 'Community of Practice' (Lave and Wenger,

1991; Eckert and McConnell-Ginet, 1992b; Cameron, 1997). A good early example of the importance of the local is Susan Gal's classic (1978) sociolinguistic study of the town of Oberwart, on the Hungarian/ Austrian border. Young Hungarian women in Oberwart spoke German in a much greater range of situations than did young Hungarian men (and older Hungarian women) and married out of their original speech community more than the men (for whom it still had something to offer). Though a clear gender tendency in Oberwart in 1974, it would be absurd to generalize this greater tendency for young *women* to use German beyond this community to others. A second example is Lesley Milroy's (1980) sociolinguistic study in Belfast, which showed that in one community, the Clonard, the pronunciation of the young women was in some respects more vernacular than that of the young men. This study was extremely useful in demonstrating that women as a group did not always produce more 'standard' speech than men (as had been found by Labov, 1966 and Trudgill, 1972, in the communities they studied).[4] Milroy's explanation lay in the fact that these women 'hung about in a close-knit group during their time away from work' (1980: 84) and that many also worked together. This made them a very 'dense and multiplex' social network – unlike their male counterparts, who were suffering from unemployment in the area. Milroy's claim was thus that vernacular use was related to network density rather than to gender *per se*. It would be possible to speculate that a similar situation might obtain in communities in which network density was similarly gendered, but not necessarily beyond these.

For the gender aspects of their variationist studies, Gal and Milroy drew on a 'gender differences' model of gender – current in academia in the late 1970s and still 'common sense' in popular understandings and deployment of gender (however, see Gal, 1995, on the theoretical shift here). As Todd and Fisher (1988: 1) observe, 'gender is an organizing principle in people's everyday experiences', and Wodak reminds us that 'biological sex is still used as a powerful categorisation device' (1997: 13). (This has to be balanced, however, against the phenomena of 'gender-blindness' and 'think male'/'male as norm', within which women and girls are invisible or at least backgrounded, phenomena often illustrated with Erich Fromm's 'Man can do several things that the animal cannot do ... his vital interests are life, food and access to females'.) Underlying 'gender differences' we can see a view of masculinity and femininity as in 'binary opposition'. This has been described (with other binaries) as a 'fictitious opposition' and a 'violent hierarchy' in need of deconstruction (Todd and Fisher, 1988; see also Davies, 1993; Gatens, 2000). Although the opposition may be 'fictitious', it has material effects which often run counter to the interests of women. Such deconstruction is therefore in effect part of the wider feminist project of gender and discourse study – and, to a smaller extent, part of the project of this book.

The 'gender differences' paradigm played an important role in early gender and language study (see Coates, 1986, 1993; Cameron, 1992; Talbot, 1998, for discussion of the problematic 'deficit', '(male) dominance' and '(cultural) difference' chronological branches). It is still at times drawn on by scholars from outside the social sciences. It also tends to be enthusiastically embraced by undergraduate students of linguistics or education interested in exploring 'gender differences' in the language of their friends, or in classroom talk. Plaintiff cries of 'I can't find anything to do with gender' or 'There's no gender' in relation to a diligently produced transcript of mixed-sex talk usually means the student has looked for differences in the talk of male and female speakers, has failed to find it, has concluded that gender is not relevant – and is disappointed. A comment similar in its thinking is 'There's only one man in the group so I can't investigate gender'.

The assumptions underlying these *cris de coeur* are now seen as problematic. Whether *gender* was seen as an 'elaboration' of a predisposing *biological sex* or as 'symbolic' of it (hence culturally variable) (see Cameron, 1997b), the equation of *gender* with *difference* meant that even with an understanding of gender as social and cultural, gender was often simply 'mapped onto' sex (consider the regrettable phrase 'the two genders'). This led – and, indeed, still leads – to circular arguments, where the researcher 'maps talk onto the gender identity of the speaker, measures gender differences in talk, and then uses gender as the explanatory variable to account for those differences' (Speer, 2002: 348). While it is now widely accepted that any gender differences in language use are not only localized, but also mediated (for example, by power and/or practice; Cameron, 1997b), the quest for 'differences' also holds good only if gender is seen as something a (sexed) person *is* or *has* (a set of attributes, evidenced by practices) – a limited and limiting understanding – as I show below.

Like other writers, in this book I do not (have not been able to) abandon the idea of gender as premised on 'difference', nor do I wish to, since it is important not to lose sight of ways in which *notions* of gender can adversely affect women's access to important linguistic resources and possibilities of expression, i.e. to discourses (Pecheux, 1982; Pavlenko and Piller, 2001) and indeed to valuable material practices. Nevertheless, I endorse the theoretical shift from 'social learning' to 'social constructionism', i.e. that gender (in this case) is produced *in large part* by language and discourse (see also Weatherall, 2002). For some, this discoursal production extends to the actual sex/gender distinction. For example:

> We…are sceptical of leaving any space for 'difference' which is not by definition social or cultural. The categories 'men' and 'women' are social categories and the 'recognition' of biological 'sex differences' on which this distinction seems to rest is itself a social and cultural practice. (Jackson and Scott, 2001)

For others, the sex/gender distinction is theoretically valid, but dynamically and problematically. For example: 'Gender builds on biological sex, it exaggerates biological difference and, indeed, it carries biological difference into domains in which it is completely irrelevant' (Eckert and McConnell-Ginet, 2003: 10; see their Chapter 1 for an excellent discussion of gender construction; see also Eckert, 1989; Gal, 1995; Bing and Bergvall, 1996; Butler, 1999; West, 2002 for examples of the prolonged debate among feminist academics about the meanings of *sex* and *gender*).

I also endorse the understanding from post-structuralism (and discursive psychology) that it is useful, productive and interesting to see gender as a *process*, something that people *orient to* and *do* – including in their spoken and written discourse. Most people are not, however, free to 'do gender' in any way that takes their fancy and care needs to be taken to encompass the idea of *transgression*, of *constraints* on what *can*, in practice, be done – linguistically or otherwise, by women, men, boys and girls – with impunity.

Given the idea of 'doing gender', against a backdrop of socially situated constraints, this book thus focuses on what people do *with language* as regards gender. What is said and written, not only by speakers' and their interlocutors about themselves, but also about women, men, girls, boys, their apparent similarities and differences, the way they do and should relate? What is seen as *important* here? To what extent is people's discourse about individual women and men, for example high-profile figures like the singers Cher and Michael Jackson with their changing appearances, to do with gender (Franckenstein, 1997)? As Eckert and McConnell-Ginet claim:

> differences in what happens to women and to men derive in considerable measure from people's beliefs about sexual difference, their interpretations of its significance, and their reliance on those beliefs

and interpretations to justify the unequal treatment of women and men. (2003: 15)

This shifts the focus from the language-using (sexed) person to our (gendered) beliefs, expressed and studied through our orientations and linguistic practices. Here, the *substance* of what is said is more important than the *style* (Cameron, 1997). And gender difference is often *a topic of talk itself*. Pregnancy, for example, these days invariably occasions not only questions about whether parents want a girl/boy or know whether the baby is a girl or boy, but also explanations on the part of parents about why they have elected, or not, to know their forthcoming baby's biological sex. Gender can thus be seen not only as process, but also, I suggest, as an *idea*, or set of ideas, articulated in and as discourse. The question then is how, as Cameron (1996) puts it, do particular linguistic practices contribute to the production of people as women and men?

A frequent collocate of *gender* is *identity*,[5] and one concern of this book is how gender identity – femininity and masculinity – is represented in spoken and written texts through different discourses. But identity is not only a question of representation. Bucholtz (1999: 4) identifies as 'the fundamental observation of discourse analysis, that speakers' identities *emerge from discourse*' (my emphasis). How does this happen and how might we conceptualize it? For post-structuralism and discursive psychology, the answer is that identity

> is not viewed in essentialist terms as something that people 'are'. Rather, identities are progressively and dynamically achieved through the discursive practices that individuals engage in. ... the emphasis is on talk and not cognition as the most important site for studying identity. (Weatherall, 2002: 138)

This is very much in contrast to traditional psychological models in which *identity* resided within an individual as an 'in-the-head' entity (Potter, 1996). Discursive psychologists' justification for their use of discourse analysis includes that it 'allows the researcher to deal with the complex content of people's representations' (Wetherell et al., 1987: 69) and because discourse analysis

> avoids the ambiguity over whether representations are constituted linguistically or cognitively (opting firmly for the former as an analytically more productive option) and emphasizes flexibility: instead of thinking of an entire representation as either present or absent, the

suggestion is that selections are made from the available themes to best suit the function to which the discourse is put ... (1987: 61)

For discursive psychology, discourse analysis may take the form of identifying culturally informed discourses, as in the post-structuralist 'strand', or close examination of small stretches of spoken data, as in CA (see also McIlvenny, 2002; Weatherall, 2002). Weatherall notes that the post-structuralist strand sees identity as 'a result of both the cultural meaning systems available and the ongoing demands of any social interaction' (2002: 123).

Discursive psychology has not been the only influence on changing understandings of gender, however. For Mary Bucholtz, 'gender identity is at once more specific than most 1970s feminism realized and more fluid than much 1980s feminism allowed' (2000: 4) – an indication of the influence of gender studies, post-structuralism and discourse analysis in language and gender's progression beyond the sometimes universalizing and limited assignment of meanings in past work.

Masculinity and femininity can be seen as both contingent and fluid (e.g. Stapleton, 2001). This results in a potential *multiplicity* of gender identity for a given individual, meaning that the plural forms *identities* (gender/sexual), *masculinities* and *femininities* (Hollway, 1984, 1995; Livia and Hall, 1997), now relatively common in the literature, can be used to refer to individuals (as well as to women and men more widely). Nigel Edley explains this potential and shifting multiplicity as follows: subject positions – 'locations' within a conversation – *are* the identities made relevant by specific ways of talking. Further:

because those ways of talking can change both within and between conversations (i.e. as different discourses or interpretive repertoires are employed) then, in some sense at least, so too do the identities of the speakers. (2001: 210)

The fluidity and continual redefinition of identity might involve also both *attributions* to the individual by others in interaction (see Todd and Fisher, 1988; Ivanic, 1998; Jaworski and Coupland, 1999), including how that individual is *addressed*; and individual *affiliation* to particular possibilities. Affiliation may take the form of a participant explicitly orienting to, 'taking up' or selecting a particular subject position in a particular context (though this will be limited by those subject positions the participant is aware of, and by material and other constraints) and rejecting others. This may depend in part on the co-participants. As an illustration, I offer West and Fenstermaker's (2002) findings from a meeting of an American university 'Board of Regents' about affirmative action. Only women of colour introduced themselves with reference to their femaleness and their colour, black men referred to their colour but not their maleness, and white men introduced themselves with reference to neither colour nor maleness.[6] The different subject positions taken up and different social identities 'performed' here thus related to gender in interaction with ethnicity.

For contemporary feminist linguistics, ideas of masculinity and femininity as somehow symmetrical, or in an asymmetrical but complementary yin–yang relationship, or even in opposition, are problematic. It is, however, possible to see men and boys *constructing* their masculinities to correspond to what they see femininities as not being – for example, if girls in a mixed-sex school seem to be doing well in foreign languages, boys might not even try (see Sunderland, 2000). Such 'boundaries' must be continually shifting. However, if in a given setting the achievements of members of one sex are valued more, and if members of that same sex are then seen as the 'norm' against which the other is measured, gender may also look very asymmetrical indeed.

Gender and discourse/gendered discourse/ gendering discourse

Eckert and McConnell-Ginet refer to 'varied discourses of gender', to mean 'the workings of a particular set of ideas about gender in some segment or segments of society' (2003: 42). Mills points to the non-uniform practices which oppress women, noting that 'feminist analysis focuses on discourses rather than a single discourse' as relevant to women's subjection because of the 'wide range of discursive and institutional structures which oppress women and which women in turn are either compliant with or resistant to' (1997: 94). *Gender* and *discourse* also appear together in the titles of several monographs and edited collections (e.g. Tannen, 1994; Wodak, 1997; Todd and Fisher, 1998; Walsh, 2002; Litosseliti and Sunderland, 2002; Weatherall, 2002); and are both central in Wilkinson and Kitzinger's *Feminism and Discourse: Psychological Perspectives* (1995) and Mills' *Discourse* (1997). Discourse analyses have shown the extent to which discourse *is* gendered, and indeed the proliferation of work here may be precisely because of the ability of discourse analysis to challenge traditional essentialist and reductionist understandings of gender (Edley, 2001).

What about the adjective *gendered*? Stronger than 'gender-related', it suggests that gender already is part of the 'thing' which *gendered* describes (and, indeed, that gender may have been *done to* that 'thing'). The '(male) dominance' (retrospectively labelled) gender and language theorists of the 1970s and 1980s would probably have taken *gendered discourse* to refer to the nature of the *interactional* dominance for which they found evidence in mixed-sex conversations: Fishman (1983), West and Zimmerman (1983) and Edelsky (1977) showed men on the whole talking more than women, interrupting more, providing fewer minimal responses, asking fewer questions and having their topics taken up more regularly. This could be said to be discourse of a very gendered kind indeed. However, in this book I am not so much concerned with this 'gendered how' of talk, but rather with substance, the 'gendered what' – the ideational rather than the interpersonal (Halliday, 1994). 'Gendered discourse' in this way can bring together the two traditional 'prongs' of gender and language study – language use and gender representation (the latter, for example, in children's books, magazines and newspapers, and of course linguistic *systems*) (see also Cameron, 1997).

Any human experience can be gendered – as can represented animal experiences (the behaviour of the 'expectant father' dog in the Hollywood version of Dodie Smith's *One Hundred and One Dalmatians*, for example). 'Being gendered' can also apply to an occupation, a written text, a leisure practice, a garment, a passing remark, meaning that, here, 'something to do with gender is going on'. School is gendered if there is a tendency for girls or boys to perform better in one subject than another. An exercise class is gendered if only women attend it. *Gender –* in the sense of *difference* – is thus more or less ubiquitous. For gender in the sense of an *idea* or *construct*, a magazine text about cooking is gendered if it *suggests* that women, or men, tend to cook in distinct ways. Walsh (2002, citing Robson, 1988) describes the lexical sets representing vocational norms for women in the Church of England as 'differently gendered'. For women these norms included 'service', 'empowerment of others' and 'a lack of interest in worldly forms of wealth and prestige'. Men, however, were judged according to 'a set of middle-class professional norms, stressing "status", "preferment", "job descriptions", etc.' (2002: 166). Walsh notes that this differential representation has continued even after women's (post-1992) right to ordination in the Anglican Church.

When women and men, boys and girls are represented and/or expected to behave *in particular gendered ways*, post-structuralism and CDA see gendered discourses as *positioning* women and men in different ways, i.e. as constitutive. Actual behaviour may – but may not – correspond to those representations and expectations, but either way people can be seen as taking up particular gendered 'subject positions', discoursally constituted (see Wetherell, 1998; Weatherall, 2002). But rather than focusing on (and ferreting out) any 'gender differences' (or tendencies), a discourse approach would see these not as an end – or the end of the investigation – in themselves, but as legitimating the 'male/female binary' and *as potentially constitutive of gender* more widely. Something which is *gendered* can thus also be gender*ing*.

Gendered discourse is frequently evaluated as unfavourable to women – as in Walsh's example, above, i.e. positioning and discoursally constituting women in particular, often conservative ways. To suggest that gendered discourse always *inevitably* constructs gender *beyond* a given spoken or written text or particular stretch of discourse would be to adopt a highly determinist stance from which analysts now distance themselves. This stance was evident in the non-sexist language campaigns of the 1970s, in which one argument for 'inclusive' language was that linguistic items like the so-called 'generic' *he* caused people to 'think male'. However, while there was some evidence that thinking could be influenced by sexist language (e.g. Schneider and Hacker, 1973), this was by no means automatic, universal or long-term (its duration was never, to my knowledge, explored). To borrow from CA, an individual's *orientation* to a particular (stretch of) discourse needs to be considered before any discussion of *construction* in relation to that individual can take place.

In another field, literature, there was a related acknowledgement that 'effect' could never be accurately predicted since there are always different ways of reading the same text (or of 'hearing' the same stretch of talk) (see e.g. Mills, 1994, on 'reader response theory'). Given a measure of *agency*, an individual can *negotiate* and *contest* what she hears and reads and can potentially *resist* discoursal subject positioning and construction. It is useful to see not only talk, but also reading/engaging with a written text, as prototypically *interactional* here.

Construction, performance, representation and indexing

Gender can be *constructed*, *performed*, *represented* and *indexed*, and these collocates are frequently found in research papers on gender and discourse (and, indeed, in this book). Often each is used in more than one way in the same text. One objective of this book is to help readers use them with appropriate reflexivity; another is to explore what might be the empirical workings of, in particular, *construction*, in relation to discourse and gender. I conclude this chapter with a brief look at each concept in turn.

Gendering: construction and performance

Associated with social constructionism and post-structuralism, *construction* and *performance* are members of the same semantic field. Lexical variations include *accomplish, achieve* and *enact*, and Bucholtz (1999) describes language as *effecting* gender.

It is commonplace to read that gender is constructed by discourse, and that speakers and writers *construct* gender in their talk and written texts. But what do we mean by *construction* (in whom, or what)? What are we looking for? Can *linguistic* evidence enable us to claim construction, and with what 'warrant' (Swann, 2002) would we make such a claim? In any talk directly or indirectly about females or males as individuals or social groups, gender can be argued to be constructed *in the words*. But is it also discoursally constructed in terms of *identity*, for the speaker, her or his addressee(s) and/or any overhearers present in a given language event? Has gender in the 'world at large' been (re)constructed in some small way? How do different theoretical paradigms address this?

Performing gender is a second conceptual way of looking at the potentially constitutive function of discourse: having *agency*, speakers/writers can 'perform' who they publicly (temporarily) 'are'. The idea of performance draws on Austin's (1962) *performative utterance* – a speech act that changes the world – which includes not only formulae such as the traditional 'I name you man and wife', but also, potentially (drawing on a 'full-blown' theory of pragmatics), *any* utterance (Thomas, 1995). *What* is performed can include a range of possibilities for gender, including various 'disturbing' ones, as in the famous 'drag queen' example (Butler, 1999; see also Barrett, 1999). *Performance* – which goes beyond language – de-privileges the idea of *identity* (Butler, 1999; see also Cameron, 1997).

The relevance of performance to gender study has been established largely by the philosopher Judith Butler and is referenced in work on gender and discourse in various ways. Stokoe and Smithson write that when gender is seen as performative, this being an 'emergent property' of social interaction, it is *discursively articulated* (2001: 218). Cammack and Kalmbach Phillips (2002) talk of what people *do with discourses*: we may 'entertain' discourses and 'try on' alternative ones (2002: 128, 131). This does not mean, of course, that we are not simultaneously being gendered *by* discourses. It is important to retain an understanding of a balance between *agency* and *constraint* here. (For more on *construction* and *performance*, see Chapter 8.)

Representation

Associated with the field of cultural analysis, *representation* can be of some*thing* or some*one*, and *representation* is usually used when the subject is 'other' rather than self. Representation occurs (and can be seen) in spoken, written and visual texts in the form of discoursal 'traces'. Stuart Hall (1997) reminds us that language itself is a representational system: signs and symbols show concepts, ideas and feelings. As another example, Hall notes the way black experience has been represented in mainstream American cinema: in the 1930s black actors were used to represent faithful servants (echoing slavery), and in the 1940s sang in black musicals. Not until the 1950s did mainstream films deal with race itself and cast accordingly. Representations may or may not be volitional – it is thus always hard to establish *intent* here, particularly since representations are often pre-formed, based on stereotypes. Representation also always involves interpretation by the 'consumer' (Stephens, 1992: 162) and there may be disagreement about what a particular representation actually *is* (see Widdowson, 1995, for a critique of Fairclough's (1989, 1992) analysis of medical discourse).

Cosslett et al. (1996) introduce the term *representation* with 'it is ... important to distinguish between our experiences and the images we meet of these in the arts, media and other cultural texts' – representation being, of course, the latter. Representation may be achieved through gender and sexual stereotyping. In a British radio programme of the 1960s, *Round the Horne*, two comedy characters, Julian and Sandy, were represented as stereotypical 'camp' gay men through the use of exaggerated intonation and lexical items and topics popularly and stereotypically (but *not* empirically) associated with effeminacy (Baker, 2002). Feminists have similarly often emphasized the *gulf* between representation and reality in terms of gendered language use, in both academic and popular texts (see also Cameron, 2003).

Representation tends not to be understood in terms of *constitutiveness*, and may imply a mediated version of a pre-existing, material reality. Within post-structuralism, Mills writes, 'the use of the term discourse signalled a major break with previous views of language and representation' (1997: 8).

Indexing

Indexing implies that one particular social meaning is signalled (often linguistically) over another. It does not, however, entail *constitutiveness*.

Language, but also visuals and physical objects, can in different ways index or 'point to' social meanings (Ochs, 1992, 1993):

> In every community, members have available to them linguistic resources for communicating such social meanings at the same time as they are providing other levels of information. This system of multifarious signalling is highly efficient. (Ochs, 1992: 338)

These signals are then interpreted by socialized, competent members of the community (Ochs, 1993).[7] A British parent might conventionally dress a boy baby in blue to index the fact that he is a boy, or in (say) yellow to index rejection either of this convention, or of the 'commonsense' status of biological sex as a category.

Linguistically, Ochs cites 'referential' indexes of gender (forms such as *Mr* and *madam*), and the much more frequent 'non-referential' indexes – 'a vast range of morphological, syntactic and phonological devices available across the world's languages' (1993: 148). These are, of course, culturally variable (see Ervin-Tripp, 2001; Weatherall, 2002) and very largely sex-preferential (what Ochs calls 'non-inclusive') rather than sex-exclusive. By 'non-inclusive', Ochs is, however, referring not only to the fact that most linguistic features *can* be used by both women and men, but also that 'many linguistic forms associated with gender are associated as well with the marking of other social information, such as the marking of stance and social action' (1992: 340). One example is the arguably sex-preferential tag questions, associated sometimes not only with female speakers but also with hesitancy and confirmation checks (but see also Cameron et al., 1989).

Performance or construction of a particular identity involves indexing. Language users, however, do not and cannot index an identity directly themselves, but do so rather *through* indexes. In Rusty Barrett's (1999) paper on performance and the speech of African-American drag queens (AADQs), *indexing* occurs as follows (emphasis added):

> (1) ... this style of speaking is only one voice used by AADQs. The *complete set of linguistic styles together index* a multi-layered identity (1999: 313).
> (2) Speakers may heighten or diminish *linguistic displays that index* various aspects of their identities according to the context of an utterance and the specific goals they are trying to achieve. Thus a speaker may use *the indexical value of language* (cf. Ochs 1992) to 'position' (Davies and Harré, 1990) the self within a particular identity at a particular interactional moment (1999: 318).

(3) *An utterance is valued because of its ability to index* an ambiguous relationship between the signifier and the signified (1999: 320).

Linguistic styles, displays and utterances can thus also achieve indexing. As attestations of linguistic indexing of *gender*, Pavlenko and Piller list 'prosody, phonology, syntax, morphology, lexicon, communicative styles, narrative styles, strategic uses of silence and use of discursive genres' (2001: 34). More broadly, *discourse* and *discourses* can also signal a *particular* gender or sexual identity or affiliation. Choices are limited, but may include *popular* and/or stereotypical views of particular forms of discourse (as in representation). Barrett observes:

> In identity performance, out-group stereotypes concerning the behavioral patterns of the group associated with the performed identity are likely to be more important than actual behavior or the group's own behavioral norms (Hall, 1995). ... [T]he language used in a performed category is likely to differ from the actual speech of those who categorise themselves as having that identity. (1999: 318)

Here, Barrett is thinking of AADQs using stereotypical but empirically unestablished, and probably inaccurate, linguistic and other forms to index that identity – *when they wish to do so*. Similarly, a gay person may choose at times to *perform* a gay identity by using language which will index that identity (as, indeed, may a heterosexual person). Clarissa Rowe (2000) illustrates convincingly how gay men at times draw on popular ideas of 'Gayspeak' in their talk: not only the 'how' of talk ('camp' intonation, for example), but also the 'what' – the topics of fabrics and fashion (a 'Design discourse?'), for example. This may not correspond at all to the talk of gay men when they do not wish to index their sexual identity.[8] In Chapters 5 and 6 we will see the 'fatherhood' discourses of 'Part-time father' and 'Father as baby entertainer'. A father's uncritical use of either may successfully index the performance of a rather traditional fatherhood identity; a critical use, the performance of a non-traditional one.

In Chapter 2 we look more closely at the nature of discourse and discourses – both what they are and what they do. We will take as examples a range of gendered (and other) discourses which can be interpretively identified in two newspaper texts, looking at the language of the texts and relations they may have with other texts. We will also look at issues of discourse *naming*.

2
Discourses, Discourse Identification and Discourse Naming

In this chapter I expand on what was said about discourses in Chapter 1, particularly in terms of relevant linguistic features, then move on to two detailed examples of interpretive 'discourse identification'. This is with a view to enabling those investigating discourse from a critical or post-structuralist perspective to interpretively identify, name and discuss the significance and workings of discourses in their own research.

Discourses have arguably been around for as long as humans have, and the genealogy of particular discourses has been explored and discussed (Foucault, 1978). Fairclough notes that 'the political discourse of the "third way", i.e. the discourse of "New Labour" [in the UK] ... is relatively less than a decade old' (2003: 125). 'A discourse', though it may be unbounded, will nevertheless be *describable*, for example in its possible linguistic traces. It may have a name or be nameable. To take an example from outside gender and language study, if the phrase *academic discourses* is used in the Faircloughian sense of discourses as 'different ways of structuring areas of knowledge and social practice' (1992: 43), then these discourses, I argue, need to be separately identified, described and differentiated, including in terms of *stance*. For example, we might talk about an 'agonistic discourse' (Tannen, 2002), as when academics confront each other in research articles, a 'modesty discourse', often drawn on in PhD theses by students wary of overstating their claims and contributions, and a 'discourse of aggrandisement', seen in personal statements of academics seeking employment or promotion.

Discourses – including gendered discourses, as I show in Chapter 3 – have been identified in different domains and within different academic disciplines. Indeed, as Fairclough observes, the identification and analysis of discourses is now a preoccupation across the humanities and social sciences (2003: 123). Many have also been not only interpretively, but also critically, named. My starting point in identifying discourses, as indicated in Chapter 1, is to see a discourse provisionally as a 'way of seeing the world' (where 'seeing' may extend beyond the receptive to actively 'thinking about'). For the analyst, this can be derived from the way people speak and write about things. Additionally, Fairclough comments on a degree of repetition, commonality and stability over time (2003: 124). While 'the way people speak and write about things' does not convey the crucial *ideologically constitutive potential* of a discourse, as in Fairclough's claim that discourse 'structures knowledge and social practice' (1992: 43; see also Foucault, 1972), it is broadly operationalizable, can be checked against the understandings of readers or listeners, and thus has useful implications for empirical research, for gender and language pedagogy and, indeed, for discoursal deconstruction and other linguistic intervention (see Chapter 9).

Jaworski and Coupland (1999) make the point that a discourse can exist only if it is 'socially acceptable' (at least to some people). To be socially acceptable it must be provisionally 'recognizable', as I suggested earlier. Recognition depends in part on certain social structures and structures of communication being in place. So, I suggest, we can now recognize an 'environmental discourse' when we see one, whereas 50 years ago we might have been thoroughly confused when faced by a text advocating some aspect of environmental sustainability, protection or repair. People do not, however, recognize a discourse, even provisionally, in any straightforward way. Not only is it not identified or named, and is not self-evident or visible as a discrete chunk of a given text, it can never be 'there' in its entirety. What *is* there are certain linguistic features: 'marks on a page', words spoken, or even people's memories of previous conversations (see Talbot, 1995a: 24), which – if sufficient and coherent – may suggest that they are 'traces' of a particular discourse. Identification of a discourse thus requires co-construction by the language user with the text and all elements of its production. The discourse is not simply 'out there', waiting to be spotted. (Here the birdwatching metaphor in the 'Introduction to Part I' begins to break down.)

Provisional recognition depends in part on *cognition*. Van Dijk (1988) observes that this includes 'strategic processes of perception, analysis and interpretation', short- and long-term memory, frames and scripts, models of communicative situations, all monitored by a 'Control System'. He explicitly relates the cognitive and the social, claiming that people's models of communicative situations are 'influenced not only by scripts but also by dominant (group) attitudes', which may in turn be 'organized by ideologies' (1988: 39). However, human psychology does not have to be understood in terms of 'inner' attitudes and perceptions. For *discursive* psychology (a branch of social psychology), as we have seen (e.g. Wetherell et al., 1987; Potter, 1996; Weatherall, 2002; Potter and Edwards, 2003), cognition can be explored through linguistic practices involving mental terms, and importantly participants' 'displays and orientations' in their talk. For discursive psychology, in Weatherall's words:

> language itself is the object of enquiry because, consistent with social constructionism, language is understood as constructing, limiting and guiding people's understanding of their worlds and themselves. (2002: 88)

Anyone who says they have recognized 'where a writer/speaker is coming from', with or without a 'close reading' (or 'listening'), and without or after negotiation of meaning, may be said to have provisionally identified a discourse. The notion of *recognizability* of discourses can also be operationalized and *empirically* explored in a *principled* way through encouraging a reader or listener (after a little 'training' in using textual and extra-textual knowledge) to 'spot' and perhaps name discourses in texts (see below).

Discourses are, of course, not only recognized, but, as we have seen, actively drawn on and produced. More discourses may be recognized than are actually taken up: language users may choose not to speak or write using language which contains traces of non-dominant discourses, for example. The path of least (discoursal) resistance is to 'access' discourses compatible with how one is being 'subject positioned' (see also Peterson, 2002): many people, for example, encountering traces of racist discourse and being positioned as someone who shares or holds racist assumptions, would choose to withdraw from the interaction rather than produce language intended to constitute and be interpreted as traces of an anti-racist, oppositional and explicitly *conflictual* discourse.

As Jaworski and Coupland point out, '*most* texts are not "pure" reflections of single discourses' (1999: 9). Within a text, *several* discourses may be apparent, some more so than others (e.g. more 'dominant' and/or with the greatest proportion of linguistic traces), some more ephemeral (e.g. marginal and/or with fewer, more obscure or more tendentious traces). Being in the same text, they must be semantically as well as grammatically related – and we can thus refer to *intratextuality*, and its importance, as well as intertextuality (see Chapter 1).

This idea of *related discourses* is important: a given text *always* has relationships with others. Fairclough writes that

> any text is explicitly or implicitly 'in dialogue with' other texts ... which constitute its 'intertexts'. Any text is a link in a chain of texts, reacting to, drawing in, and transforming other texts. (2001: 233)

and that 'Texts ... set up dialogical or polemical relations between their "own" discourses and the discourses of others' (2003: 128). To this we can add Bakhtin's 'Our speech ... is filled with others' words, varying degrees of otherness or varying degrees of "our-own-ness" ' (1986: 89). Similarly, Kristeva (1986) sees this intertextuality as the property a text has of being full of 'snatches' of other texts. Accordingly, any (say) written text will probably bring to mind other texts to which it is similar in some way, or in explicit contrast (i.e. in an oppositional relationship). For a discourse to be even provisionally recognizable, its linguistic traces must also exist – however marginally – in *other* texts. If discourses were not related (and pre-existing individual speakers), we would be able to make little sense of them. Though not assuming conscious intention, in this sense a particular text can be seen as a *reaction* to previous texts, and also a 'drawing in' of those texts through the way it adopts comparable (or oppositional) propositions or styles. (Bakhtin, 1986, adds that utterances are also related to *subsequent* utterances, since a text anticipates reactions.)

As we saw in Chapter 1, a 'hybrid' discourse is a broadly balanced articulation of two or more discourses. *Interdiscursivity* can be seen as 'the complex interdependent configuration of discursive formations' (Fairclough, 1992: 68), as in the 'hotel towels' example. (It thus contrasts with 'manifest intertextuality', i.e. drawing in the actual words of another text, for example, direct reported speech.) Interdiscursivity, which ensures discourses' continuing fluidity, may be key to both discoursal change *and* social progress, and can also be seen as dialectically (sometimes retrospectively) 'transforming' texts through encouraging a rethinking of their meanings.

Interdiscursivity may involve 'appropriation' of one discourse by another, to the point where traces of the 'appropriated' discourse are foregrounded (the *Animal Farm* scenario). Alternatively, the 'appropriated discourse' may be diluted, and Caldas-Coulthard notes with regret 'the mis-appropriation of the feminist discourse of sexual liberation' by women's lifestyle magazines such as *Marie Claire* (1996: 267). The theoretical alternative is *colonization*, i.e. that a given discourse has not *appropriated* but has rather *been colonized by* another (Chouliaraki and

Fairclough, 1999). Have advertisements which draw on the notion of the financially independent career woman to sell cars 'appropriated' a discourse of feminism for commercial gain (Goldman's (1992) 'commodity feminism', for example), or has feminism discursively (and usefully) 'colonized' such ads? (see also Mills, 1997: 102). Intertextuality can thus be used as a strategy in linguistic intervention (see Chapter 9).

It is possible to see linked, related, *networked* discourses as constituting an 'order of discourse' (the term has been adapted from Foucault). Fairclough defines this as 'the totality of discourse practices within an institution or society, and the relationship between them' (1992: 43, 71; see also Fairclough, 2003). Configuration relationships include dominance/ marginality, mutual support, opposition, foreground/background and hierarchy, where one discourse 'overarches' several others. In Chapter 5, 'Fatherhood discourses in parenting magazines', for example, I use an 'architectural' metaphor to represent one gendered discourse overarching several others (see also Sunderland, 2000a, 2002). I originally referred to these as 'bricked together', but borrowing from Potter's developed 'construction site' metaphor (1996: 103), I now see these bricks as 'soft and vague', only 'snap[ping] into shape as they are cemented into place'.

Associated 'overarched' discourses are not necessarily mutually supporting, however (Pecheux, 1982). *Contesting* or *competing* 'counterdiscourses' have the potential to 'disturb' a given discoursal order, which is 'put at risk by what happens in actual interactions' (Fairclough, 2001: 235). An order of discourse remains an open system. Even a single utterance of a reader or speaker can thus contest – and disturb, or at least undermine – the legitimacy of a given discourse.

Discourse and linguistic features

Mills notes that we can 'detect a discursive structure' because of 'the systematicity of the ideas, opinions, concepts, ways of thinking and behaving which are formed within a particular context' (1997: 17). All these may be manifested – systematically – in language. But, given that discourses are interpretively identifiable in part through linguistic 'traces', we need to know what traces might be relevant. Critical discourse analysts typically draw on linguistic features such as nominalization, passivization and sequencing (Jaworski and Coupland, 1999; Fairclough, 2003; see also Halliday, 1985), but I will also refer to the more recent, related work of van Leeuwen (1996, 1997) on 'social actors' and 'social action'. These notions include ideas, knowledge, beliefs and practices (including linguistic practices). I also consider possible consumer addressees, and the question of what Walsh calls the text producer's 'affinity with, or distance from, the ideas of represented subjects' (2002: 39), i.e. her explicit or implicit evaluation of those ideas, knowledge, beliefs and practices. Varying with genre, 'affinity' raises different issues for analysis of media texts (Chapters 5 and 6) and fiction (Chapter 7).

As regards 'labelling' practices, I look at lexical choices, especially repeated lexical choices, in how social actors are referred to (e.g. in noun phrases). For 'social action' I look at verb types, verb phrases, and activization/passivization. As Fairclough (2003) notes, although lexis may provide the most obvious distinguishing features of a discourse, grammatical features can characterize and differentiate discourses too. For both I look at collocations, and at 'absences' as well as 'presences', i.e. at what possibilities do not appear, but could have done (van Leeuwen, 1996, 1997), and, from a feminist perspective, arguably should have done. (In other CDA-oriented work, the analytical focus is on modality and transitivity choices; see also Fairclough (2003) on semantic relations such as hyponymy.) Such traces facilitate the text-based part of identification of *discourses*, in particular of *related discourses* within the same text (*intratextuality*) as well as in different texts. But since linguistic traces can be 'manifestly intertextual', and can show evidence of interdiscursivity I focus on intertextuality too.

I am assuming a measure of *authorial choice* – though not necessarily intentionality, and not free, unlimited choice (see Toolan, 1996). Authorial choice may be particularly relevant to 'absences' and 'presences': to syntagmatic choices – what words, phrases, sentences, paragraphs and discourses, are 'chained' together (or not), how, and in what order, to constitute whole spoken and written texts; and to paradigmatic choices – what has been selected for a given 'position' in the chain.

'Discourse identification' has been referred to elsewhere as 'detecting discourses' (Cammack and Kalmback Phillips, 2002; see also Mills, 1997; Edley, 2001, on the identification of 'interpretative repertoires'). After a little guided practice, conscious discourse identification and naming can be done independently by students through close reading of culturally familiar texts, if they are willing to think systematically and linguistically – (intra)textually, intertextually and interdiscursively, in short, to bring to bear understandings from outside the text to the text itself – as well as critically.

Two examples of 'discourse spotting'

I start with examples from two 2002 British newspaper texts to show how gendered discourses can be provisionally and interpretively identified, or 'spotted', and named. In the examples, I focus on some of the linguistic features referenced above. I hope to make the identification process as explicit and transparent as possible. This is partly in response to Potter, who observes that 'the relation of Foucault's notion of discourse to any particular instance of talk or writing is not always well specified' (1996: 87), and to Francis (1999), who problematizes the question of discourse categorization. I chose these texts as they are clearly 'gendered' (they are about humans, and gender figures explicitly as a category in both), and because I have used them successfully for 'discourse spotting' purposes in postgraduate teaching in the UK, and in a workshop of language educational professionals in the US.[1] Some of the discourses described here were produced in these events.

It has to be said that the discourses are not only interpretive and provisional, but are also an effect of 'Western' co-construction. They are also a *partial* set, in that still others could have been identified. Discourses are non-ubiquitous, produced within particular educational, social and political contexts. Different discourses are accordingly likely to be 'spotted' by different social groups of readers and analysts – for example, those who favour a feminist perspective and those with a more traditionalist perspective – even when looking at exactly the same textual set of linguistic traces (see Christie, 1994). This will depend in part on what seems self-evident, 'common sense' or simply salient to given readers/listeners. A covert racist discourse may be spotted and named by anti-racist campaigners (and spotted and differently named by advocates of racist practices!) but may not be recognized as such by those who simply don't care. Alternatively, members of different 'Communities of practice' (say) may 'spot' the same discourse at the same time, but evaluate it differently. A 'Discourse of fantasy', for example, can be viewed positively ('your dream may come true!') or negatively (a cynical distraction, ideologically blinding women and men to what is really 'going on').

The first text, from my local weekly newspaper, the *Lancaster Guardian*, was found on the 'Wedding Album' page. Entitled 'Tie the knot at Leighton Hall – A dream wedding', it tops the page. (Leighton Hall is a country house in Lancashire, parts of which are open to the public.)

Contained in the three short columns of 'Tie the knot at Leighton Hall' I suggest are linguistic traces of a variety of discourses. Those co-constructed by myself, the postgraduate students and the language education professionals are listed – and thus named – below. Some of these we can describe as 'descriptive' (in the 'Specific context' sense of *discourse*). Others we can see as discourses in the 'interpretive' sense (see Chapter 1). We can divide this second group into *general* and *gendered* discourses. (These 'types' may overlap.) We are not too concerned

Tie the knot at Leighton Hall

A dream wedding

FAIRYTALE dreams can soon come true for North Lancashire brides now Leighton Hall has been awarded permission to host civil wedding ceremonies.

The historic house with its spectacular backdrop and Gothic towers and turrets, has been a popular wedding reception venue for the last ten years but the increase in competing venues having wedding licenses has spurred the owners to apply for their own.

Couples can now exchange vows at Leighton, as well as cele-

by Gayle Rouncivell

brating their special day within the most romantic and idyllic of settings.

Suzie Reynolds, owner of Leighton Hall, personally supervises the hall's weddings.

She said: "Modern couples want to get married somewhere extra special and a bit unusual - historic settings, such as Leighton, are increasingly popular.

"More people are enjoying the convenience of getting married, taking photographs and celebrating their reception at the same venue so we decided

it was time that we too were able to offer this full service.

"We are looking forward to giving couples the wedding days about which they have always dreamed!"

Brides can choose one of two rooms for their ceremony - the music room, which overlooks the Victorian walled garden and enjoys spectacular views of the parkland, or the main hall with its 'flying' staircase, down which the bride can make a breathtaking entrance.

For more information contact Leighton Hall on 734474.

Figure 2.1   From *Lancaster Guardian*, 11 January 2002.

at this stage about the mechanics of discourse *naming*, but I have used 'scare quotes' for the names of interpretive discourses to indicate their interpretive nature.

Descriptive discourses:

(a) an architectural discourse
(b) a legal discourse

Interpretive discourses:
(a) General:

> (i)   a 'Promotional discourse'
> (ii) a 'Consumerist discourse'
> (iii) a 'Discourse of late modernity'

(b) Gendered:

> (i)   a 'Discourse of fantasy'
> (ii) a 'Biggest day of a woman's life' discourse
> (iii) a 'Compulsory heterosexuality' discourse

These will be discussed more fully below, but readers may first wish to return to the text to identify possible linguistic 'traces' of these, together with reminders of – relationships with – other texts and discourses.

The second example comes from a national UK broadsheet, *The Times*. It is entitled 'Why women are just first class', and reports how, for the first time, in 2001, more first class (undergraduate) degrees were awarded to women than to men.

Interpretive discourses
(a) General:

> (i)   an 'Informational discourse'
> (ii) a '*Horse-race* discourse'

(b) Gendered:

> (i)   a 'Battle of the sexes' discourse
> (ii) a 'Gender differences' discourse
> (iii) a 'Poor boys' discourse
> (iv) a 'Gender equality now achieved' discourse

Readers may again wish to return to the text before continuing, to identify linguistic traces of these discourses as well as intertextual links.

Why women are just first-class

By Glen Owen
Education Correspondent

WOMEN are racing ahead of men in the battle to secure the most first-class degrees, new figures show.

Last summer 12,400 women were awarded firsts, compared with 11,300 men — marking the first time that they have recorded a substantial lead at the highest degree level. It follows years of being outperformed in university examination halls, and completes their dominance at all levels of the academic system.

Traditionally, men have always secured more firsts: six years ago they led by 1,800. By 1999 their lead was down to just 300, and in 2000 the two sexes were neck and neck. This year's results reflect the fact that the number of women gaining firsts annually has trebled in ten years.

Girls started to surpass boys at GCSE level soon after they replaced O levels in 1987,

and in 2000 they gained more A grades at A level for the first time. These advances have led to higher numbers entering university. Last year they comprised more than 55 per cent of the 265,000 first degree students sitting their final exams.

However, the figures, released by the Higher Education Statistic Agency, show that while they have overtaken boys in absolute terms, the proportion of women students who gain firsts is still lower: 8.46 per cent, compared with 9.5 per cent of male students. But they are closing this gap too — the boys' lead, at this measure, of 1.04 per cent compares with a lead of 1.28 per cent in 2000.

Teachers believe that male results are suffering because they are subjected to a "laddish" culture which regards academic success as "uncool".

Overall, the figures showed that 9 per cent of all students secured a first, compared with 8 per cent in the previous year.

Figure 2.2   From *The Times*, 12 January 2002.

Linguistic traces, intratextuality and intertextuality

We will now look more closely at the linguistic traces of the discourses apparent in these texts. Although most people use the language of texts to co-construct discourses unsystematically and unconsciously, the discourse analyst can do so systematically and consciously.

'A dream wedding'

While looking broadly at 'social actors' and 'social action', we can look specifically not only at lexical items, in particular noun phrases and verb phrases, but also at collocations and recurrent items.

Descriptive discourses:
(i) An architectural discourse
This discourse is realized principally by distinctive 'semi-specialist' lexical traces in the form of nouns and noun phrases:

> *historic house*
> *backdrop*
> *Gothic towers*
> *turrets*
> *Victorian walled garden*
> *'flying' staircase*

These resonate with both the 'fairytale' image of weddings at Leighton Hall, and with the ideas of consumerism and choice, Leighton Hall's unique architecture providing it with a particular marketing niche. The third paragraph of the third column, in which we read about *the music room, which overlooks the Victorian walled garden and enjoys spectacular views of the parkland*, resembles (has links with) a real estate or realtor's description of a property which is for sale – not surprising in a text which also has a promotional function (and which may indeed have drawn on existing promotional literature; see also Fairclough, 2003). This can be seen as a 'hybrid' discourse – and a good example of (almost 'manifest') intertextuality.

(ii) A legal discourse
There are two legal issues here – marriage, and the licence needed by institutions that 'host' civil wedding ceremonies. Lexical traces include the slang (but polite) verb phrase metaphor *tie the knot* (i.e. the legal registration of the marriage); the idea of *permission* which has been (rather formally) *awarded* to Leighton Hall, after the owners had *applied* for it; and the lexical item *wedding licences*.

Interpretive discourses:
(a) General
(i) A 'promotional discourse'
Leighton Hall is nominalized as a *venue*, which operates alongside *competing venues* wishing to obtain wedding licences. Also evident is a trace of a

related possible 'mission statement' discourse (arguably a 'sub-discourse' of contemporary promotional discourses): the verb phrase *offer this full service*. This text is not formally an advert, but effectively functions as one, with the glowing representation of Leighton Hall as a wedding venue (and note the telephone number!). Also interpretively identifiable as a 'marketing discourse', this discourse is closely affiliated with that of consumerism. The stereotypical, unselfconscious text draws heavily on consistently positive and superlative adjectives within noun phrases: the *spectacular backdrop*, the *most romantic and idyllic of settings*, *spectacular views* and the bride's *breathtaking entrance*. There is also the personal involvement of the owner of the Hall, Suzie Reynolds. The words attributed to Reynolds (presumably a financial beneficiary of any weddings) are, however, low-key, rather general and even detached, the advertising *effect* coming from the words of the reporter, Gayle Rouncivell. It is not possible to infer exactly how this 'text production' arrangement came about, but this particular distributing of words (which discoursally backgrounds Reynolds' own commercial interests) may have been seen as more persuasive than the other way round.

Also 'advertised' is the 'convenience factor': 'More people are enjoying the convenience of getting married, taking photographs and celebrating their reception at the same venue ...'. This discourse can thus be seen as related to the 'Consumerist discourse' (and, by implication, part of the wider 'Discourse of late modernity', in which time and commodification are key elements; see Chouliaraki and Fairclough, 1999); discourse *as ideology* is apparent here.[2] 'Behind' this discourse it is possible to see almost psalimpsestically a 'Discourse of economic diversification': Leighton Hall is a large country house standing in several acres of parkland, which makes it expensive to maintain (see also below).

(ii) A 'Consumerist discourse'
Related to the 'Promotional discourse', this discourse is suggested not only by possibility of a clearly *expensive* event, but also by the idea of consumer choice, phrasal traces of which permeate the text (see Giddens, 1999, on the 'modernity dilemma' of 'personalised versus commodified experience'). Couples have chosen Leighton Hall for wedding receptions in the past (it is a *popular wedding reception venue*), *where* to get married is reportedly an important issue for many (*somewhere extra special and a bit unusual*), and *brides can choose one of two rooms for their ceremony*. There is also the underlying idea of choice between a religious and a civil wedding ceremony – Leighton Hall being marketed implicitly as a venue for the latter. In the British National Corpus, the word *venue* includes among

its top fifteen collocates *popular, chosen* and *favourite*, which links this lexical trace particularly closely to the idea of 'choice'.

(iii) A 'Discourse of late modernity'

The 'Discourse of late modernity' (a name adapted from Chouliaraki and Fairclough, 1999; see also Giddens, 1999) for me was suggested primarily by the implicit intertextual links with a 'Discourse of economic diversification' (in the UK, often drawn on in the context of struggling organizations, such as farms). I also co-constructed it from the notion of *civil* wedding ceremonies (note the absence of religious references in the text), and the noun phrases representing social actors: *modern couples*, and even *couples* (consider the available – but absent – paradigmatic alternatives, such as *bride and groom, husband and wife-to-be*, or *future husband and wife*).

(b) *Gendered* discourses

The three discourses in this category are interpretively named from a feminist perspective.

(i) A 'Discourse of fantasy'

This discourse is recognizable through several noun phrases: *fairytale dream, dream wedding* and *most romantic and idyllic of settings*, which sit neatly alongside the *Gothic towers*. There are intertextual associations with the women waiting in their towers in *Rapunzel* and *Sleeping Beauty*. Members of the discussion group referred to a 'fairytale discourse' and a 'Hollywood discourse' – the latter not only because of the fantasy element, but also because Leighton Hall is represented almost as a theatre for the wedding (among other things, it has a *backdrop*). Interestingly, absent is any reference to the marriage of which the wedding is the beginning – like fairytales, the wedding here is all-important.

(ii) A 'Biggest/best day of a woman's life discourse'

This idiomatically and ironically named discourse is suggested by the idea of 'dreams coming true' for *North Lancashire brides*, who *make breathtaking entrances down the flying staircase* and choose the room for *their* ceremony. (This *their* could in principle refer to 'the couple', though this requires something of a 'reading against the grain', sandwiched as it is between two occurrence of *bride*.) Interesting here is the lexical absence of *bridegroom* as an independent social actor. He could have been mentioned, since he is entailed in the recurring (thrice mentioned) *couples*, but is not. *Brides* are the subject and agent of *can choose* and *the bride* is the actor in the final subordinate clause of the same sentence: *down which [staircase] the bride can make a breathtaking entrance*. (These are cases of the 'can of possibility' – rather than 'of ability' – which dovetails with the overall consumerist stance of the text.) This *breathtaking entrance* entails being the object of gaze – traditionally, the *male* gaze (in particular, of the bridegroom and her father) and the *envious* female gaze. The groom is subjected to nothing like the same visual evaluation. Interestingly, *bride* in the British National Corpus collocates mainly with content words (*blushing, prospective, dress*), *groom* with functional words. It is also syntagamtically and atypically first in the male/female 'pair' *bride and groom*, and unmarked (like *widow*). *Bride*, with its collocational 'load', can thus be seen as almost functionally reproducing certain discourses (Paul Baker, personal communication).

In this discourse two propositions are evident: (1) marriage (of which the wedding is the symbol) is more important for women than for men (really, the only way to make sense of this text), and (2) marriage is more important for women than anything else. Together, these constitute the implicit traditional representation of a woman as a (future) *wife*, the fairytale wedding the return for a future relatively circumscribed identity. 'Behind' this discourse, then, lies a *patriarchal* discourse. This is not explicit (there is nothing, for example, about the bride's father 'giving her away', or about the best man speaking 'on behalf of the bridesmaids', as is traditional in Anglican church weddings, and these *absences* may even be seen as faint traces of a competing 'Late modernity discourse'). A patriarchal discourse is, however, suggested by intertextually linked *absences*: if the groom is backgrounded in this 'fairytale' text, his important, grounded, 'real life' concerns must be elsewhere.

(iii) 'Compulsory heterosexuality'

Adrienne Rich's 'compulsory heterosexuality' (1980) discourse (see Chapter 3) can be seen in 'Dream Wedding' in that there is no suggestion that couples who might be interested in 'exchanging vows' (with or without legally 'tying the knot') are anything other than heterosexual (*bride* entails *bridegroom*), despite three mentions of *couples*, and despite the fact that religious constraints would not obtain. This also resonates with 'fantasy/fairytale' discourses (again as enthusiastically endorsed by Hollywood), and fairytales are replete, as noted above, with heterosexual weddings, the couple subsequently (we are often informed) unproblematically living happily ever after.

'Why women are just first class'

Let us now look at the discourses and linguistic features of 'Why women are just first class', from the London *Times*. There is an obvious ambiguity in the *just* of this title. It may be intended as an intensifying adverb, or as a modifier (*only just*); alternatively, the ambiguity may be intentional.[3] (And, for a given reader, its meaning may change prior to, while and after reading the article.)

Though some descriptive discourses may be apparent – educational and assessment discourses, for example – this time I look only at interpretive discourses, both *general* and *gendered*.

Interpretive discourses
(a) General
(i) An 'Informational discourse'
At first sight, the article appears to be objectively and straightforwardly informing readers about the facts and details of a particular educational achievement on the part of women undergraduates, as well as of girls at school. There are percentages and other figures, accompanied by a range of verbs and verb phrases in the simple past and present perfect tenses (*were awarded, have recorded, have always secured, started to surpass, gained, have led, comprised, have overtaken*). There is also a series of comparisons of the academic achievements of women and girls with those of men and of boys.

Women and girls (or their pronominal referents) are subjects of the following sentences, and, with the exception of the second example, their *agents* as well:

Women are racing ahead of men ...
Last summer, *12,400 women* were awarded firsts ...
Girls started to surpass boys ... and in 2000 *they* gained more ...
Last year, *they* comprised more than 55% ...
But *they* are closing this gap too ...

Men are the subject (and agent) of the sentence only in

Traditionally, *men* have always secured more firsts ...

And in the clause

the boys' lead ... of 1.04 per cent compares with a lead of 1.28 per cent in 2000.

it is the *lead* which is the subject and agent (the clause in fact occurs after a dash, and follows the 'But they [girls] are closing the gap' clause).

There is, however, disingenuity here, in the guise of factual information. More women were indeed awarded first class degrees – but later in the article we are told that (since more women than men now enter university), more sat their final exams (55 per cent were women). All things being equal, then, we would *expect* more women to receive more of *each* degree class. The statement late in the article that a lower (though decreasing) proportion of women than men still gain firsts rather clouds the triumphalism of the first paragraph.

This syntagmatic arrangement of the text and this 'Informational discourse' dovetail *intratextually* with the following *'Horse race* discourse' in ways which act to shore up familiar 'Gender differences' discourses (see below).

(ii) A *'Horse race* discourse'
This lexical metaphorical type of discourse is realized by the verbs and verb phrases *racing ahead, closing the gap* and *overtaken*, and the adjectival and noun phrases *neck and neck* and *the lead*. (Warrington and Younger, 2000, report a similar news headline about boys being 'lapped by girls'.) As a member of the discussion group pointed out, it is in fact possible to read the whole article as a race: men were in the lead – now women are in the lead, but for the first time – then men again (since 'the proportion of women students who gain firsts is still lower'). Finally, the emphasis is implicitly on the success of girls, though this is not apparently something we should be entirely happy about since male results are 'suffering'. Drama and sensationalism are thus not only the province of tabloid newspapers, and women may be the more 'newsworthy' sex for tabloids and broadsheets alike. In representing the gaining of first class degrees as a *competition*, the 'horse race' metaphor implies a 'Battle of the sexes' discourse. Discoursally, *as a metaphor*, it can be seen to disguise what is a clear deployment of the broad 'Gender differences' discourse (see below; see also Chapter 3; and Fairclough, 2003, on 'lexical metaphor').

(b) Gendered
(i) A 'Battle of the sexes discourse'
Linguistic traces of 'Battle of the sexes' include *years of [women] being outperformed [by men] in university examination halls, completes [women's] dominance, Girls started to surpass boys ...*, and, of course, the *battle* to *secure* the *most first class degrees* of the first sentence (emphasis added). The emphasis here is thus not just on individual competition, but on an essential *social* tension between female and male students (and by implication women and men more broadly). Of the media, Walsh (2001: 22) notes that 'Where women are included as represented subjects, gender stereotypes abound, including those which dichotomize the sexes in

crudely antagonistic terms ...'. I suggest that 'Battle of the sexes' is an extremely recognizable discourse globally, evidenced by different traces and types of traces even within the same language, but also that it is *enjoyed* by many (as are other 'gender differences' discourses; see Chapter 3). 'Battle of the sexes' despite (or perhaps because of) its traces often being allegedly humorous may reflect a patriarchal fear of women 'winning' the battle. Implicit here is the sexist construct that any gains of one group must be at the expense of the other.

(ii) A 'Poor boys discourse'

Evidenced mainly in the penultimate paragraph, the discussion group members all saw 'Poor boys' as salient. Interestingly, the name of this discourse can be used ironically, from a feminist perspective to mean an overstatement or misrepresentation, or 'straight', and is apparent in texts in which boys and men are quickly represented (these days) as the ones in need of pity and understanding. The verbal linguistic traces here are also interesting. 'Teachers [all teachers?] believe that male results are *suffering* because they [boys] are *subjected* to a "laddish culture" which regards academic success as "uncool" ' (emphasis added) – subjected by other male students, or somehow by other males, one supposes.[4] However, because of the classic 'agentless passive', this is not indicated, leaving boys as put-upon victims. If there is a 'laddish culture' in the classroom (connoting messing about, being rude to the teacher, exhibiting sexist behaviour and actively resisting working hard academically), this is likely to disadvantage female students as well. However, this point is saliently absent.

The 'Poor boys discourse' has been identified elsewhere in expressions of teacher sympathy for boys who 'struggled to cope with emancipated women and very successful girls who made them feel inadequate'! (Warrington and Younger, 2000: 506; see also Epstein, 1998; and see Chapter 4). Warrington and Younger see expressions of sympathy as misplaced and/or ignoring the facts that girls still have problems in educational institutions – and indeed after school do not command the higher salaries which might have been predicted by their alleged educational advantages. Dramatic press headlines identified in a range of newspapers have included boys being 'lost', 'in terminal decline' and described as 'the failing sex' (Warrington and Younger, 2000: 494). There are links here with educational texts on both sides of the Atlantic on boys' 'failure' at school. Boys' reading and (now, especially) writing have been a particular object of concern and have prompted a range of remedial programmes, including the 'Dads and Lads' reading programme in Lancashire ('Lancashire Dads

Read with Their Lads'). Other (problematic) programmes have aimed at attracting men as role models to work alongside boys in elementary and high school classrooms (Epstein et al., 1998; Gertzman, 2000; see also Cameron, 2003).

(iii) A 'Gender equality now achieved discourse'
This discourse may be a relatively tenuous one; certainly, the largely American discussion group found it difficult to recognize. 'Gender equality now achieved' can, however, be provisionally seen as a combination of triumphalism, self-congratulation and denial. Traces here may include the *absence* of women being shown as doing worse than men when it comes to getting *proportionately* more first class degrees (that they are doing worse is made clear in the second column) – together with *their representation as if they are doing better*. If women are apparently doing well, there is no problem, no glass ceiling, no one need feel guilty and no one need do anything further, except perhaps reassure themselves that it is in *other* (i.e. less advanced), far-off countries that women and girls suffer discrimination and educational disadvantage.

As indicated in the penultimate paragraph, to drive home the point, it is apparently *boys* who now deserve our concern. 'Gender equality now achieved' thus has close inter- (and intra-)textual links with 'Poor boys'. The problematic but possibly intended inference here is that if only boys are (represented as) having problems educationally, then girls must be doing well.

(iv) A 'Gender differences discourse'
All three gendered discourses discussed above draw on an underlying/ overarching, 'common-sense', dominant 'Gender differences discourse'. This is an 'easy' discourse to represent in media reports, since it dovetails with popular and, I suggest, widely *enjoyed* understandings of gender as *difference* (evidenced by the sales figures of John Gray's *Men are from Mars, Women are from Venus*, and the like). To take 'Battle of the sexes' as an example, not all women did better than all men in their final examinations, but the fact that these are gender *tendencies* is not acknowledged. Though there are some hedged references, we are still told about 'women', 'men', 'boys' and 'girls', for example:

Women are racing ahead
Girls started to surpass
while [*girls*] have overtaken boys ...
The *boys*' lead
male results

We are thus left with a strong impression of bipolarity and of gender as a clear case of a masculine/feminine binary opposition. It could, of course, be argued that in each example the phrase 'as a group' or 'on the whole' is implicit, but while some readers will see it this way, others will not.

* * *

These two newspaper articles illustrate how linguistic evidence of several provisional discourses of different types – *descriptive, interpretive general* and *interpretive gendered* – can frequently be found, and the discourses thus argued for in a given text. Some discourses may be dominant (and widely recognizable), others peripheral or marginal (and less widely recognizable, though suggested by intertextual links or faint linguistic traces). If, on a first reading, a discourse seems apparent, linguistic traces, however faint, should also be evident. In 'Tie the knot at Leighton Hall', for example, we found evidence for a range of discourses in lexical items in noun phrases, particularly those referring to social actors. Conversely, salient linguistic traces may themselves suggest a discourse which in this text they are locally 'realizing'. While remembering that discourses are not simply 'out there' waiting for identification, it is possible provisionally and interpretively to identify discourses by considering both linguistic and wider discoursal relationships within and outside the relevant text, and the language of the text itself.

Relationships between discourses

The analyses of these two newspaper texts illustrate how discourses crucially exist in constellations, networks or 'orders' of related discourses. Some 'members' of a given discourse network will always be produced outside a given text, creating 'intertextual' links. Discourses will thus often be both inter- and intratextually related, some relationships being ones of similarity, others oppositional. As such, discourses may support or oppose each other, and may also 'feed off', 'seep' or 'leak' into each other. And, as we saw in the 'hotel towels' text in Chapter 1, discourses can be actively *appropriated* by writers for their own purposes, raising the alternative possibility of discoursal *colonization*.

A discourse takes meaning from its network(s), and readers/listeners use networks to make sense of the discourses in a text. In these two newspaper articles there were no obvious, actual examples of 'manifest intertextuality', i.e. where words are 'lifted' wholesale from one text and put into another (though this may have happened in the production of

'A dream wedding'). There were, however, several examples of interdiscursivity (Kristeva, 1986). 'Gender equality now achieved', for example, can here be seen as carrying echoes of the 'Poor boys discourse' – the sting in the tail, suggesting that women's and girls' equality has been achieved *at someone else's expense*. At other times two or more discourses may be seen as overlapping (examples here are the Promotional/Consumerist discourses apparent in 'A dream wedding').

As regards oppositional, contradictory discourses within an 'order', on an *intra*textual level, 'A dream wedding' seems largely free of contradictions. The 'Biggest day of a woman's life discourse', traditionally bound up with religious discourses, can be seen as having been smoothly appropriated by discourses of late modernity and consumerism. Yet in terms of *gender relations* there is a contradiction between the notion of *modern couples*, marrying in a civil ceremony, and the 'Biggest day' discourse.

'Why women are just first class' includes at least two contradictions: an underlying tension between women having and not having achieved equality; and whether female or male students tend to be the more disadvantaged in educational contexts. The text is certainly not a straightforward endorsement of women's achievements to date. These sorts of contradictions may be characteristic of 'hybrid' media texts which 'function to expose sexism, yet often reproduce it in covert forms' (Walsh, 2001: 22). This text is ostensibly celebrating an end to sexism in one particular sphere, but is at the same time reproducing it covertly, through its linguistic traces of the 'Battle of the sexes', 'Poor boys' and underlying 'Gender differences' discourses (see Chapters 3, 8 and 9 on contradictions and change; see also Cameron, 2003).

Discourse naming

Although readers and speakers are always *interpreters* of texts and discourses, most have no interest in explicitly identifying and naming discourses. However, anyone *can* name a discourse. As Chouliaraki and Fairclough note, 'there is no "closed" list of ... discourses, and there are relatively few that have stable names for analysts or for participants' (1999: 56). There can, therefore, never be a 'typology' (or *Dictionary of Discourses*) – perhaps other than an electronic three-dimensional 'virtual reality' one, which indicates relationships and is in a constant state of flux.

Naming of discourses can be done conceptually and formally. Conceptually, here I use the distinction between 'descriptive' discourses (e.g. classroom discourse) and 'interpretive discourses' (e.g. a 'Poor boys discourse') – the subject of this book. Within a context- or domain-related understanding of discourse, *descriptive* discourses often take descriptive names such as *classroom discourse, courtroom discourse, legal discourse, architectural discourse, informational discourse,* or *public* and *private* discourse. For interpretive discourses, the names which the analyst from a particular standpoint provides are also interpretive (e.g. a 'Sexist' discourse). Some interpretive names refer not to substance, but to how one discourse relates to others (*mainstream, competing, mutually supporting, dominant*), or, importantly, to what it is seen to *do* (*a repressive discourse, a liberating discourse*). And such names may combine, so that we might have, for example, a 'Competing discourse of masculinity'.

Discourse identification and naming of discourses from an interpretive, critical perspective are thus not neutral activities, but rather say something about the 'namer' as well as the discourses. To some, a pornographic written text or visual image might represent a 'Discourse of misogyny'; to others (including some women), a 'Discourse of liberation' (connoting, for example, freedom from censorship and repression). It is thus important for the (feminist) discourse analyst to recognize and acknowledge these and to retain a measure of explicitness and reflexivity about her own analytical and naming practices – explicitness in her documentation (e.g. that she is adopting a feminist perspective) and reflexivity in terms of her willingness to consider the name, what it entails and what would be the grounds for reconsidering it (see below). Ideally, identified, named discourses should be offered up for scrutiny by a group of informed others (those whose area of work is not gender and language as well as those in the field) to ensure the analysis is not solely the product of the analyst's particular interpretive proclivities.

The exercise with the two newspaper texts also suggests different *formal* ways of discourse naming. One pattern is 'adjective + *discourse*'. This is applicable to descriptive discourses, such as *courtroom discourse*: these are both discourses and discourse *names* that most readers would probably accept. However, the 'adjective + *discourse*' pattern can, I suggest, also be used for 'interpretive' discourses – a 'Feminist' discourse and a 'Maternal' discourse, for example. It can further be used to indicate relationships between discourses (a 'subordinate discourse'), and what a discourse may *functionally* achieve (a 'liberating discourse').[5]

I have used two other ways of formally naming interpretive gendered discourses. The first is the 'a Discourse of + abstract noun' pattern ('a Discourse of late modernity', 'a Discourse of fantasy'), which could equally well be referred to as a 'late modernity discourse' and a 'Fantasy discourse'. Here, *substance* is important. Writers who wish to describe discourses in relation to others tend not to use 'Discourse of', probably because, say, a 'Discourse of opposition' suggests a particular, unintended *content* (an 'oppositional discourse' may not be a 'Discourse of opposition').

The second formal way is by using a *specially created* adjectival phrase preceding *discourse*: the 'Biggest day in a woman's life discourse', the 'Battle of the sexes discourse'. These names are less easily 'reversible', though partly for stylistic reasons ('Discourse of the battle of the sexes?').[6] The scare quotes, used here for all interpretive discourses, additionally remind us that the phrase is being used in a special, perhaps ironic, perhaps stylistically odd and/or clumsy way. These 'analyst's names' may not be self-explanatory or even recognizable – although the *discourse* to which each refers should be. These are the *most* specific and interpretively named discourses (and see Fairclough, 2003, on 'levels of abstraction' in talking about discourses). Discourse names such as these require a particular degree of reflexivity and explanation on the part of the analyst.

Existing named discourses

In Chapter 3, I review in some detail a selection of gendered discourses which have been explored to date. I will conclude this chapter by listing some of the many gendered discourses which were included and thus named in the index of *Gender Identity and Discourse Analysis* (Litosseliti and Sunderland, 2002). Each of these was mentioned once or more, by one or more contributors to the book. Contributors developed their own discourse names *and* cited those 'coined' by others.[7]

The descriptive discourses, which in the main text of the book formally took the pattern of adjective + *discourse*, included:

| classroom |
| cultural |
| official |
| teenage |

The interpretive gendered discourses of substance, which formally took the patterns of 'adjective + *discourse*', or 'a *discourse* of + abstract noun' (for most discourses these are alternatives), included:

birth
childhood
conservative gender relations
corporeality
femininity
fertility control as beneficial
gender-blindness
identity
lost identity
masculinity
maternal
parental identity
patriarchal
resistance
sexuality
subversion
teenage femininity

The interpretive *relational* discourses, which formally took the pattern of 'adjective + *discourse*' included:

alternative
coexisting
companion
competing
dominant
mutually supporting
oppositional

The interpretive *functional* discourses, the first of which also formally took the 'adjective + discourse' pattern, the second two 'a *discourse* of + abstract noun' pattern, included:

liberating
resistance
subversion

The gendered interpretive 'Specific discourses', which took the form of 'X discourse', included:

'compulsory heterosexuality' discourse
'equal opportunities' discourse
'father as baby entertainer' discourse
'father as line manager' discourse
'father as mother's bumbling assistant' discourse
'father's full investment in childcare as *desirable*' discourse
'God's will' discourse
'have and hold' discourse
'male sexual drive' discourse
'mother as main parent' discourse
'new mother who also works outside the home' discourse
'nurturing' discourse
'part-time father' discourse
'permissive' discourse
'privileged femininity' discourse
'privileging of appearance – in women' discourse
'pro-natality' discourse
'women beware women' discourse

Many of these will be referred to in this book.

In Chapter 3, the gendered discourses I look at include some famous ones, including those proposed by Adrienne Rich and Wendy Hollway, which are frequently cited, and some less famous but telling ones. This will provide a background to Part II and its chapters on gendered discourses relevant to the classroom (Chapter 4), fatherhood in 'parenting' magazines (Chapter 5), media reports of celebrity fatherhood (Chapter 6) and award-winning children's books (Chapter 7). Readers are also encouraged to study their own gendered texts (which are not hard to find) and to identify provisionally and broadly name the discourses they recognize in them, considering inter- and intratextuality, and 'traces' of these discourses in the form of relevant linguistic features (absent as well as present). They may then wish to show the texts and their discourses to friends (linguistically inclined, and otherwise) to see just *how* recognizable their identified discourses are.

3
Some Gendered Discourses Identified to Date

Though relatively few are documented, gendered discourses abound. As an example, I offer a motherhood discourse which we might call 'Good mums stay at home with their children'. While I am not aware of this discourse being named *as such*, it is a familiar discourse frequently voiced in relation to family and professional life. It is exemplified in an 'essay' in the *Sunday Sun* of 21 May 2000, in which the writer expresses the opinion, in no uncertain terms, that Cherie Booth, wife of British Prime Minister Tony Blair, should stay at home with new baby Leo (i.e. not continue to work as a barrister). Entitled, 'Cherie, try some Leo-natal care', the 'essay' concludes 'What the soap [i.e. Downing Street life as a soap opera] needs now is a slice of real life ... a new mum who puts her career on ice for a while and gives baby her all.' (For more on Leo Blair, but in relation to his father, see Chapter 6.) It is possible to see this discourse as maintaining a wider, *conservative*, discourse of motherhood.

In this chapter I present a *selection* of documented gendered discourses, which have been provisionally identified and expounded on within different disciplines. Some have achieved canonical or near-canonical status in that they are often drawn on in discussion of new empirical data. Several have critical (and sometimes ironic) names. These have been selected from work on named gendered discourses *per se*, and because together they represent a considerable range and diversity of contributions to gender and discourse study.

I do not fully critique these papers. The main purpose of this chapter is to describe some important, interesting and influential identified gendered discourses, including what they (potentially or actually) *do*. A second purpose is to consider the methodology and analytical approaches used to identify these discourses, including where (i.e. in which epistemological sites) these have been found, and naming considerations. Data come from written and spoken texts, the latter including both solicited and naturally occurring talk. The majority of the studies I report in this chapter are, however, not primarily linguistic in focus – the role of close linguistic analysis varies in part with discipline – but, arguably, could have been enhanced by a linguistic dimension. Where appropriate, I make suggestions as to how this could be done.

I start with the overarching 'Gender differences discourse', and then move on to discourses concerning sexuality, women's health (the menopause) and employment, and discourses produced by some very young women.

The 'Gender differences discourse'

This dominant discourse underpins (or overarches) much of the discourse circulating (to my knowledge) *globally* both today and in the recent and distant past. It is a significant 'lens' for the way people view reality, *difference* being for most people what gender is all about. Once its 'common-sense' status has been contested, 'Gender differences' can be *seen* as such. (Arguably, any discourse on gender is premised on difference *in some sense*.)

'Gender differences' is probably the most frequently invoked 'popular' gendered discourse: as Cameron observes in relation to a particular stretch of a transcript of men's talk, 'the behaviour of men and women, whatever its substance, may happen to be in any specific instance, is invariably read through a more general discourse on gender difference itself' (1997a: 48). This discourse also seems to be enjoyed, reassuring and indeed important to many people's sense of self (Cameron, 1996). Whole book-length textual traces of 'Gender differences' include Tannen's *You Just Don't Understand!: Women and Men in Conversation*, Gray's *Men Are From Mars, Women Are From Venus* and, most recently, a series by Pease and Pease starting with *Why Men Don't Listen and Women Can't Read Maps*. 'Differences' may be celebrated or derided, but in this discourse 'gender' is given *de facto* explanatory status. However, I suggest that this 'gender lens' is employed particularly where *women* are concerned: How often is football hooliganism seen as an issue of masculinity? Circulating with 'Gender differences' is therefore what we might call a 'Male as norm' or 'Think male' discourse, a trace of which is gender-blindness.

We have already seen the 'Gender differences' discourse in Chapter 2 in *The Times* article on examination results, where linguistic traces included 'Girls started to surpass boys at GCSE level ...'. Predicated on the *existence* of magazines for women and girls, traces of 'Gender differences' also include those features in women's and girls' magazines which are based on an assumption that women and men are so different that we cannot understand each other – at least not without the help of the magazine. Such features claim to enlighten the female reader about the mystery of what her boyfriend/male partner/husband *really* wants, thinks or means by what he says or does. From *Cosmopolitan* of May 2003:

> His Baffling Dialling Code Behaviour Explained – Cosmo listens in on men's all-too-confusing telephone behaviour.

> Sexposé: What His Favourite Position Really Says About Him: How his in-bed cravings can be a clue to his dating style.

> What Men Really Think… about masturbation.

And from the British 'girls' mag' *Sugar* of the same month:

> Boywatching: We find out what makes sexy surfer sorts say 'I love you'. Does he charm or smarm? Suss out your crush.

Such features appear at times in men's magazines too, though from different angles. I call this member of the 'Gender differences' order of discourse 'Mutual incomprehension of the sexes'. It may be argued that no one takes this sort of thing seriously (though empirical studies of *consumption* are needed to assess this properly). However, this discourse still maintains essentialist thinking – that women just *are* like this, men just *are* like that[1] – in a more general sense. The connection between 'Gender differences' and heterosexuality seems evident, and 'Gender differences' has been seen as *produced* by dominant heterosexuality discourses (Rich, 1980; Hollway, 1984, 1995; Davies, 1989b; Butler, 1999: 'Preface'; and see below), although it is unclear how this plays out cross-culturally. However, many *new, lower-order* 'Gender differences' discourses can be seen as helping to maintain essentialist thinking: for example, Cameron writes that the current discourse on women as good communicators and men as deficient ones does 'the usual ideological work of affirming the existence of fundamental differences between women and men' (2003: 461; see also Cameron, 1997a).

Other 'lower-order' 'Gender differences' discourses range from what we might call *Vive la différence!* to explicitly sexist legal discourses enshrining women's rights as radically circumscribed relative to those of men. More subtle sexist discourses include those documented by West et al. (1997: 125) in advertisements in Singaporean newspapers promoting marriage between well-educated Asians which, addressing women, proclaim: 'It's wonderful to have a career and financial independence. But is your self-sufficiency giving men a hard time?' (see also Lazar, 2002).

The 'Gender differences' discourse itself can be considered as *implicitly* sexist, not only in terms of making unnecessary category distinctions but also, more seriously, in the sense of working against women's interests. Politically, the one-time feminist slogan 'Different and equal' or 'Different but equal' was viewed with scepticism by many other feminists. Academically, 'Gender differences' has been characterized as a 'Hierarchical female/male duality' (Peterson, 2002: 252; see also Gatens, 1990; Lloyd, 1990),[2] and the feminist understanding of *patriarchy* has been important here (see Stacey, 1993). However, 'Gender differences' has also been a *critical* discourse. Feminist '(male) dominance' language and gender theorists of the 1970s and early 1980s (Zimmerman and West, 1975; Edelsky, 1977; Fishman, 1983) may have been producing a discourse which suggested (to many) that gender differences existed as a result of discoursal and other socialization – but this was with a view to exposing, documenting and deriding any differences found in mixed-sex talk, in order to promote progressive change for women and girls. Less critical was the discourse of feminist '(cultural) difference' language and gender theorists of the 1980s and early 1990s (exemplified in different ways by Tannen, 1990 and Holmes, 1995), who variously saw the 'dominance' studies as representing women as powerless victims and wished to *celebrate* differences. *Both* groups of theorists, however, looked at 'sexed individuals' and, regardless of their intentions and real value of their findings, were lending credibility and indeed ammunition to a conservatism and sexism underpinned by the assumption that women and men *just are* different (Cameron, 1992).[3]

For some people, of course, 'Gender differences' is not an ideological cover-up, but simple 'common sense'. This view points to the strength of the discourse as a *particularly* recognizable 'way of seeing the world', its popularity resulting in continuing discoursal recycling and recontextualization, production and reproduction (Cameron, 1996). To the extent that it in one way or another it seems to be virtually 'part of the system', universally, 'Gender differences' seems almost reified. The apparent 'common-sense' quality of 'Gender differences' is presumably one reason for the citing of evident biological differences in its defence *outside* the academy. Cameron (1997b: 32) refers to the 'translation' model of gender (i.e. that gender is relatively straightforwardly translated from sex, and 'anatomy is destiny'). However, how *important* biological differences are (i.e. are made to be = *gender*), is socially constructed. The *significance* of biological sex, for example, as Davies (1989a: 135) observes, 'has been extended far beyond the reproductive function'. Without denying dimorphism, we can ask *which* biological differences are *treated* as meaningful and important. Eye colour, for example, is biologically determined, but has been largely irrelevant socially (Cameron, 1997b, cites the additional example of blood group). At certain times and in certain places, 'race' (with biological skin colour a salient feature) is important, but biological sex much less so. And consider the *variability* of the importance attached to having a particular set of genitalia. When women are required to fight in wars, this becomes less salient than in peacetime practices. And though biological sex may be more important for children attending multicultural schools than skin colour in whom they associate with, when children play together *outside* school, gender often loses its salience (Thorne, 1993).

Adrienne Rich's 'Compulsory heterosexuality discourse'

Adrienne Rich is not a linguist and has never used the word 'discourse' to describe 'Compulsory heterosexuality'. Her article 'Compulsory Heterosexuality and Lesbian Existence', which appeared in *Signs* in 1980, is largely theoretical and few explicit lexical traces of 'Compulsory sexuality' are suggested (though see below). Yet this is probably the most famous *critical* gendered discourse, referred to frequently in the literature, and *dominant* outside academia.

Given that 'women are the earliest sources of emotional caring and physical nurture for both female and male children', Rich writes, it is logical to ask '*why in fact women would ever redirect that search*', and concludes that heterosexuality thus 'needs to be recognized and studied as a *political institution*' (1980: 637, emphasis in original). She cites Gough's (1975) 'characteristics of male power' which 'enforce' heterosexuality. Those which add to 'the cluster or forces within which women have been convinced that marriage, and sexual orientation toward men, are inevitable, even if unsatisfying or oppressive components of their lives' are:

> The chastity belt; child marriage; erasure of lesbian existence (except as exotic and perverse) in art, literature and film; idealization of heterosexual romance and marriage – these are some fairly obvious forms of compulsion, the first two exemplifying physical force, the second two control of consciousness. (Rich, 1980: 640)

Rich also critiques four books 'all presenting themselves, and favorably reviewed, as feminist' (1980: 632): *The Reproduction of Mothering* (Nancy

Chodorow), *The Mermaid and the Minotaur: Sexual Arrangements and the Human Malaise* (Dorothy Dinnerstein), *For Her Own Good: 150 Years of the Experts' Advice to Women* (Barbara Ehrenreich and Deirdre English) and *Towards a New Psychology of Women* (Jean Baker Miller). In none of these, Rich writes, 'is the question ever raised, whether in a different context, or other things being equal, women would choose heterosexual coupling and marriage', and in none 'is compulsory heterosexuality ever examined as an institution powerfully affecting [mothering, sex roles, relationships, and societal prescriptions for women]' (1980: 633). Here, Rich is in effect providing empirical support for 'Compulsory heterosexuality' by pinpointing these discoursal (interrogative) absences, in precisely those texts where this question might reasonably be expected to be asked.

It is not easy to miss linguistic traces of 'Compulsory heterosexuality', perhaps especially in media discourse. Consider, for example, the claim in a British tabloid newspaper article on gender relations that 'The mature woman feels free to fantasize about men of any age group' (*Daily Express*, 21 April 2000) and note the unifying definite article before *mature woman*. A second (reconstructed) example is the words of a male contestant on *Blind Date* (that British primetime TV icon of heterosexuality), who informed Cilla Black, the presenter, that 'I attended an all-boys school, which was next to an all-girls' school, and we all whistled at the girls, *of course*' (emphasis added). Needless to say, this was not contested. And 'Compulsory heterosexuality' dominates 'lifestyle magazines' for women, young and old – though not in a problematizing way. Feature titles, from *Cosmopolitan*, include:

Want to date him again?

'Wow! You're Amazing in Bed': why keeping your eyes open during sex will have him begging for more

New Man is Dead (And *Cosmo* Helped Kill Him) – Why fun, fearless females prefer a 'Strong Man' to a 'New Man'

The *Cosmo* world appears to be overwhelmingly heterosexual.

'Compulsory heterosexuality' enables heterosexuality to be normative and thus in effect socially prescriptive. It means that whereas, say, opposite-sex affection in public may be unremarkable, same-sex affection normally entails risks. Discoursally, it means that many people, on hearing a woman refer for the first time to a partner, will soon ask about *his* job. For the gay female professor or teacher (unlike her straight colleague), referring to her social life or domestic situation in class will almost always be potentially transgressive (Nelson, 1999; Morrish, 2002).

As indicated, 'Compulsory heterosexuality', together with its associated social practices, can be seen as spawning the 'Gender differences' discourse. (This is implicit in Rich's discussion.) Wendy Hollway (1984) sees heterosexual relations as the *primary site* for the reproduction of gender difference and indeed for hierarchization here. For Hollway, the biological difference on which heterosexual relations are based

> *overdetermines* individuals' positionings, both historically and in present interaction. Couple or sexual relations add the extra dimension of 'desire for the Other' ... which I believe makes salient the power relations. (1984: 260; emphasis added)

Using herself as an example, she writes:

> Ever since I had grown up I had been in a couple relationship with a man, and however well I succeeded in doing things, they were always there – men who knew more than me, men whom I could learn from – to guarantee my femininity. (1984: 230)

I look more closely at Hollway's influential own work on the discourses of heterosexuality (1984, 1995) in the following sections.

Wendy Hollway's 'Heterosexuality' discourses

(1) Gender-differential subject positions

Working on heterosexual relations from a psychological perspective, Hollway was interested in theorizing 'the practices and meanings which re-produce gendered subjectivity (what psychologists would call gender identity)' (1984: 227). *Re-production* (with a hyphen) indicates the possibility of change, not just maintenance (reproducing the same thing). Hollway draws in part on post-structuralist theory, on its recognition of the self as non-unitary and its constitution as ongoing, and on the constitutive importance it affords to discourse, including discoursal positioning and self-positioning ('Speaking as a parent ...', 'I'm not a feminist, but ...').

Hollway sees heterosexuality as constructed by the way in which

> at a specific moment several coexisting and potentially contradictory discourses concerning sexuality make available *different positions and different powers for men and women*. (1984: 230, 236; emphasis added)

Hollway was thus acknowledging (critically) the 'Gender differences discourse', its workings and its inherent hierarchy. Though the differentially gendered discourses she identifies can be seen as part of what we might see as the 'Gender differences' *order* of discourse, Hollway was simultaneously *challenging* the 'male–female dualism' inherent in 'Gender differences' by emphasizing the instability of all discourses, the contradictions in those identified here, and the momentariness of any positioning.

Hollway's methodology was interviews, i.e. her data were transcripts of solicited rather than naturally occurring talk. The interviews were with heterosexual women and men on the topic of sexuality. Hollway identified three 'discourses of heterosexuality' (though claims, probably rightly, that it would be relatively easy to identify others). One was a 'Permissive' discourse, i.e. the validity of sexual activity outside monogamous marriage. In her data this discourse did not create different subject positions for women and men. (In the decades prior to the women's liberation movement and the advent of the contraceptive pill she would however probably have found a 'Transgressive' discourse for women, and at other times and in other places for men too.)

The other two heterosexuality discourses, in contrast, positioned women and men very differently. These were the 'Male sexual drive' and 'Have/hold' discourses. 'Male sexual drive' is explicitly about men and implicitly about women. It is evident in the offering and sometime acceptance of excuses for rape ('She led me on'; 'No means yes') and the concept of the sexual 'point of no return' (for men, which women should know about, and have the responsibility to obviate; see also Rich, 1980). It can also be seen in the need felt by some men continually to 'enact' their heterosexuality, in part by discoursally differentiating themselves from women and, particularly, from gay men (Cameron, 1997a). 'Male sexual drive' can be seen as having links with a wider 'Boys will be boys' discourse, in which there is greater tolerance for boys' transgressions than for those of girls, for example, in the classroom, as shown by the findings of such educational researchers as Sadker and Sadker (1985) and Epstein et al. (1998). Hollway writes that 'Male sexual drive' is entertained as 'common sense', including by many psychologists and sociobiologists. Such an understanding must be anti-woman – and hence potentially damaging (see Chapter 9) – since, in the absence of competing discourses, it releases men from *controlling* and *taking responsibility for* whatever drives they may experience.

Hollway comments on the evident 'gender-differentiated positions' of the 'Have/hold' discourse, i.e. that women are the 'object' of the 'having and holding', men the 'subject'. 'Have/hold' has as its focus 'the Christian ideals associated with monogamy, partnership and family life' (1984: 232). For men, this may appear to conflict with 'Male sexual drive'. Hollway suggests that the contradiction is, however, 'resolved' when men visit it upon women: 'Either women are divided into two types [wife/mistress, virgin/whore, Mary/Eve], or more recently a woman is expected to be both those things' (1984: 232). For teenage girls, the former manifests itself in the 'slags or drags' dilemma (Cowie and Lees, 1981). For women, Hollway indicates that *Have/hold* entails either their having a dangerous sexuality (producing irrational male jealousy, so that this sexuality must be controlled through subservience), or a lacking sexuality (to be compensated for by the joys of family life).

Analytically, Hollway arrived at these three discourses 'through a combination of my own knowledge and what was suggested by the data' (1984: 231), identifying this approach as 'grounded theory' (Glaser and Strauss, 1967), and adding that 'Clearly my own assumptions and those of [my] research participants share a common historical production; they will also be recognizable to most readers.' Use of one's own social and political knowledge is standard for qualitative critical analysis, of course, but 'what was suggested by the data' is from a linguistic perspective vague, and we would expect to read linguistic 'traces' of each discourse in the interview transcripts. Hollway's concern is *not* linguistic traces; indeed, she is more concerned with 'the use I make of these three [discourses] in my analysis of the effects of gender difference in positioning subjects' (1984: 231) than with providing empirical support for the discourses themselves. However, linguistic traces could, I suggest, be sought and found. Here I cite the example of 'Will' whose talk Hollway uses to exemplify 'Male sexual drive':

> in adolescence I felt that there was a very impersonal sexuality .... It was my need – as it were – that did it to me .... And that's what I mean by feeling quite enslaved to an abstract impersonal sexuality. (1984: 233)

Note the repetition of 'impersonal sexuality', the paradigmatic choice of the verb phrase *enslaved*, and in particular the verb phrase 'my need – as it were – *that did it to me*' (emphasis added). Will is showing considerable, perhaps critical, awareness of his adolescent psychosexual processes, and is not claiming licence to carry out whatever sexual practices that might occur to him. Nevertheless, he is positioning himself retrospectively as *not* the agent of his own adolescent sexuality; the agents are 'my need' and an 'impersonal sexuality'. Similar critical text analysis could be carried out on the rest of Hollway's interview data.

What is the wider significance of this analysis of this fragment? What more can be inferred? Materially, 'Male sexual drive' may play an important *legitimating* role, constitutive perhaps of Will's understandings if not his behaviour. Theoretically, however, this raises issues of Will's *agency* and of the *status* of discourse. Is Will's adolescent sexual drive solely discursively constituted? What about the *extra-discursive* considerations of adolescent hormones, Will's likely capacity to impregnate large numbers of women in the context of the evolutionary adaptation of reproductive arrangements in the human species, and so on? In part, answers depend on the theoretical approach adopted (see Chapter 9).

For certain 'Western' contexts, multiple traces of a rather different 'Have/hold' discourse are evident in many magazines for women and adolescent girls, in which how to 'get' your man and then 'keep' him ('he chased me until I caught him') are directly or indirectly, from one angle after another, the topic of the text. In the May 2003 issue of *Cosmopolitan*, for example, we read about 'Flirt-With-Me-Fashion'. Here, at least in one sense, men are the 'object' of the 'having and holding', women the 'subject'. This version of 'Have/hold' overlaps with 'Compulsory heterosexuality' (and might be seen as in part a 'subordinate' or 'lower-order' discourse here), but *also* constitutes what we might call an 'Incomplete woman' discourse (i.e. until she meets a Mr Right).

(2) Women's heterosexual desire

In a later, 1995 study, Hollway looked at discourses of women's (lack of) heterosexual desire. Her concern was to theorize sex as signification, in a way that contested the given 'contours' of 'male dominance through heterosexuality'. Hollway's 1995 paper starts:

> There is no emancipatory discourse concerning women's hetero-sexual desire; that is, there is no currently available way of conceptualising women's pleasure and sexual desire (active sexual wants) in heterosexual sex which is regarded as consistent with principles of women's liberation. (1995: 86)

In support of this, Hollway cites Foucault's (1978) four nineteenth-century discourses of sex. Three of these – *the masturbating child, the homosexual* and *the hysterical woman* – she sees as regulative. The fourth, *the reproductive heterosexual couple*, Hollway claims left adult heterosexuality as 'a hallowed space, protected from public intervention, in the name of a man's right to rule in his own domain' (1995: 91). Adult heterosexuality was thus not talked about. In less patriarchal times, social traces of this discourse can still be seen in the relative recency of the acknowledgement of non-consensual marital sex as rape, i.e. a crime worthy of investigation and prosecution. (In some countries it is still not a crime, and even where it is, there may be little point women reporting it.) Similar observations can be made about domestic violence.

Hollway writes that the second wave of the Women's Movement brought about a range of 'discourses of unpleasurable heterosex', with American and British feminism concentrating on 'the oppressiveness of male sexuality as manifest in rape, pornography, prostitution and sexual harassment' (1995: 87). Feminist discourse likewise sees love as 'captured by the discourse of [heterosexual] romance', for which any claims of love simply mask domination (1995: 98). Here Hollway cites Rich's 'Compulsory heterosexuality discourse', and Sheila Jeffreys' (1990) concept of *heteropatriarchy*, as 'amplifying' 'the dominance of heterosexuality in reproducing women's inequality' (1985: 90). She also identifies as contributory the concept of 'sleeping with the enemy', and ideas and slogans (prevalent in the 1970s) such as 'Anyone can be a lesbian.' To these we can add the 1970s' slogan 'Feminism is the theory, lesbianism is the practice' and the ideas (challenged by some feminists, but held by others) that lesbians were the vanguard of the second wave of the Women's Movement, and that penetrative heterosexual sex was, in effect, rape. Susan Brownmiller wrote in *Against Our Will* (1975: 15) that rape 'is nothing more or less than a conscious process of intimidation by which *all men* keep *all women* in a state of fear' (her emphasis) – a claim of considerable symbolic importance, but, I suggest, an essentialist overstatement as regards lived day-to-day experience.

Hollway's analysis is complex and discourse analysis (in a 'close linguistic' sense) plays only a relatively small part. However, analysis of her interview data led her to find *no* evidence of an emancipatory discourse of heterosexual sex. She writes that two *political* effects of this absence may be

> the distancing of many heterosexual women from feminism, and the colonization of issues concerning heterosexuality by the right wing without much of a struggle, because the feminist agenda has recently been unable to incorporate any positive emancipatory discourses about heterosexual relating. (1995: 101)

It is interesting to speculate whether Hollway's pessimism is justified in 2004 and whether there is (still) no emancipatory discourse of women's heterosexuality. Is that not what the successful TV series *Sex and the*

City is largely about, for example? (Though we should balance this against the distinctly non-emancipatory discourses of heterosexuality in the equally successful *Bridget Jones* productions.) And was there really no modern emancipatory discourse of women's heterosexuality when, and before, Hollway was writing? The 'permissive sixties', for example, was surely not *only* seen as creating problems for those women involved (I am not denying that there were such problems), or experienced as positive only by heterosexual men? I think we have to assume that what Hollway regrets is the lack of an emancipatory discourse of heterosexuality, which is *explicitly* informed by feminism.

In a discussion of the *extra-discursive* (see also Chapter 9), Hollway claims that an *absent* discourse does not mean that what there is no discourse around does not have meaning. 'Emancipatory heterosexual practice is [thus] possible, even though an emancipatory discourse of heterosexual sex does not exist' (1995: 100). It is made possible, for Hollway, by *contradictions* between discourses, individual histories and meanings. These contradictions achieve significance through the unconscious, and/or extra-discursive positive heterosexual practice (1995: 100) – though this is, of course, to see sex as non-discursive. If positive heterosexual experiences, carefully considered and intuitively endorsed, do not correspond to 'discourses of unpleasurable heterosex' for feminists (as indeed they do not for Hollway), they may be *experienced* as emancipatory from a feminist perspective and may contribute to the production of new, positive heterosexuality discourses.

Margaret Wetherell, Hilda Stiven and Jonathan Potter's 'Discourses concerning gender and employment opportunities'

The gendered discourses reported in Wetherell et al. (1987) made this paper an important and frequently cited forerunner in the field for both psychology and discourse analysis. Wetherell et al. were writing from a social psychological discursive perspective, which looks not at fixed or 'inner' characteristics and traits, but rather at 'the systems of making sense available in … society' (1987: 59). These 'systems' the authors describe as 'collectively shared practical ideologies', where ideology refers to 'systems of belief or thought which maintain asymmetrical power relations and inequalities between social groups' (1987: 60). Both 'systems of making sense available in a society' and 'collectively shared practical ideologies' correspond broadly to the way 'a discourse' is used in this book – except that Wetherell et al.'s 'systems' are negative, non-emancipatory ones.[4]

Like Hollway, Wetherell et al. took their data from interviews. One of the interview topics was equal opportunities and constraints on these.[5] The interviewees were British female and male undergraduates. Like Rich and Hollway, Wetherell et al. did not carry out *close* linguistic analysis of the transcripts and were quite explicit about this:

> The particular analysis presented in this paper ... is not concerned with the fine-grain examination of discourse, with describing and comparing, for instance, the rhetorical devices, metaphors or tropes developed in the construction of each version of events. (1987: 60)

Rather, they identified 'the broad *types* of versions [of events] accessible to our respondents, the themes and theories they use to structure and formulate a world view for these interview topics ...' (1987: 60).

Wetherell et al. identified various 'dominant themes' in the students' discourse. Two particular 'themes' they called 'equal opportunities' and the limiting 'practical considerations' (1987: 62). These could, I contend, be referred to also as *discourses*. 'Equal opportunities' and 'practical considerations' both co-occurred in the talk of *most* of the students: as the authors write, 'Egalitarian discourse does not magically wipe out non-egalitarian discourse' (1987: 66). The ideological contradictions were, however, rarely noted by the students.

Like Hollway, Wetherell et al. place a good deal of stress on such contradictions. Here, they say, contradictions may enable the 'force and continuation' of these discourses of employment and gender because 'the commonplace adoption of practical considerations talk serves to naturalize and justify inequality' (1987: 69). More generally, Wetherell et al. see contradictions as *essential* to the maintenance of an ideology. This contrasts with Hollway's view of contradictions in (heterosexuality) discourses as *emancipatory* (see also Chapter 9).

My final point about this important paper is methodological. Interviews, which produce elicited rather than non-naturally occurring spoken data, of co-constructed talk, may be seen as not the best 'sites' to identify discourses. However, being broadly *focused*, interviews can be used to collect data on particular 'key' discoursal fields (such as equal opportunities). Interviews also have advantages over questionnaires here. (This is the reason for focus groups.) Wetherell et al. point out that since discourse analysis can deal with extensive bodies of material from the same participant, lengthy and detailed interview transcripts enable the description of contradictions. In contrast, 'the inconsistencies and flexible moment-to-moment adoption of different themes would tend

to be edited out or obscured in traditional survey or attitude question-
naire methods' (1987: 69).

Justine Coupland and Angie Williams' discourses of the menopause

Coupland and Williams (2002) identified gendered discourses in three
written genres: pharmaceutical brochures, popular media texts and 'articles and popular books representing emancipatory feminism', mostly
from 1995–97. Their focus was contemporary 'Western' discourses on the
menopause. Menopause is an interesting site for gender and language
study given the importance in Western cultures attached to youth and
sexuality, the prominence of the fashion and cosmetic industry, which
target women at the younger end of the market, and the traditional association between attraction and sex, and sex and reproduction/
reproductive ability. Analytically, Coupland and Williams 'take[] a critical
discourse analytic approach' to their texts, 'draw on social constructionist
theory to reveal how these texts formulate entrenched and emergent ideological discourses about the menopause and its potential sociocultural
meanings' and describe 'the discursive and semiotic means by which
menopause emerges as a heavily politicized lifespan identity construct'
(2002: 420). They do not, however, carry out close linguistic analysis.

Coupland and Williams identify three discourses, which interdiscursively are closely related. The first, evident in the pharmaceutical
brochures, is a predictable 'pharmaceutical' discourse. This represents the
menopause in pathological terms, with frequent reference to hormone
replacement therapy (HRT) as a corrective. There are several discursive
and semiotic 'strategies' here, including presenting interpretations of the
menopause as uncontentious facts, leaving authorship ambiguous (independent doctors? pharmaceutical companies?), constructing menopause
as a 'problem' with (pharmaceutical) 'solutions' and use of metaphors of
'deficiency, loss and breakdown'. On the topic of hot flushes: 'It's as if
your body's thermostat control has developed an intermittent fault.
Don't worry, normal service will eventually be resumed for most
women ...' (2002: 425). Coupland and Williams also cite 'argumentative
strategies', i.e. the implicit contestation of non-pharmaceutical
solutions: 'There is no "natural" substitute for HRT because no other
treatment replaces the oestrogen your body is lacking. Any claims made
for a non-prescription treatment acting like HRT should be viewed
with caution ...'. Such rhetorical traces constitute textual evidence for the
existence of competing discourses.

The second discourse is 'alternative therapy', evident in magazines, newspaper articles and high-profile books. This represents menopause as a problem (and ageing as degenerative), but not an illness or disease, and the emphasis is on individual action, principle and 'taking control' independently of medical intervention. There is, however, explicit rejection of pharmaceutical or medical models of the menopause; there are thus contesting discourses here too, but 'alternative' ones.

The third is an 'emancipatory feminist' discourse which 'works to empower through more fundamental [i.e. more fundamental than the other two discourses] ideological transformations' (2002: 442). It is the only menopause discourse which tries to define female midlife in positive, even liberating, and sometimes 'normal' terms. For example, from Gannon, a psychologist:

> After approximately 30 years of menstrual cycles in order to provide transitory fertility, ovarian serenity is restored, oestrogen once again becomes stable and levels return to normal, menstruation ceases. The woman experiences release from reproductive pressures and is able to participate fully in her career, social and family activities as she need no longer be concerned about the problems associated with menstruation, birth control and pregnancy and is no longer at heightened risk for endometriosis, uterine fibroids and breast cancer. (1996: 243)

There might also even be a hint of a discourse of positive heterosex here! (Juliane Schwarz, personal communication).

Such linguistic traces (among others) show this discourse to be intertextually contesting both the previous discourses. Supporting, 'overarched' discourses include celebration of women's different bodily states (Coupland and Williams characterize this as a form of 'essentialist feminism'), and also a materialist feminist discourse, critical of sexist ideas such as women's value residing in youthful attractiveness (i.e. the sometime emphasis in the pharmaceutical discourse on HRT as able to promote younger-looking skin).

Coupland and Williams document insightful 'ways of speaking' about menopause, pointing to discursive and interdiscursive elements which 'play and replay themselves, albeit with variable commitment and emphasis' (2002: 421). The interdiscursivity and mutual contestation point to current and ongoing discoursal shift, with implications for constitutiveness. 'Linguistic' discourse analysts may wish for closer reading in this investigation of what are essentially 'discursive and semiotic' *strategies*. Coupland and Williams' study could, however, be broadly replicated using linguistic analysis of a selection of *representative* or of 'telling' texts rather than this large dataset of often long texts.

Jennifer Coates' 'Consciousness-raising discourse' in the talk of teenage girls

The last study concerns discourse 'acquisition' in teenage girls. Coates (1999) looked at the gendered discourses used by teenage girls (four friends) during their adolescence, from age 12 to 15. Coates assumes that girls do not (yet) share the speaking practices of women, and her focus was discursive practices in the process of development.

Coates' study was unusual in being a longitudinal one: as she says, 'We know very little about the ways in which children become gendered speakers' (1999: 123; see also Francis, 1999). Also, unlike the other researchers we have looked at, she used as data *naturally* occurring talk: the girls 'agreed to turn on a tape recorder when they were together, and they were free to delete any portions of their talk that they did not want me to hear' (1999: 124). Analytically, 'Discourses were initially identified by content alone, then later examined for linguistic characteristics' (1999: 125). Coates' study is thus the most 'linguistic' of the discourse analyses in this chapter. As I suggested in Chapter 2, it is possible to provisionally 'recognize' a discourse, and then 'confirm' the identification with a study of what seem to be its linguistic traces or intertextual links.

Coates sees girls as 'performing' femininity, and in doing so experimenting with a range of discourse styles. She identifies a wide range of discourses in the girls' early talk, including what she calls 'Factual/Scientific', 'Pseudo-scientific', 'Maternal', 'Repressive', 'Romantic love', 'Liberal' and 'Resistant/Feminist' discourses. In their talk when they were 14 and 15, Coates identified an additional 'Consciousness-raising' (or 'Self-disclosure') discourse:

> characterised by the expression of information of a highly personal nature. It is a subjective discourse, in contrast with others in the girls' repertoire. In other words, although other discourses may touch on topics such as bodies or boyfriends, they do not involve intimate self-disclosure. The new discourse makes the girls vulnerable in a way the others do not. Not surprisingly, then, it is also characterised by reciprocity: sections of conversation where it appears normally involve two or more girls in mirroring self-disclosure. (1999: 126)

Coates cites lexical repetition, collaborative overlap and the frequent use of well-placed minimal responses as some of this discourse's other interactional traces.

An example of Coates' 'Consciousness-raising/Self-disclosure' discourse is:

J: well, when I started fancying him in the Second year/I fancied him ever since then/

L: yeah/ I [s]- I knew that/ sort of/

J: yeah you sort of guessed/ [...]

J: and then/ the real sort of clincher was ((still xx))   and I suddenly-

V: <pp LAUGHS>

J: because I suddenly sort of fancying – you know people say love's blind/ I think I

V: oh but d'you

J: thought he was perfect apart from the ((obvious things))/ and I just suddenly have seen

L: yeah

V: think–   mhm

J: how awful he is and horrible/ <PEAL OF LOUD LAUGHTER = release of tension>

L: yeah/

V: yeah/   <MATCHING LAUGH>

H: yeah/   <LOW CHUCKLE>

'Matching self-disclosure' is seen as an expression of the support the girls seek from each other, and indeed the above may appear more like 'self-disclosure' than 'consciousness-raising'. Coates, however, has a principled reason for making the latter the primary name for this discourse:

> I use the label *consciousness raising* with the deliberate aim of calling attention to the similarity between this mode of talk and its antecedents in the consciousness raising of the Women's Movement, particularly in the 1950s and 1960s, when women would meet in groups for the express purpose of talking about our personal experience, to become empowered through an understanding that our experience was not unique but was shared by other women under patriarchy. (1999: 126)

As regards the interesting question of the *origin* of this discourse in these girls, she adds:

> It is noteworthy that the girls have mothers who were themselves teenagers in the 1950s and 1960s [and who would thus have been of the age of many Women's Liberation Movement activists in the 1970s], and although I am not saying that mothers have explicitly taught their daughters a particular way of talking, it is certainly the case that these girls, like many others of their generation, are growing up in households in which feminism is as routinely accepted as wholemeal bread. (1999: 127)

Coates notes that, in general, the girls' talk at 14 and 15 is highly complex and heterogeneous, in part because of the different 'voices' in it, one of which is the 'maternal' voice. It is also heterogeneous because of the range of discourses deployed – Coates gives as an example a long stretch of talk about menstrual periods. 'Consciousness-raising' is just one of three dominant, intertwined discourses produced and within which the girls are positioned. The other two discourses are a medical discourse, instantiated by the choice of lexis such as *bad back* and *backache*: 'periods are understood in a frame of ailments or ill-health, with *back rest* and *hot water bottles* coming from a lexical set pertaining to possible cures' (1999: 136), and a repressive (or patriarchal) discourse, 'realised in part through syntax':

> The girls represent themselves as affected rather than as agents (*hot water bottles help me*); the proposition *x helps me* presupposes *I need help* .... The only agentive verb ... occurs in conjunction with the negated modal *can't* ['backaches – I can't go like that/and I can't go like that/'] where *can't* means *not able/not possible* ... (1999: 136)

The originality and contribution of Coates' study lie in how (gendered) discourses can be identified not only in terms of theme but also, with more delicacy, through close linguistic analysis. 'Consciousness-raising' and the other discourses provisionally identified here are as a result more *substantiated* than others in this chapter. However, such linguistic analysis is not unproblematic in terms of interpretation and claims about the *significance* of the findings (see Potter, 1996): does the paucity of agentive verbs really mean the speaker feels controlled rather than in control, for example?

Coates observes with regret that as the girls get older, 'the continuing intertextuality found in their talk seems to constrain rather than liberate them'. With the emergence of the serious 'Consciousness-raising/Self-disclosure' discourse, 'the ludic aspect of their talk decreases' (1999: 137). Their talk is now more sophisticated, but resistance and subversion of discourses decline and there is less evidence of agency. Articulation of 'Consciousness-raising' is accompanied by medicalized talk about their bodies. There is, however, also negative talk about their bodies, and self-naming as 'bad': *'I'm a bitch/I'm really horrible'* (1999: 138). Coates asks 'whether these young white middle-class girls – a privileged group, who will be the professional women of the next generation – are in fact liberated', and wonders whether 'although they think they are speaking, they are in fact being spoken' (1999: 138). This may, of course, be taking an over-determining view of discourse and underestimating individual (senses of) agency; it may also be to overprivilege the perspective of the *analyst*.

Conclusion

The 'Gender differences discourse' is widely produced and can be considered as an 'overarching' or 'higher-order' discourse, 'sheltering' a range of 'subordinate' discourses (though some can be seen as being produced in part under the 'Gender differences' 'umbrella', and in part outside it). Many of the other gendered discourses identified would seem to be weakly or strongly interdiscursively linked – with each other, and/or with those described in other chapters and elsewhere. I have, however, resisted the temptation to create a diagrammatic 'model' of discoursal hierarchies and relationships (showing contradictions and 'competing discourses'), since the static and two-dimensional nature of this might suggest closure and a modernist idea that these discourses do not need to be co-constructed or produced, but, rather, are straightforwardly 'out there'.

The significance of discoursal *contradictions* has been raised by Hollway and by Wetherell et al. (see also Francis, 1999). As regards whether contradictions are a conservative or an emancipatory force in discourse, presumably they have the potential to be both, and this is clearly a topic worth pursuing, at both the empirical and theoretical levels (see Billig et al., 1988; and Chapter 9).

Part II

Gendered Discourses:
Empirical Studies

Introduction: the 'fruitful epistemological site' for gender and discourse study

The following four chapters each explore 'sets' of gendered discourses in some detail. Chapter 4 looks at gendered discourses in the classroom. Chapters 5 and 6 explore discourses of *fatherhood as institution*. Chapter 7 investigates gendered discourses in award-winning children's literature. The classroom, fatherhood and prize-winning children's literature can all be seen as *epistemological sites*, and I consider each to be a *fruitful* epistemological site for the study of gendered discourses.

The epistemological site is an important notion for any study involving discourse analysis. It might *literally* be a site in the sense of a specific physical setting – a Starbucks coffee shop to investigate the production of complex noun phrases, for example – but the notion of epistemological *site* is much broader than this.

All data can also be seen as *selected from* a particular epistemological site, and how interesting and relevant those data are depends in part on the site itself. The question is what *are* the most fruitful sites, i.e. those that might yield particularly telling data. West and Fenstermaker (2002), investigating 'the ongoing accomplishment of gender, race and class in social interaction', address this in a very direct way. They *explicitly* ask of their chosen epistemological site (the University of California Board of Regents on affirmative action policies): 'In what sense … does this meeting constitute a logical place to explore the ongoing accomplishment of gender, race and class in social interaction?' (They then provide a three-part answer to this important question in a very substantial paragraph (2002: 542).) The data selection process is, however, not always documented fully in research papers: although we are normally told where data came from, we are not always provided with a rationale for *why*. Here I concur with Stephanie Taylor, who, in a discussion of discourse analytic research, writes: 'For every project, the researcher must establish the justification for the data being used, even if this is done cryptically through reference to a previous study' (2001: 28). Establishing this justification may involve acquainting the reader with the range of *potential* sites considered (and rejected).

For any study, it is always useful to consider what might constitute an 'ideal' epistemological site and data, i.e. what data from what site could be expected to provide the best answer to a given research question? The *best* data would be that which not only enabled the answering of the research question, but also enabled the study to contribute theoretically to the field more widely. In this, it would constitute 'interestingness'

(Barton, 2002), and this is likely to be reflected in any justification. In the real world, of course, the researcher must consider what the best data are she or he can reasonably get, given constraints on data collection. This necessarily requires epistemological consideration of the extent to which the 'actual' data obtained represent a compromise, and in what way they might limit claims that can be made about the status, generalizability or relevance of the findings of the study.

Any study of gender must involve humans[1] (as opposed to, say, agent-obscured accounts of scientific processes), and any study of discourse has to involve *language in use*. But what would constitute a particularly *fruitful* epistemological site for gender and discourse research? Pavlenko and Piller (2001) note how the 'primary unit' where language and gender research is conducted has shifted from interpersonal encounters and speech communities to 'Communities of practice' (e.g. Eckert and McConnell-Ginet, 1992a, 1999). Relatedly, site depends in part on the specific research question – put simply, what is being investigated? The discourse analyst might be concerned with a concept, phenomenon, topic, genre, domain, speech act, group of people, event or setting, which she feels is revealing and fruitful in some way: this *is* the epistemological site. An epistemological site is that where data are drawn from, and not the data as such: 'material only becomes data through certain considered processes, including selection' (Taylor, 2001: 24). And, of course, some epistemological sites ('fatherhood', for example) cannot even be considered as material (though *fatherhood texts* can be).[2]

Broadly, it is possible to make a distinction between sites in which we might expect gender to be represented in a traditional way, and those in which we might expect it to be represented non-traditionally. Predictable, for example, is the discourse of 'Wedding Album' pages of local mainstream British newspapers, which tend to report in a highly formulaic way who married whom, where, what their occupations are, who gave the bride away, what she wore, who the bridesmaids were, who the best man was, and the location of the reception and honeymoon. Such sites should, however, always also be explored for traces of less traditional gendered discourses. Potentially fruitful epistemological sites for *non*-traditional gendered practices may include those in which women and men 'transgress' traditional norms: when men become pre-school teachers or 'escorts' for women (Taylor and Sunderland, 2003), for example, or when women become combatants in the army or police officers with traditionally masculine responsibilities (McIlhenny, 1995). Here, while some non-traditional gendered discourses might be expected to be evident in the text (depending on its purpose and the affinities of the text producer), it would not be at all surprising to find traces of thoroughly traditional gendered discourses as well.

I will now look briefly at five examples of studies on what for the researchers concerned have been 'fruitful epistemological sites' for the investigation of gender and discourse, and which have included justifications for these sites. The first example comes from Chapter 3. Coupland and Williams (2002) justify the epistemological site of the menopause (as phenomenon and topic) as worthy of study since, in recent social scientific research, it has been 'subject to a complex and variable set of representations, all ideologically loaded, politicized and subject to cultural variation' (2002: 420). Here we have a case of what Taylor describes as an 'implied or stated argument that the origin or context of the material relates it to wider social practices' (2001: 25). Often a rationale for an epistemological site is that it has not been explored before. This is not true of Coupland and Williams' study. As they say, neither menopause nor menopause texts are new epistemological sites. However, 'up to now, close qualitative analysis of discursive constructions of the menopause has been limited to a very few texts ... or to examination of women's own talk about their experiences of the menopause' (2002: 419, 420). The originality of their study lies in the size and range of their written corpus (which takes data from texts of three types – pharmaceutical brochures, popular print media texts and feminist texts).

Second, Susan Speer's (2002) study has as its epistemological site gender and leisure, more particularly, women's and men's non-participation in certain sport and leisure activities, and more particularly still, 'arguments about possible injury [used] to justify women's *non*-participation in leisure activities such as boxing and rugby' (2002: 351). Speer justifies this site as follows: 'By identifying the resources that participants use to produce and challenge [these] sexist assumptions, it is hoped that the study of gendered and sexist talk will be taken in productively new directions.' She thus sees this site as enabling her study to contribute to gender and discourse study more generally, in terms of how sexist assumptions are (a) discoursally produced, and (b) challenged (see also Kitzinger, 2000).

For other researchers, the epistemological site may be *who, doing what*. The third example comes from Mary Bucholtz's *Reinventing Identities: the Gendered Self in Discourse* (2000). In her theoretical introduction to this collection, Bucholtz advocates the study not of 'good girls' (normatively female white, straight, middle-class women) – although this may have been necessary as a starting point for gender and language study, it also excludes many groups and practices – but rather of 'bad girls' (to investigate, for example, how girls use language to experiment with transgression and 'badness'). Bucholtz also advocates the study not only of such 'anomalous femininity' but also 'anomalous femaleness' (exemplified by drag queens), in order to 'pose problems for neat theories' (2000: 9). Bucholtz's rationale for this 'bad girls' epistemological site is thus primarily a theoretical one.

The fourth example, also of a theoretically focused rationale, is Kay Wheeler's (2002) work on 'candidates' most able to show evidence of the construction of gender (a topic I return to in Chapter 8). Wheeler's chosen candidate was the epistemological site of *small-group conversation*. She saw gender construction as essentially interactional, something that could be achieved only through negotiation and possible contestation of meaning. Wheeler writes: 'the dynamics of multi-voiced interaction allows for a broader and more diverse (multi-layered) analysis of the warrants that may be used to claim the possible construction or co-construction of gender identities' (2002: 20). Wheeler's multi-voiced interaction data came from the non-naturally occurring but unsolicited talk[3] of a group of four friends, postgraduate students at a British university. Though two were men and two women, Wheeler was not interested in 'speaker sex', but rather in what in their talk could be construed as 'gender construction'.

The fifth and last example is the work of Clare Walsh, whose *Gender and Discourse: Language and Power in Politics, the Church and Organisations* (2002) includes a study of the pre- and post-ordination period of women priests in the UK. Walsh notes that this epistemological site

> *affords an ideal opportunity* to explore the tensions between women's construction of themselves, as both campaigning outsiders and as recently ordained insiders, and the sometimes very different ways in which they have been constructed by others, including the media. (2002: 165; emphasis added)

This choice of an 'event' as an epistemological site is interesting but challenging. An event may be brief or relatively lengthy (as this was). It may be that the researcher knows a certain event is coming and prepares for it (again, as in Walsh's study). It may be that it is unexpected but is recognized as a serendipitous and fruitful epistemological site (the death of Princess Diana and the events surrounding it are a good example here) – though whether it corresponds with the researcher's research timetable is another issue. A similar epistemological site would be the talk of one specific individual, on the grounds of wider significance or ramifications (Taylor, 2001) – for example, Fairclough's (2000) *New Labour, New Language?*, which focuses on the rhetoric of Tony Blair.

How are the sites in Part II this book – the classroom, fatherhood and award-winning children's literature – epistemologically fruitful?

The classroom (Chapter 4) provides learning opportunities and constitutes a continuous and lengthy social experience, characterized by a vast range of practices (see also Walkerdine, 1990, on the classroom and subjectivity). It is also a domain replete with concerns about and tensions surrounding gender, suggested by the 'Why women are just first class' text in Chapter 2. The study of discoursal contradictions is particularly well served by this epistemological site, where the critical '(Male) dominance discourse' on classroom interaction may compete with the 'Poor boys discourse' and also with an overall acceptance of gender differential wage and salary paths after school (Wetherell et al.'s (1987) 'Practical considerations' discourse).

Fatherhood (Chapters 5 and 6) constitutes an interesting epistemological site in that, in a climate of continually changing gender relations, and indeed what might be called one of post-feminism,[4] parenthood more generally may interdiscursively produce new gendered discourses and discoursal tensions. In many contexts, parenthood is now expected not only to be a responsibility of, but also a source of pleasure for, fathers as well as mothers (though not necessarily in equal measure). Fatherhood texts produced for consumption in this climate are thus likely to constitute interesting data. Several parenting magazines now have titles such as *Parents* rather than *M and M (the magazine for the mum-to-be and new mother)*. These materials beg the question of whether they really are for parents, or mainly for mothers. A second 'sub-site' is media treatment of 'Celebrity fatherhood'. I look at this in relation to the birth of Leo Blair, the high-profile baby of British Prime Minister Tony Blair and Cherie Booth. Media representation of this event is epistemologically interesting since Tony Blair was seen as a dynamic, modern and in many ways progressive leader, but also because Cherie Booth is a barrister who had no intention of renouncing her career after Leo's birth.

Children's literature (Chapter 7) can be seen as an important epistemological site for discourse analysis in relation to gender since books are part of many young children's lives. Stephens (1992: 5) writes: 'it is through language that the subject and the world are represented in literature, and through language that literature seeks to define the relationships between child and culture'. In particular, children's literature is often written with the intention that it has something to *teach*. The discourses flowing through what children read, or have read to them, position them in particular ways, which they may enjoy or resist (or both!).

Lastly, children's books may be experienced widely by young children during a possibly important period of 'early discourse production' (Francis, 2000). (Young children *themselves* and their linguistic practices can also be argued to constitute an important epistemological site for discourse and gender study.)

As regards gender, like media texts, children's literature needs to acknowledge in some way social change and challenges – though the desiderata here have gone beyond the provision of 'positive role models' for women and girls advocated by some feminist literary critics in the 1970s (for example, Register, 1975). As regards *award-winning* children's books, these are reviewed and get a great deal of publicity; often their covers are embossed; sometimes they have a special status in children's libraries, where they may automatically be purchased (perhaps in multiple copies) and displayed and/or shelved in a special section. They may also be systematically selected for purchase by parents and school librarians. Because of their special status they may be dramatized or filmed (as has, *Holes*, a Newbery winner). Presumably, all this exposure enhances their chances of being read by children, and by parents and teachers to and with children.

As will now be clear, the notion of *epistemological site* and its associated data for a given study has a hierarchical dimension. Children's literature provides a good example. Having identified this as the broad epistemological site, and contemporary American award-winning children's literature as the 'sub-epistemological site', I had to select the actual materials or 'data sources' (recent Newbery and Caldecott medal winners) and to decide how many award-winning books, from which years, to analyse. I also had to identify certain passages from each book – 'telling' or representative cases – as 'samples' for analysis or principled illustration. Using Taylor's (2001) distinction between *materials* and *data*, it is possible to see all Newbery and Caldecott medal winners as *materials*, and the chosen books as *data*.

Chapter 4, on the epistemological site of the classroom, is in a way a continuation of Chapter 3, in that it describes a range of gendered discourses, identified in a variety of ways, and cuts across talk and written text. Chapters 5, 6 and 7, on the other hand, deal entirely with discourses produced in written texts, each chapter focusing on a single study.

4
Gendered Discourses in the Classroom

In this chapter I describe a diverse selection of gendered discourses which have been documented in relation to classrooms – mainly, but not only, foreign language classrooms. Some were apparent in talk, some in written texts. Most of these discourses are non-classroom (and non-education)-specific, and indeed not *predictably* instantiated in classroom discourse, but were nevertheless flexible enough to be reproduced in classrooms. (This is a 'tribute' in particular to the robustness and fluidity of 'Gender differences' discourses.) In addition to this description of gendered classroom discourses, I aim also to indicate how emancipatory, or otherwise, particular gendered discourses are for girls. (For a discussion of learning in the *community* in relation to gender, see Pavlenko and Piller, 2001.)

In the background: the broad 'Gender differences' discourse

Although looking for gendered discourses in the classroom may be a relatively new endeavour, the study of gendered classroom discourse is not. Classroom talk has been a focus of feminist work since the start of the second wave of the Women's Movement, and the concept of 'gendered discourse' was used in classroom research well before the term came into circulation.

In the 1970s and into the 1980s, there was a tendency – understandable in the light of the sociopolitical concerns of the time – for feminist researchers to search for, report and thus expose interactional differences seen as sources of educational disadvantage for girls. In Anglo-American classroom studies, epistemological sites included 'public' teacher-talk to students, student-talk to the teacher, and student-student talk (usually on-task pair- or group-work). Differences were not always found and were not always statistically significant (Boersma et al., 1981; Dart and Clarke, 1988). Overall, however, one picture was of teachers at all levels of education talking more to male than to female students (Kelly, 1988). In so far as male students sometimes tended to be asked not only more questions, but also more *challenging* questions, and to be praised and encouraged more, some researchers claimed that male students also received *better* teacher attention. This was not and should not be seen as 'bias' or favouritism, but rather as a result of male students either being perceived as needing this attention, or as 'soliciting'[1] it. In a recent study, Jule (2001) found that one reason boys took up more 'linguistic space' than girls was because the teacher engaged with their contributions more. However, much of any extra attention paid to boys is *disciplinary* (e.g. Kelly, 1988) and thus as likely to hinder as help them educationally.

Another picture was of male students at all levels talking more than their female peers – both to the teacher and in pair- and group-work (e.g. Dart and Clarke, 1988; Kelly, 1988; Swann and Graddol, 1988). Again, this was sometimes seen not only as more talk from, but also better learning opportunities *for*, boys (e.g. French and French, 1984; Sadker and Sadker, 1985).

Underlying these studies was, of course, a familiar, but *critical* 'Gender differences' discourse,[2] 'differential teacher-treatment by learner gender' and 'gender differential opportunities for student talk' entailing both comparison and contrast. One frequently documented 'subordinate' discourse was 'male dominance' (to name it retrospectively, since it was not referred to as a discourse *per se*), used mainly in reference to gender imbalances in student talk.[3] The 1970s and early 1980s were, of course, when the '(male) dominance' explanation of gender differences in language use generally was pervasive (see Chapter 3). Critiquing the amount and type of boys' talk however and inevitably to an extent positioned girls as powerless victims, and traces of a 'Girls as victims discourse' were evident. Wolpe in turn critiqued studies which 'have been concerned to demonstrate that boys behave in a dominant way detrimental to girls' academic progress and development of self-esteem' since this has resulted in the establishment of 'a stereotypical profile of boys' behaviour and how girls are said to respond' (1988: 12). (This was partly redressed in later work, such as that of Arnot et al., 1998, who pointed out sensible compensatory strategies that girls tended to use, like asking the teacher questions after the lesson; see also Baxter, 2003.)

Boys' classroom domination is now often seen (for example, in the press) in terms of a 'laddish anti-learning culture'; where this exists, of course, it can adversely affect girls as well as boys (Warrington and Younger, 2000; see also Vandrick, 1999; Francis, 2000; Skelton, 2001). While 'Gender differences' classroom interaction *studies* are less evident, gender tendencies in education continue. As regards achievement, girls are now performing academically better than boys on a wider variety of measures (e.g. Arnot et al., 1998; Epstein et al., 1998) – at least at secondary schools in the UK. This is not necessarily a paradox, of course: logically, girls can be seen as performing well *despite* their relative silence; without (some) boys dominating classroom talk, they might perform even better. Girls' particular achievements have contributed to the 'Poor boys discourse' (see Chapter 3, and later).

We have already seen several education- and classroom-related gendered discourses in Chapter 2, in *The Times* article reporting problematically that women were being awarded more first class degrees than men at British universities (recall that more women sat the exams). One discourse I suggested to be 'flowing through' this article was 'Battle of the sexes'. This discourse was also independently documented by Francis (1999) as produced by primary (elementary) school children. Citing 'Boys think they're better than girls, and girls think they're better than boys', seven-year-old Lynn's explanation of classroom sexism, Francis notes '[Battle of the sexes] presents the genders in conflict or competition. It is identified grammatically when "the girls" and "the boys" are presented in antagonism' (1999: 305). It can also imply that the gain of one 'gender' automatically entails a loss for the other.

The 'Equal opportunities discourse'

Gender differences – or, more accurately, tendencies – found in the Anglo-American classroom studies have largely been represented as negative and a reason for suspicion. Something to do with gender was 'going on' – something which broadly entailed disadvantage. To my knowledge, nowhere was it claimed that the teacher should treat all students the same, but the desideratum seemed to be that there should be no interactional differences between female students as a group, and male students as a group. This 'Equal opportunities discourse' was drawn on in the UK in Equal Opportunities policies of schools and county-level Local Education Authorities. The Equal Opportunities policy of one comprehensive school in the north-west of England included in its 'Action' list:

> The school prospectus and other appropriate documents will make mention of relevant Equal Opportunities policy, as well as themselves avoiding sexism and racism in the selection of language, examples and illustrations.

and

> [A]ll name-calling and bullying will be seen within the context of equality of opportunity, and will always lead to a response from staff.

The Languages Faculty policy of the same school included:

> there may be aspects [of discrimination] which relate more specifically to the foreign language lesson. Boys, for instance, could be disadvantaged more here by teachers' expectations e.g. that girls are better at languages. Because speaking is a skill central to foreign language learning, we can identify speaking as an area where problems might especially arise e.g. girls could be selected more often for dialogues and role plays.[4]

The 'Equal opportunities' discourse, which extended to class, ethnicity, disability and sexual orientation, thus had implications for classroom language as well as for issues such as access. It had considerable credibility in Anglo-American educational institutions.

However, 'Equal opportunities' is *profoundly* culturally and historically situated. In some cultural contexts it may be unfamiliar or peripheral; in others it may even be non-legitimate (other than perhaps in government/NGO rhetoric and documentation, or in women's groups). In many non-Western cultures, 'Equal opportunities' is associated with feminism, often seen as anti-men and anti-family (hence anti-woman); or with 'permissiveness' and single teenage mothers (something many non-Westerners look on with concern and disapproval).

Most classroom studies have been done in British, American, Canadian, Australian, New Zealand or continental European settings. So, not only is more known about gender and classroom discourse in those parts of the world, but also the paradigms and critical perspectives which those studies have adopted, explicitly or implicitly, have precluded understanding of paradigms and critical perspectives which may operate in other cultural contexts. Where there is non-acknowledgement of 'Equal opportunities', this is not the same as endorsing educational disadvantage for women and girls. An example follows.

An alternative gendered discourse of education: 'Privileged femininity'

'Privileged femininity', identified and named by Kitetu (1998; Kitetu and Sunderland, 2000), can be seen as a pro-female discourse, a form of positive discrimination. Kenya has recently witnessed several campaigns for gender equality in education. In government policy, gender differentiation is largely seen in terms of parents educating their sons and marrying off their daughters at an early age. However, a section of the Kenyan Government's Development Plan of 1994–96 acknowledges that

> females are disadvantaged at all levels of education in terms of access, participation, completion and performance ... there remains a striking gender gap influenced by bias which exists in the education system in favour of boys ...

and vows that

> the Government will endeavour to ... *overcom[e] different treatment of girls and boys* ... initiate the gradual removal of all stereotyping of gender roles in educational materials and textbooks ... (p. 255; emphasis added)

Kenya's struggle for gender equity in education thus draws on what we can see as an 'Equal opportunities discourse' in its official documentation. The question is whether the government's representation of gender differential treatment and intentions to overcome it are in line with Kenyan cultural thinking, i.e. whether this discourse competes with other, more traditional ones (see also Vavrus, 2002, on tradition and girls' education in Tanzania).

In Kenya, as elsewhere, gender differentiation tends to be seen as normal, unproblematic and not associated with disadvantage. Questions have been raised about whether, in the drive for equality, women are seeking to become men, and whether men will be expected to give birth to babies. It has also been argued that in traditional, patriarchal cultural practices the rights of individuals were safeguarded on the basis of their gender (Pala, 1987).

I will illustrate the 'Privileged femininity' discourse with reference to a study of a physics lesson in a Kenyan secondary school (Kitetu, 1998). The students, a mixed-sex class of fifteen- and sixteen-year-olds, were learning about 'structures', and constructing these from wire. They did this in six groups – two consisting of girls, two of boys and two mixed. The (male) teacher tried to help one, apparently struggling, group of girls. An extract from Kitetu's fieldnotes reads:

Teacher moves around checking on students' work.

Girls' group (4) making an airing rack. Struggling with the wire.

Group (1) making spectacles. The girl is watching.

Teacher with boys' group 1.

Girls' group (6) making a bed little progress. They sit idly.

Boys' group (2) making stool. Group 3 making a bed, group 5 out of view.

Teacher goes to girls' group (6), goes back to his table, returns to group 6 with plastic straws, thread and needles.

Girls' group (6) given straws, take the plastic straws, thread and needle from the teacher. Start making a chair.

Boy from group 3 helps girls' (only) group (4) to cut their wire.

Teacher watches the girls start again with the new material comes to where I am sitting, says 'they know how to use knitting needles', referring to girls' group (6).

Despite its stereotypical appearance, the teacher's action can be read as a form of positive discrimination: he was going out of his way to help the girls, to make sure they were doing something constructive, and making use of their existing skills. In a subsequent interview with Kitetu, he said, again, '[the girls'] fingers are soft and they are used to handling knitting needles'. He also claimed categorically that he did not differentiate between girls and boys (perhaps interpreting 'differentiation' as 'discrimination').

But was this really doing the girls a favour? Kitetu interviewed five of them:

K: I saw the teacher helping you by giving you straws instead of wires, how do you feel about that?

G5:   Do it ourselves.

K: So you do not want to be given anything different?

G5:   No.

K: You want to do what everybody is doing?

G1: The teacher will not always be there so you have to learn yourself.
K: We should not differentiate the materials you use?
All: No.
G4 It depends on the materials, like the wires we were using were so hard ... so he can give us some other tool.
K: But you also want to fight your way like everybody else.
G1: The serious thing is if you are given different tools in the main exam we are given the same tools ... we shall not be given special anything ... that ... these are girls give them this and these are the boys give the other.
K: One other thing, do you see equality in your schooling?
G2: I think girls are higher ... think we are ... OK sort of favoured.
K: In this school?
G5: Yes in this school ...

(Kitetu, 1998)

With the possible exception of G4, these girls were apparently claiming that they did not want special treatment. And was it really the case that they could not handle 'hard materials'? Perhaps they could – but 'Privileged femininity' should be seen against the backdrop of other circulating gendered discourses. One such, here, was the importance of girls' domestic roles and responsibilities and related practices. The following is a typical 'diary' of one non-school day written by Chebet, aged sixteen:

---

6 o'clock – wake up and do house work like sweeping.
7 o'clock – make breakfast and take it with family members.
8 o'clock – fetch water and finish housework like washing utensils.
9 o'clock – boil githeri if any and make tablecloths well.
10 o'clock – make tea and take it to the people working in the shamba.
11 o'clock – work in the shamba for a short while.
12 o'clock – run home fast and get lunch ready.
1 o'clock – take lunch and feed my younger brothers.
2 o'clock – wash utensils and sweep the kitchen again.
3 o'clock – go for firewood 2 km away.
4 o'clock – bring cattle from the field and milk them.
5 o'clock – wash my younger brothers and also take a bath. I visit my friend Cherono.
6 o'clock – make supper vegetables and ugali.
7 o'clock – all take supper.

Continued

> 8 o'clock – wash utensils, sweep the house and chat with my brothers and sisters.
> 9 o'clock – study.
> 10 o'clock – read the bible, pray and sleep because I become tired.
> 11 o'clock – in deep sleep and may be dreaming by the [sic] time.

Chebet's day involves a lot of physical work, after which it is hard to believe her hands are soft! 'Privileged femininity' thus may really be about giving girls an easier time at school in recognition of the work they typically have to do at home. These traces of 'Privileged femininity' have links elsewhere in this context, in the form of social practices. Kitetu notes that girls, unlike boys, could not be given corporal punishment, and that girls entered the dining room before boys (possibly in response to the East African practice of men and boys traditionally eating before women and girls). Further interdiscursive links might be seen with traditional 'chivalric' and 'charitable' Christian discourses, which obtain – if not ubiquitously – internationally.

'Privileged femininity' and gender differentiation more generally thus need to be understood as historically and culturally situated. The same is true of *progress*. Practices largely disapproved of by conventional Western feminism – beauty contests, men holding doors open for women – may sometimes represent a step forward for women, as indeed may 'Privileged femininity'. 'Privileged femininity' is, of course, problematic. However, it needs to be weighed against 'Equal opportunities'. Equal opportunities policies may aim to help, but may lack credibility, subject positioning women and girls in culturally alien ways; such policies may even be seen as dangerous if they do not come with safeguards. In particular, if all students have the same, wide-ranging freedoms, it is nevertheless girls who risk pregnancy and may then face barriers in continuing their education. As a teacher interviewed by Kitetu said: 'the moment you allow [girls] a lot of freedom ... because they are ignorant [they] may mess with boys who are a bit more experienced ... and [in] the final analysis they are going to be the losers'. With such understandings, 'Equal opportunities' is unlikely to 'work' as a discursive strategy. When there is a genuine commitment to the education of girls and women, discourses such as 'Privileged femininity' may be more productive, and may represent the most effective (perhaps short-term) way forward. 'Privileged femininity' may not constitute a range of emancipatory possibilities for girls, but may contribute to bringing about a 'critical mass' of girls and young women in secondary and higher education.

I conclude this section with a documented episode from a secondary school classroom in Eritrea. Here, fewer girls than boys go to school, especially in the rural areas; there are greater drop-out and 'year repetition' rates for girls; and girls do less well in exams. Disadvantage seems rife. But consider these field notes on a lesson in a secondary school in Asmara, the capital city (Ogbay, 1999):

> While I was at the back seat recording the lesson ... a girl at the front seat was restless and trying to attract the attention of the students around her. She was writing something on a small piece of paper and passing it to the students behind her. They read it and laughed. She repeatedly did that. Then she put a sharpener which had a small mirror on the back of it. Using the pencil to hold the sharpener, she could see what was going on behind her. Then we had our eyes locked together as I was trying to figure out what her aim was. She did not seem to be bothered. The teacher did not see any of this.
>
> 21 March 1997

Here we have a girl creating discipline problems. Ogbay in fact reports a considerable amount of teacher attention devoted to reprimanding girls. Here (as anywhere) this may reflect institutional and teacher attitudes rather than actual student behaviour; it may be tied to the thinking in many African contexts that 'good girls' do not make nuisances of themselves.[5]

These classroom practices may illustrate the multiplicity of discourses that can be at play in a given classroom event, positioning girls (and boys) in different ways; they may also illustrate the impossibility of any straightforward, 'culture-blind' interpretation of what may be gendered behaviour. One additional, traditional discoursal desideratum in Eritrea is that a good woman is silent (this, of course, does not sit well with girls asking questions, giving oral presentations or practising speaking a foreign language). However, the issue is not that Eritrean classrooms are not being dominated by boys (Ogbay's study suggests they are), or that one sex has a monopoly on classroom disruption, but that girls may actively *resist* the educational process. In Eritrea there is an extremely powerful discourse about the importance (and inevitability) of marriage – rather than higher or even secondary education – for women. The 'pencil sharpener' episode needs to be understood in the context of prevalent social and discursive practices. Here salient traditional discourses compete with modern educational, institutional and even constitutional discourses of gender equality.

* * *

Neither 'Equal opportunities' nor 'Privileged femininity' is a specific 'classroom discourse', or even a 'discourse of education', though traces of both may be *produced* in the classroom. This chapter continues with a description of some other 'non-education-specific' gendered discourses. Circulating outside the classroom, these discourses are reproduced and recontextualized within it, mediated by generic classroom processes. The chapter concludes with examples of gendered classroom discourses that pertain *specifically* to education.

Non-education-specific classroom discourses

(a) 'Boy-as-OK/Girl-as-not-OK'

'Boy-as-OK/Girl-as-not-OK' is a 'Gender differences' discourse, which I named interpretively after observing an unusual classroom event and studying the relevant small stretch of classroom talk (Sunderland, 1995). The event took place in a German language classroom in a comprehensive (state secondary) school in the UK.

The students are eleven and twelve years old and in their second term of learning German. They have been writing German dialogues in single-sex pairs (their usual choice – or response to social constraints?). The teacher is asking pairs of students to 'perform' their dialogues. She is aware of research that shows that more teacher attention characteristically goes to boys and is carefully alternating between pairs of boys and pairs of girls. It is now the turn of two boys:

T:	we're going to have two more boys I think. two more boys . what about Ray and Max
Ray/Max:	no.
T:	no. Why not
Lia/May:	we're boys
Kay/Bea:	we're boys
Kay:	we're boys miss
T:	all right we'll have two more girls and then we'll see if the boys have got any courage

No one laughed at the girls' words, and the teacher selected Lia and May to perform their dialogue. Perhaps because there were no linguistic traces of an obvious 'sexist discourse' here, there was no challenge. As I wrote in an earlier paper, 'There are few clear implications here for teacher intervention, or even for whether intervention is appropriate' (Sunderland, 2000b: 168). Yet two of the boys in the class, whom I later interviewed, were both emphatic that 'no way' would they ever have said 'we're girls, miss', because 'boys have a limit [to] what they can do', and if they had, 'everybody [would have] laughed their heads off'.

This episode, and the boys' views, could be explained by the fact that *girl*, in English, in some contexts (mixed-sex secondary schools in the UK, for example), is an insult for a boy – meaning that no boys would say 'we're girls' without risking extreme ridicule from their classmates. Epstein (1998) claims that at primary school, which these children would have attended two terms previously, *girl* is the worst thing a boy can be called. *Boy*, on the other hand, is not used to insult a girl (even the outdated *tomboy* is relatively mild). I suspect, however, that this episode deserves a fuller, more social and more sensitive explanation, of which the semantic derogation of *girl* forms only a part. Such an explanation is hinted at in the words of the boys who were interviewed.

These boys were representing (and perhaps understanding) gender as a clear male/female binary. They were also illustrating how gender (masculinity/femininity) is in many ways asymmetrical – girls (here, at least) can cross some gender boundaries with impunity; boys cannot, or at least not with impunity. The fact that the boys cannot temporarily 'become' girls – even temporarily, strategically and jokily – shows that some boundaries of masculinity are more rigid than those of femininity. However, this entails there being more 'wrong' with being a girl than with being a boy: my reason for the name 'Boy-as-OK/Girl-as-not-OK'. This is a particularly problematic, non-emancipatory discourse since the girls can only be 'winners' here by exploiting an essentially anti-female discourse. Yet as we can see the name indicates a masculine perspective, but ironically so; although it may be all right in some senses to be a boy, boys' behaviour is clearly constrained relative to that of girls. Boys have to work hard at being boys; they cannot 'play' with gender identities.

In this episode there were thus traces of other discourses – 'Oppositional masculinity' (masculinity is what femininity is not), and a 'Bounded masculinity/Unbounded femininity' discourse. The latter is highly situated. In many cultural contexts, for example, femininity is as bounded as masculinity, if not more so, in that transgression of normative traditional feminine practices may be far more serious than transgression of normative traditional masculine ones (adultery may be a case in point).

This episode, which can be seen as a 'telling case' (Mitchell, 1984), illustrates how the critical '(Male) dominance' explanation/discourse, referring to verbosity, asking questions, interrupting, and so on, may be irrelevant to the understanding of much gendered classroom talk. Here, more relevant is the way boys and girls (those shown here and their classmates) 'subject positioned' each other and indeed themselves by producing traces of 'Boy-as-OK/Girl-as-not-OK' in and about this episode.

(b) Gendered classroom discourses in a study of 'Teacher-talk-around-the-text'

Several gendered classroom discourses were suggested by a study of 'Teacher-talk-around-the-text': an exploration of how foreign language teachers actually used 'gendered textbook texts' of both a progressive and a traditional nature (Sunderland et al., 2000a,b, 2002).

Data were collected first at a British Council English language school in Portugal. The students were adults. One text, from *Upper Intermediate Matters* (Bell and Gower, 1992), about wedding customs, focused on the wedding of an Indian man and a Swedish woman. Clive, the teacher, used the text as a springboard for comparison of Portuguese and other wedding customs. Referring to British Anglican ceremonies, Clive says:

> the bride (.) usually (.) if it's especially for the church wedding will wear white (.) and (.) the bridesmaids (.) she will often choose the (.) the outfit for them (.) usually she chooses something horrible so they (.) don't look as good as her

Clive may have intended to be humorous, ironic, or even to critique the traditional English wedding set-up. However, his words may not have been thus read by his Portuguese students. Clive was clearly distorting traditional practices in his representation of femininity (indeed no one could blame Bell and Gower for this spin on their text). Of interest here however is the gendered discourse Clive was articulating to do this. This discourse might be called 'Women beware women': women cannot trust other women, are jealous of them and are preoccupied with the possibility that they might steal the show on their Big Day (note the intertextual links with the 'Biggest day of a woman's life discourse' identified in Chapter 2). There is nothing predictable about 'Women beware women' for the classroom, and its occurrence there may point to its robustness and, for some, its legitimacy.

A second set of data was collected in a private English language school in Athens. The lesson was based on a unit from the textbook *Highflyer* (Acevedo and Gower, 1996), called 'It takes all sorts', about ideas of beauty in different parts of the world. This could be seen as a 'non-traditional text', since it associated beauty with both sexes and used an equal number of pictures of women and men. Two teachers, Martha and Anna, were observed.

Martha asked the girls whether they found the men good-looking, and the boys the women, giving feedback such as 'OK that's how you feel'. At the end of the lesson, she returned to the title, highlighting the idea of differences being part of life. Christina Leontzakou, who observed these lessons, saw Martha as endorsing the non-traditional stance of the text and articulating an emancipatory (if clumsily named) 'Appearance as equally salient for women and for men discourse'.

In most contexts, this discourse is peripheral, competing with a dominant and in many ways non-emancipatory discourse of 'Privileging of appearance – in women'. The latter is evidenced socially by the number of women's magazines about fashion, hair and make-up; the proportion of the contents of 'general' women's magazines addressed to these topics, in contrast to the contents of magazines for men; and practices such as beauty contests and fashion parades. Consider also the proportion of their income women and men spend on clothes, hair and make-up, and the proportion of women and men who opt for cosmetic surgery.[6] Relatedly, there exist the distinctly non-emancipatory (and often damaging) slimming practices and serious eating disorders in women and girls. In a chapter entitled 'Femininity as discourse', Dorothy Smith refers to the 'forever imperfect actuality of the body to be groomed, dressed and painted' (1990: 202; see also Naomi Wolf's *The Beauty Myth*, 1991). Goldman (1992) calls this 'commodity feminism' (a pun on the Marxist concept 'fetishism of commodities'). The 'Privileging of appearance – in women' discourse is not only 'in women' as opposed to 'in men', but we can also paradigmatically contrast *appearance* with *intellect*, for example. Time and energy spent on fixing one's appearance is time away from more sustainable and productive concerns.

To return to the English class in Athens: Martha's colleague, Anna, dealt with the text rather differently. Anna asked a male student which of two pictures of women, a model and a singer, he preferred. The student replied, 'the model', and was followed by another male student who said (in Greek) 'none'. This was followed by:

T: in English
S: nothing
T: none of them (.) why not (.) don't you like blonde
S: so what [translated from Greek]

This student can be seen as refusing to be caught in the hetero-normative trap of expressing preferences for one woman over another, and in particular for a blonde-haired woman. Anna, however, was asking the question in a way that draws on recognizable gendered stereotypes. Relative judgements about women in terms of their appearance can be seen as traces of 'Privileging of appearance – in women'. Unlike her colleague, Anna was not articulating a competing and emancipatory 'Appearance as equally salient for women and for men' discourse, and did not do so anywhere in her lesson. She can be seen as producing traces of a subversive gendered discourse in relation to 'It takes all sorts', which in effect contests the presumably progressive intentions of the text writers (who may well have considered themselves to have been drawing on the 'Equal opportunities discourse').

Many foreign language textbooks have to date been analysed for gender representation (see Sunderland, 2000, for a review). Yet gendered discourses in teacher-talk-around-the-text may be more relevant than those in the text itself, in terms of subject positioning and gender construction (see Chapter 8). With the wisdom of hindsight, then, it might be more worthwhile to look at what is *done* with gendered representations in class. Teacher- (and student-) talk around educational texts will, I predict, be recognized as a fruitful epistemological site in future discourse and gender study.

Education-specific gendered classroom discourses

Three gendered classroom discourses which can be seen as education-specific are what we might call 'Neat girls', 'Girls as good language learners' and the familiar 'Poor boys'.[7] These may have a particular bearing on gendered academic identity and educational attainment, positioning female and male students *as students* in particular ways. Each, however, also has identifiable intertextual links with gendered discourses circulating outside the classroom.

(a) The 'Neat girls discourse'

'Neat girls', though not to my knowledge hitherto named as such, has been explored in relation to school literacies. It expresses the idea that girls are expected to write 'better' than boys, not only in terms of content, but also with higher standards of neatness (White, 1986, 1990; Millard, 1997). 'Neat girls' is related to the familiar 'Boys will be boys' discourse – boys being expected to be untidy, grubby and messy in their persons and in their written work, exemplified by the rather dated British prototype of William Brown in Richmal Crompton's *Just William* books. It can be seen as part of the 'order of discourse' shared by 'Privileging of appearance – in women'. 'Neat girls' may in some ways be advantageous for girls, 'neatness' in writing having obvious benefits: neat work may, for example, result in positive teacher responses (Clark, 1988). However, if neatness (which is of course presentation) is stressed and celebrated at the expense of substance, this must ultimately be counterproductive.

(b) The 'Girls as good language learners discourse'

Worldwide, girls tend to perform better than boys in the language class-room (see Sunderland, 2000c). Despite this – and see Pavlenko and Piller (2001) for exceptions – the discourse of 'Girls as good language learners', i.e. that girls 'just are' the better language learners, remains and, in my experience, is produced by many language teachers around the globe. No satisfactory neurological support for this claim exists, however (see Klann-Delius, 1981; Hirst, 1982; Sunderland, 2000c). Indeed, one inves-tigation into innate sex differences in second language learning con-cluded that cultural factors could explain almost all the behavioural variation here (Ekstrand, 1980; see Pavlenko and Piller, 2001, on motivating factors for women). In the UK, foreign languages are more popular with boys in single-sex than in mixed-sex schools, which lends support to this (Cheng et al., 1995; Sunderland, 2000c). This discourse is in many ways a non-emancipatory one, leading (as it often does) women on to low-paid jobs in foreign language teaching.

Any gender differences in achievement in additional languages are then likely in large part to reflect socially constructed gender differ-ences. However, the (reconstructed) utterance 'girls just are better' is an interesting trace of this discourse, not only because it rejects a need to explain (drawing on a 'common-sense' idea of gender differences), but also because of the implied traces of 'Boys are poor language learners (relative to girls)' and the non-emancipatory 'Girls are not as good at other subjects (as languages)' (see also Stanworth, 1983). This discourse may have a bearing on language teachers' expectations and behaviour: girls may be treated in subtle ways more encouragingly than boys (the 'Pygmalion effect'), or ignored if teachers feel they need less attention.

An intertextually-related discourse is 'Girls are better than boys at language and communication in general' (including first language acquisition) – an interesting reversal of the older idea that women's speech is 'deficient' in some way relative to men's (see Cameron, 2003). Traces of this would include claims about girls developing language earlier than boys – because they are girls (see Nichols, 2002). Related practices may include girls who are perceived as being good at English as a first language being channelled into this at the expense of other school subjects. Again, this success may not play out beneficially in their future education and employment (White, 1986; Swann, 1992). However, girls' superiority here may be more discoursal than actual. Hyde and Linn, in a meta-analysis of 165 studies of gender differences in verbal ability, concluded that '[T]he magnitude of the gender difference in verbal ability is so small that it can effectively be considered to be zero' (1988: 64).

Interestingly, Hyde and Linn (among others) document a decline in the degree of reported gender difference in studies of verbal ability done between the 1950s and the 1980s. They concede this may be to do with publishing practices (i.e. an increased willingness to publish studies which do not find statistically significant differences). However, they identify another possible reason: 'with increased flexibility in gender roles beginning in the 1970s, boys have been permitted or encouraged to engage in more activities formerly reserved for girls, and these activities foster verbal ability' (1988: 63). The social and discoursal practices around this flexibility (which I tentatively name 'Feminization of education' since this is sometimes used in this connection – and not necessarily negatively) compete with the next (familiar) discourse.

(c) The 'Poor boys discourse'

Boys' underachievement at school has become a familiar and international theme (see Epstein et al., 1998; Francis and Skelton, 2001; Skelton, 2001; see also Chapter 2). Warrington and Younger see traces of 'Poor boys' in expressions of teachers' sympathy. They quote a female Head of Department:

> I have to say that I feel genuinely sorry for the boys: it is expected that they achieve and perform.... I really wouldn't come back as a man. I think they have so many things to face, so many demands made of them. (2000: 506)

'Poor boys' is usually produced in relation to boys' difficulties at school, often seen to include communication skills, in particular reading and writing. However, in this discourse boys' difficulties exist in part because girls in humiliating contrast seem to have less trouble with these (see Nichols, 2002: 128, on the apparently gender-neutral discourses produced by parents which nevertheless 'constitute girls and boys as differently gendered and differently literate').

'Poor boys' extends to communication skills beyond school – call centres, for example, tend to prefer women employees for their perceived superiority in talking to the public (Cameron, 2000) – and to attainment more generally. However, traces of this discourse can be seen as constituting or contributing to something of a 'moral panic', and Epstein (1998) notes the 'passion' generated by issues of boys' 'underachievement' in contrast to the relative lack of interest generated by (and indeed gender-blindness about) well-documented boys' behaviour problems. Further, as Warrington and Younger (2000) point out, citing an *Independent* article of 1998, 'the statistical underachievement of boys in schools is nothing compared with the statistical over-achievement of men in life' (2000: 495).

'Poor boys', like any discourse, is not isolated. Epstein et al. (1998) note that one related set of discourses is that drawn on by 'Men's Movement' arguments, i.e. claims about how men have lost control of their lives because of assertive women; and how this plays out in boys' education through the 'damaging' practices of women teachers, mothers and/or feminists. Another related discourse is 'Boys will be boys' (seen in Chapter 3), which somehow exonerates boys from academic effort. Epstein (1998) cites the importance of hegemonic, heterosexual masculinity here, writing that during the years of compulsory schooling, there 'seems to be a particular set of discursive strategies within which boys can "do boy" without risking homophobic and misogynist abuse; and visibly working at school work is not one of these' (1998: 103).

These three gendered classroom discourses can be seen as thriving under, and in turn 'shoring up', a hospitable (if partial) 'Gender differences' discourse – which is, as we have seen, not emancipatory for women and girls. In addition to positioning female and male students in particular ways *as students*, then, they can also be seen as performing an ideological function (as seen in Chapter 3) of affirming apparent fundamental differences between women and men, boys and girls.

Post-structuralism and gendered classroom discourses

For post-structuralism (as in CDA), discourses have an ideological function. (Most) boys may in fact be doing better at reading, writing, articulating their ideas, foreign language learning and presenting their work than 'Neat girls', 'Girls as good language learners' and 'Poor boys' allow. As Epstein *et al.* point out:

> There is more overlap between the attainment of boys and girls than there is difference; there are significant differences in the relative attainments of boys and girls in different subjects and at different levels; and, while there are many boys who are not performing well at school, there are many others who are doing very well indeed. (1998: 10)

These discourses may, however, not only be doing men and boys a disservice. Ideologically, discourse about women's alleged superiority may also be intended (in some sense) 'to distract attention from factual evidence suggesting that in material reality women are still "the second sex" ' (Cameron, 2003: 457).[8]

Whereas the 'Gender differences discourse' can be seen as essentialist, determinist and as representing girls as 'victims' or as members of a monolithic group (e.g. Wolpe, 1988), post-structuralism has been attractive to some feminist researchers for alternative discourses of gender and education. Post-structuralism *privileges* discourse over existing material structures and categories. Seeing the social world as continually constituting individuals through discursive processes, and in turn 'constantly being constituted through the discursive practices in which individuals engage', is of considerable interest since it challenges *inter alia* the notion of the *inevitability* of the male–female dualism (Davies, 1989a). In particular, post-structuralism has been used to problematize *girl* as a dichotomous element:

> Girls become 'girls' by participating within those available sets of meanings and practices – discourses – which define them as girls.... And the discourses which provide the available positions ... shift in contradictory ways. There is no one way in which girls as a group, or as individuals, can be fixed in our understanding. (Jones, 1993: 159)

I will try to unpack this a little. Discourses define and provide available positions not of their own volition, of course, but rather as they are produced – sometimes intentionally, usually not – by language users. Discourses 'shift' in that they continually jostle, overlap and give way to each other. This discoursal shift must entail both gaps and contradiction, with its potential for both maintaining the status quo and for social transformation (see Chapters 3 and 9). As an example, I cite Judith

Baxter's (2002b) 'collaborative talk' and 'gender differentiation' classroom discourses (see below). Baxter writes that a post-structuralist analysis would identify contradictory positioning of female speakers here: collaborative talk values supportive speech and good listening skills, whereas, within gender differentiation, girls are expected to be good listeners. What is expected may not be perceived as valuable. Jenkins and Cheshire (1990), for example, show how girls' listening skills during an assessment of students' oral skills are indeed apparently not fully valued. This contradiction may help transform the status quo if it is noted as a contradiction, and contested (see also Chapter 9 on discursive intervention).

Baxter has developed 'Post-structuralist discourse analysis' (PDA) and 'Feminist post-structuralist discourse analysis' (FPDA) (2002b, 2002a respectively; see also 2003) in relation to gender and classroom talk, but deals with principles important for gender and discourse study more widely. Baxter's aim is to combine the privileged status of discourse (and the de-privileging of the material) in post-structuralism with the empirical thrust of discourse analysis, and she critiques studies of discourses which do not 'get[ ] down to the business of what is actually uttered or written'.[9] Aspects of Baxter's paper on PDA – mainly the way she deals with conversation analysis (CA) – have been critiqued by Candice West (paper and critique appearing in the same (2002) issue of *Discourse and Society*, together with Baxter's response to West).

Baxter's specific concern is shifting power relations in the classroom, and (drawing on Foucault) how these are 'constantly negotiated through the medium of *competing* discourses' (2002b: 829; emphasis in original). It is not difficult to see classroom power as continually shifting – between teacher and students, most obviously, but also within and between other groupings (girls and boys being just two). PDA is not 'sociologically-neutral' (Baxter's characterization of CA), but nor does Baxter see power through a lens of what she calls the 'benevolence of a single paradigm' (her characterization of CDA). PDA supports social transformations, focusing on 'the free play of multiple voices... the voices of silenced, minority or oppressed groups need to be heard', but is wary of an 'emancipatory agenda' in the form of a 'grand narrative' that 'becomes its own dominant discourse' (2002b: 831).

In her study of public talk in the classroom, Baxter (2002b) identifies five intertextually-related discourses: *peer approval, teacher approval, a discourse of fair play,* and two we have already seen: *collaborative talk* and *gender differentiation. Gender differentiation* refers to 'established' gendered tendencies within interactional styles – for example, girls conforming more to classroom rules for talk, and boys tending to undermine the girls – tendencies which appeared to be 'deeply embedded within the structures of classroom discursive practice' (2002b: 833).

Focusing on the spoken interactions of two girls, Anne and Rebecca, Baxter conducted her analysis of excerpts of her classroom transcripts on two levels. The first was a 'denotative micro-analysis' of the verbal and non-verbal interaction, to establish linguistic evidence with which most discourse analysts would agree. The second level, an avowedly and 'more connotative analysis', was based on the first. This included accounts of the participants (produced in interviews) and of Baxter herself (2002b: 833). I exemplify this using a fragment of one of Baxter's excerpts. The class (fourteen- and fifteen-year-old girls and boys) is discussing 'desert survival' and considering the value of a compass:

TEACHER:	Anne?
ANNE:	If you didn't go the, er, habitat [*sic*], you're not going to be able to survive with just the water and say, the overcoat (JOE INTERRUPTS FROM 'SAY')
JOE:	You can still go there, can't you?
REBECCA:	Yes.
ANNE:	Not if you haven't got a compass because you are south-west.
JOE:	Yeah, but if you are going to be travelling during the day.... (SEVERAL OF THE BOYS TRY TO ADD ON, REINFORCE JOE; BOYS SPEAK LOUDLY WITHOUT BEING NOMINATED BY THE TEACHER; A NUMBER OF GIRLS HAVE THEIR HANDS UP)

In the 'denotative micro-analysis', Baxter shows how Anne and Rebecca struggle to complete a sentence or develop a point of view. For the 'more connotative analysis', she uses the different identified discourses to 'read' the interaction. Potentially contradictory and competing, Baxter shows that through their constant interplay, the discourses alternate in positioning boys and girls as effective public speakers, or otherwise (hence 'multiply locating' them). The discourses thus allow different analytical readings. Within the discourse of *gender differentiation*, 'it can be argued that female linguistic interactions may be circumscribed by the dominant definitions of femininity shaping the subject positions available to girls like Anne and Rebecca' (2002b: 837),[10] and Baxter also points to aspects of the talk in which within the discourse of *teacher approval*, Rebecca can also be seen, and be perceiving herself, as relatively powerless. However, within the discourse of *peer approval*, she can be seen as *powerful*: the people who are selected by the teacher, Rebecca claims, are 'boffy', people 'who are real good at work', where *boffy* (from *boffin*), Baxter claims, is a 'put-down', not associated with popular or likeable students.

In Baxter's paper 'Feminist Post-structuralist Discourse Analysis' (FPDA), the feminist thrust of her work is more focused. She writes: 'The post-structuralist quest ... is to create spaces to allow the voices of marginalised groups, such as women ... to be heard with ringing clarity' (2002a: 8). Baxter is trying to 'mak[e] sense of the relative powerlessness of "disadvantage" experienced by silenced or minority groups' *and* 'argue that females are multiply located and cannot be dichotomously cast as powerless, disadvantaged or as victims' (2002b: 839, 840; see Chapter 9 for pedagogic implications here). Baxter refers to this as a 'tricky juggling act'.

As regards the actual identification of the five discourses, these 'emerged ethnographically' through the process of long-term observation, videorecording and interviewing. This suggested that certain governing factors were constituting the patterns of speech and behaviour in the classroom. Baxter then coded the transcript by noting all meta-language ('where explicit attention was drawn to a discourse by a participant'), key words and phrases that seemed to indicate a discourse, and para- and body language apparently indexical of a discourse (e.g. when boys jeered at a girl's contribution). Importantly, however, Baxter's main objective was not to identify discourses, but rather to make sense of classroom linguistic practices (including gendered ones) through a post-structuralist lens (Judith Baxter, personal communication).

FPDA is an interesting development, in particular challenging post-structuralism to look more closely at linguistic data, and to deal positively with the question of 'value', and perhaps challenging CDA practitioners to consider more variable and shifting notions of power and its locus. Baxter makes clear that she does not see 'feminist post-structuralism' as an oxymoron, and cites others (e.g. Walkerdine, 1990; Davies and Banks, 1992) who have worked in this way. There are, she reminds us, different understandings of post-structuralism, and indeed of its relationship to feminism. Post-structuralism *can* have values, but practitioners need to be constantly on guard and reflexive about these. If women's and girls' 'disadvantage' is not to be lost in the swirl of discourses and positionings, and the recognition of their strengths, agency and capacity for resistance, the juggling act may be worth learning: there must be a readiness for a less defensive, more multi-faceted and resilient version of feminism, one that retains connections with its founding principles, yet is simultaneously capable of critiquing, informing and undermining itself with new insights and possibilities (Baxter, 2003: 29).

Conclusion

In this chapter I have presented a range of gendered classroom discourses. Most notably, some – 'Appearance as equally important for women and men', 'Equal opportunities' and perhaps 'Privileged femininity', for example – seem potentially emancipatory for women and girls. Rather more – including 'Boy-as-OK/Girl-as-not-OK', 'Women beware women', 'Privileging of appearance – in women' and of course 'Gender differences' – seem relatively conservative. Second, only a few of the discourses are specifically about education, the remaining majority thus technically not being 'classroom discourses' at all, but have nevertheless been *produced* in the classroom – a reminder of gendered discourses' crucial fluidity. Clearly, different combinations of discourses will multiply position different students in different gendered ways (within a differently gendered 'nexus') at different times – the point behind Baxter's *feminist post-structuralist discourse analysis*. Nevertheless, this ideological 'imbalance', together with this discoursal fluidity, provides sobering contemporary support for Sara Delamont's claim that

> schools develop and reinforce sex segregations, stereotypes, and even discriminations which exaggerate the negative aspects of sex roles in the outside world, when they could be trying to alleviate them. (1990: 2)

This of course happens in a range of (discoursal) ways.

In the next three chapters, I look at some newer empirical studies of gendered discourses, in texts on fatherhood, and in award-winning children's books. These are all studies of *written* texts. This requires us to see discourses as being 'co-constructed' by the reader, together with the text itself and in particular, at least in principle, everything that contributed to its production.

5
Fatherhood Discourses in Parenting Magazines

In this chapter and the next I examine some gendered discourses surrounding fatherhood in written texts. We are thus not looking at *actual* fatherhood practices, but rather at the discourses that seem to be drawn on in their textual representation. Like motherhood, fatherhood can be viewed as both experience and institution (Rich, 1976). As institution, it is an interesting epistemological site since the social practices that together and variously constitute fatherhood (and motherhood) are, in many cultural contexts, in a state of flux, a flux corresponding to that in gender relations more widely.

Fatherhood is represented in a range of fictional media genres – soap operas and Hollywood films, for example. *Mass*, often global, media may be a particularly potent cultural site in the way these subject position women and men (though this does not equate with *influence*), and for the reproduction of normative gendered identities and relations (see Walsh, 2002; also Bergvall, 1999; though see Sutton, 1999, on the question of the linguistic relevance of the media as data for language and gender research). Here, we are concerned with the representation of fatherhood in the non-fictional print media genres of commercial parenting magazines and newspaper editorials on and reports of 'celebrity fatherhood' (Chapter 6). In media texts, the relationship between the text producer and text consumer/interpreter is 'mediated by' that text, but unidirectionally: the roles of producer and consumer/interpreter do not alternate, unlike in most talk. Any negotiation of meaning can therefore take place only through the consumer/interpreter cognitively *engaging* with the text.

Parenthood discourse is not a new area of research. Before moving on to the epistemological site of parenting magazines and the topic of fatherhood, I therefore briefly review four related studies, the first two of motherhood, the second two motherhood and fatherhood.[1]

In a study of conversations between women friends, Jennifer Coates took as her starting point that the range of discourses to which we have access 'enable us to perform different "selves"' (1997: 291); this can be seen as *self-positioning*. She identified two competing discourses of maternity. The first was a 'dominant' discourse, 'which says that children are "marvellous", and as part of which all mothers take pride in their children's achievements'. Coates saw a linguistic trace of this in a mother's response to a question about how her child performed in an end-of-term play: 'yes ... he was marvellous/he was marvellous/every kid in it was marvellous'. The second, 'alternative' discourse 'asserts that not all children are likable and ... it is not compulsory for adults to like all children' (1997: 294). Coates cites a conversation in which one woman, Sue, says, 'I still quite often don't like children' and another, Liz, responds, 'Actually, I think you particularly dislike your own.' While there is laughter, from Sue, after what she says and before Liz responds, and while we do not have to read this bit of talk 'straight', Coates is, I think, right to claim that this is a very subversive discourse. It is made more so, here, since Sue and Liz are both mothers and are in effect contesting the idea of women as 'loving, caring, nurturing beings for whom having children is the ultimate experience of their lives' (1997: 294). Sue and Liz are actively producing this alternative discourse of maternity (femininity?) and are not unthinking victims of the dominant one. However, though there is no documented instance of Sue or Liz also producing traces of the 'dominant' discourse of maternity, there is no reason to think they have never done so given their access to this, and the documented frequency of production of conflicting discourses and of individuals' 'interpretive repertoires' (e.g. Wetherell et al., 1987; Edley, 2001).

The other three studies are of *representations* of parenthood in written texts and visuals. The discourses 'identified' can be seen as 'co-constructed' by the analyst in conjunction with the text itself and all that contributed to its production.

Harriette Marshall (1991) used a 'discourse analytic approach' to identify 'recurrent themes and constructions of motherhood' in a selection of parentcraft texts and manuals from 1979–88. She refers to these themes and constructions as 'accounts', which can also be seen as *discourses* (she does refer to a 'missing' discourse). From an implicitly critical perspective Marshall writes:

> Given that the same phenomenon could be described in a number of ways, discourse analysis examines social texts, both spoken and

written, to see which linguistic constructions are selected and which are omitted. (1991: 67)

This is to see as important what is not said, as well as what is (see also van Leeuwen, 1996, 1997; Fairclough, 2003). The reference here is to traces of discourses, but it is possible *explicitly* to extend this idea to absent *discourses* (see also Chapter 7). Marshall's accounts include the (ironically titled) 'Motherhood as ultimate fulfilment', 'Mother love as natural' and 'Sharing the caring'. Echoing Lazar, Marshall points out that 'sharing' usually means that the father is responsible for the most positive aspects of childcare and the mother for the maintenance work. She also identifies 'Anything goes' (the 'Flexibility' account) and a 'Happy Families' account (the assumption that the child is living with its biological parents, a contented heterosexual couple, and that only the mother's role is crucial). These two accounts clearly compete. The 'missing' discourse is

> one that gives consideration to depression associated with the social environment and changes in women's lives as a consequence of having children, including their financial situation, dissatisfaction with medical intervention or giving up employment outside home. (1991: 82)

Michelle Lazar (2002) looked at both motherhood and fatherhood in TV and print ads aiming to persuade 'better educated' Singaporeans (in particular women) to marry and start families – of more than one child. In one ad, the print version includes 'there's one precious gift, which only you can give – a brother or sister'. Using a critical Hallidayan framework, Lazar notes that the TV version 'concretely plays this out through the deployment of a transactional action process, whereby the mother, the Actor, gives a new-born baby, the Goal, over to the delighted boy, the Beneficiary' (2002: 122), and identifies what she calls the construction of the mother's 'other-centredness' in this motherhood discourse. 'Other-centredness' is also exemplified in representations of a mother cheering on a child in a race and holding the float of a child attempting to swim. Lazar notes:

> The gendered nature of the mundane care-giving tasks the mother performs is emphasised in contrast to what the father is shown doing at the same time … whilst the mother [above] is represented as watching over the safety of her young son at the beach by holding onto his float, the father, although also represented as an Actor, is engaged in an activity entirely different in nature from the basic care-giving function performed by the mother. The father performs a popular,

entertainer role whereby he plays with and makes funny faces at the child ... (2002: 122)

Lazar observes that despite her other-centredness *and* bearing the prime onus of parenting in these ads, the mother is rarely the focus of the *child*'s attention. In the above example, the child's attention is on the entertaining father. It appears that 'the other-centredness of mothers is taken for granted as part of their maternal "nature" and, therefore, as something quite unremarkable' and that '[p]art of being other-centred ... is represented as contentedly watching from the margin the bonding that goes on between the father and children' (2002: 123). Lazar cites both the advertisement genre and the 'discourse of conservative gender relations' as constituting the primary subject position offered to women here: 'consumers of all-consuming personal relationships' (2002: 124).

I too looked at both fatherhood and motherhood discourses in British parenting manuals, magazines and National Health Service literature of the early 1990s (Sunderland, 2000a, 2002). Through linguistic analysis, including of the verbs *play, help* and *share*, the nouns *play, help* and *fun*, and the 'social actor' nouns *mother/father* and substitution forms such as *someone else*, I interpretively identified 'Mother as full-time parent/Part-time father' (broadly equivalent to Marshall's 'Sharing the caring') as an 'overarching' discourse. I similarly found that this was (to use an architectural metaphor) 'supported by' related, 'bricked together', discourses which I called 'Mother as line manager of the father', 'Mother as wife/partner', 'Father as baby entertainer', 'Father as mother's bumbling assistant' and 'Father as line manager' (see Potter, 1996: 103, for a similar 'brick' metaphor). This cluster of fatherhood discourses was not coincidental; rather, the part-time nature of this represented fatherhood *entails* activities which are non-essential to the baby's survival and thus allows a measure of relative incompetence.

* * *

This study: parenting magazines

One recent development in popular texts on childcare has been the advent of glossy magazines with such titles as *Parents, Parenting, Practical Parenting, Parentwise* and *Baby Years: For Parents of Children from Birth to Age Five*.[2] These magazines are particularly interesting sites for the study of fatherhood discourses. In contrast to, say, *Mother and Baby*, the UK's best-selling parenting magazine, magazines with such titles might be *expected* to address and represent mothers and fathers alike; whether they do was the topic of my study and the focus of this chapter.

Mothers and fathers may not be *equally* prominent: for one reason, in breastfeeding, fathers cannot do more than be part of the 'breastfeeding team' (perhaps feeding with expressed milk); for another, women-specific topics may include ante- and post-natal exercise, maternity wear and diet; and, third, single mothers are likely to figure in the target audience. However, we could logically expect fathers to be 'co-addressees' and be represented in a wide variety of parenting practices in a significant proportion of the magazine features.

At first glance these parenting magazines would seem to bear more similarity to women's 'lifestyle magazines' than to 'men's magazines' (which tend to feature 'special interests', soft porn, or both – see *Snowboarder*, for example). Light but serious (non-ironic) advice features concerning human relationships are immediately evident. The persona of the writers is friendly and the tone of their features informal, with use of *you* and *your* frequent (see Talbot, 1998).

There is also a large number of advertisements for consumer products. These are *commercial* magazines, and the role of advertisements is important, since promoters expect magazines to provide a 'hospitable environment' for their ads. Talbot writes:

> As a matter of necessity, magazines have become saturated with the genre of advertising (advertising has been the main economic support of the magazine industry since the end of the nineteenth century; the cover price of a present day 'glossy' would not cover the cost of the paper it is printed on). Because of pressure from manufacturers and their advertisers … it has become increasingly difficult for magazine editors to include anything that is not directly related to promoting products. (1998: 173)

There are thus adverts for *and features on* (post-)maternity wear, children's clothes, equipment for baby and toys galore. For example, an article in *Baby Years* on 'A germ-free environment' is juxtaposed on the facing page with an advertisement for a sanitizer. Sponsorship thus shapes the content and tone of a magazine. In the women's magazines analysed by Dorothy Smith (1988), women and girls were positioned as consumers through the combined missions of the fashion, cosmetics and publishing industries. If most women's magazines thus draw on a discourse of 'consumer femininity' (Talbot, 1995b, 1998) operating within 'consumer capitalism' (Fairclough, 2000), these parenting magazines draw heavily on a discourse of 'consumer parenthood' – or rather, as we shall see, 'consumer maternity'.

Data and preliminary observations

The magazines sampled for the study were an issue of each of the American magazines *Parents* (November 2002), *Parenting* (November 2002) and *Baby Years* (October/November 2002).[3] All three magazines present a similar, cheerful, rather simple picture of family life in which everyone means well, and though child rearing is not easy, problems can always be overcome – often through welcome advice. Shared values seem to be assumed (see also Talbot, 1998: 186). Some families are one-parent, some children have learning or behavioural difficulties and some children are adopted – from within the US or overseas. However (at least in the issues chosen for analysis), there is no hint of anything other than heterosexuality. The target readership is different, but only slightly: *Baby Years* looks at children from 'preemies' (premature babies) up to five years, *Parenting* at children from birth to twelve years, and *Parents* at embryohood to age thirteen.

Lifestyle magazines are heterogeneous genres, and these three include both advice and non-advice genres, the latter including 'Out of the mouths of babes' (the cute things little children say), celebrity profiles, 'true life' personal narratives and letters to the editor. This heterogeneity extends beyond genres to discourses, and Talbot gives examples of 'journalism, discourses of economics, the family, fashion, science (selectively drawn on in the health and beauty sections) and, very selectively, feminism' (1998: 177). Magazines are also *multi-voiced*, not only in terms of multiple authorship, but also because individual articles are sometimes populated by various characters. This is true of the majority of the childcare advice articles in each of *Parenting, Parents* and *Baby Years*, 'voices' including not only that of the writer, but also quoted 'experts' and parents.

In terms of gender, a quick flick through the pages reveals visuals (in advertisements and otherwise) featuring fathers; an examination of the written texts reveals references to *parents*. At first sight, most features seem gender-neutral. The Contents pages of *Baby Years*, for example, include advice features such as 'Disciplining your toddler' and 'Spotting and treating ear infections'. Some features are, however, explicitly oriented to mother or father, for example, an article on breastfeeding ('Two at a time'). In the parallel 'Time for Mom' and 'Time for Dad', the former is entitled: 'Keeping up Appearances' and subtitled 'Improving your child's body image', but 'Time for Dad' is entitled 'Dads on the Move' and subtitled 'A guide to the rock-climbing trend'. The 'Parent to Parent' feature is entitled 'Empty: How it feels when a mother's arms are no longer full'.

The titles in *Parenting* and *Parents* are also largely 'gender-neutral' – although the 'Work and Family' feature entitled 'How Your Working Affects Your Child' turns out to be about *mothers* who work outside the home, and 'Single parents: involving your ex' has as its focus the single mother. In *Parenting* the explicit exception is the 'Essay', 'Have husbands joined a bedroom conspiracy?' (i.e. to sleep on the side of the bed away from the bedroom door). There is, though, a feature entitled 'Parenting as a team' (see below). In *Parents*, the exception to the gender-neutral titles are 'Healthy mom' and the 'Healthy mom handbook'. The three-feature section entitled 'Time for you' has as the titles of its first two features 'Simple beauty' and 'Best face forward'. (The third feature is 'Sex and marriage'; there are in fact two articles on parental sex in this issue, the second being entitled 'Behind the bedroom door'.) There is also an article entitled 'Emergency guide: first aid for babies' – though on the cover the corresponding by-line is 'Lifesaving moves moms must know'. Though gender-neutrality and apparent inclusiveness may extend from the magazine title to the feature title (an editorial requirement of consistency?), it may stop there.

For this study, I chose to focus on 'advice' features (henceforth 'articles') that concerned parental *childcare*.[4] The ostensible purpose of these articles is to shape actual parenting behaviour in a helpful way, and they therefore seemed to provide the greatest scope for study of representation (and possible construction) of 'desirable' childcare-related fatherhood practices. The number of childcare advice articles in each of the three magazines was as follows: *Parenting* – 11, *Parents* – 7, *Baby Years* – 13, a total of 31.

Critical Discourse Analysis (CDA) provides a suitable framework for looking for discourses, including *competing* discourses, here, in part through an examination of the linguistic features for representations of social asymmetries, and in part through identification of salient absences. I also draw on the Althusserian notion of 'interpellation' ('hailing') in order to look at who is really being addressed by texts on 'parenting', and on the notion of reader response (here, Mills, 1992).

The language of parenting

How might a magazine genuinely promoting full-time or hands-on fatherhood, or 'shared parenting', index this linguistically? Editors and writers would presumably consider both *address* and *representation*. For the latter, I suggest we would find few verbs describing the father's actions which might be seen as linguistic traces of the 'Part-time father' discourse – verbs of the *helping out, entertaining* and *bumbling* semantic field variety (Sunderland, 2000a, 2002). *Breastfeeding* might be frequently mentioned, but so would the father's role in providing support, together with the alternative or supplementary practice of *expressing milk* (milk which can then be given to a baby by the father or other carer).

For *address*, Althusser's (1984) notion of *interpellation* is useful. Usually glossed as 'hailing', the most frequently cited example of interpellation is someone who hears a police officer call out 'Hey, you!' and turns round. The police officer has constructed (or 'subject positioned') the person in a particular way (subject to authority and possibly guilty of something), and the person who turns round (assuming she is not simply curious) can be seen as sharing that recognition and the person being 'hailed' can even be seen as constructing/positioning herself as guilty. One can, though, be interpellated by more than just upholders of the law, including by what Althusser calls 'ideological state apparatuses'. These include the media, which 'through a constant barrage of images and information … map out the role of the subject' (Mills, 1992: 186). They do this, according to Mills, to reproduce the conditions of production within a society, since 'in order for a capitalist society to continue to function, workers must be made to recognise their position within that society and accept those roles' (1992: 186). Applying this to childcare, a socialist feminist analysis might claim that, under capitalism, women's main role (as daughters, wives, mothers) is twofold: to *maintain* male workers, for example by making sure they are well fed, clothed and rested (and not at the state's expense), so that they can continue production, and to *produce* new workers. In (late) modernity, this analysis is dated in many ways. However, vestiges remain, for example in the well-documented male–female division of domestic labour, and gendered tendencies in full-/part-time patterns of paid employment.

If parenting magazines can be seen as *potentially* part of the ideological state apparatuses of the media, we can look at their patterns of interpellation in this light. A study of 'direct interpellation' might begin with occurrences of *you* and the possessive adjective *your*. If shared parenting is being encouraged, we would expect recurring plural *you* (and few occurrences of *your husband*, for example). *You* is, of course, ambiguous: felicitously so, perhaps, for the practice of slipping from plural *you* to a singular addressee – in principle, father *or* mother. Other pronouns can also interpellate a reader. *We* may be inclusive of the reader, but which one(s)? Again, there can be slippage here. What begins life as 'we parents' might later change to 'we mums', for example.[5]

Linguistic features other than pronouns can also interpellate *indirectly* – in fact, there is what Mills calls 'an unending series of hailings' (1992: 186). We can, for example, look at how parents are *lexicalized* in noun phrases. If shared parenting is being encouraged, we would expect recurrences of *parent[s], mum and dad,* and their equivalents. Importantly, if such lexical representation can function as interpellation, representation can also be seen as a form of address. Yet again, however, there may be slippage – despite being in principle 'common gender', *parent* may start by (potentially) meaning either parent, but later mean *mum* or *dad*.[6]

Interpellation goes beyond noun phrases and pronouns. When main verbs are in the passive, the 'agent' may not be indicated, for example: 'A hot baby needs to be ...'. And consider participles, for example: 'Providing stimulation for a baby ...'. Here, either or both parents can be seen as textually 'backgrounded' – perhaps for stylistic reasons, the agent(s) being self-evident from the rest of the text, *or* deliberately deselected. It is then up to the reader to supply an 'agent' or 'social actor', drawing not only on her views and experiences (including of other texts outside the magazine), but also on other cues within this text and magazine. Such cues include the overall 'environment' of the magazine as well as the language of the particular advice feature. 'Indirect interpellation' in a consistent direction in all these ways, together with the use of singular *you,* may mean the 'ideal reader' of these texts is not father and mother equally.

The broad research question for this study was thus whether the magazines constituted a 'shared parenting' environment, or at least a 'father-friendly' one. This required looking at the different 'voices', references to breastfeeding, gender stereotyping, any representations of 'shared parenting', salient textual absences of the father and visuals – as well as formal linguistic features. In this way it was possible to co-construct several discourses of parenthood, discourses which may positioned fathers and mothers in particular ways, and to identify the addressee(s) of the advice features (mother, father or both), within this broad understanding of interpellation.

Analysis and discussion

In all three magazines, the representation of fatherhood can at best be described as 'mixed' and at worst as distinctly unencouraging. This was apparent from both the formal linguistic features and, more widely, in what can be called the mother-friendly environment of the advice articles. (In the following sections, *Baby Years, Parenting* and *Parents* are referenced by BY, P and PS, respectively; the following number refers to the relevant feature in each dataset.)

Formal linguistic features

Starting with pronouns and referents to parents, phrases such as *you, your baby, your tot, your doctor, your child, your children, your kids,* and *your new-born* are commonplace, most articles allowing readings of *you* as male parent, female parent or both (with no slippage later). 'Common gender' phrases involving *parent[s]*, including *single parent*, are also frequent, and writers have apparently tried to be inclusive here. There are, however, instances of what can charitably be interpreted as slippage: *Parenting*'s 'Work and Family: How your working affects your child' opens with 'For working mothers ...' [P2]. Similarly, *Parents*' '0–12 months: Pucker up!' begins: 'You've undoubtedly been smooching your baby and saying things like "Give mommy a kiss!"...' [PS7a].

And the linguistic absence of father is salient. Despite the frequent occurrence of *parent[s]*, explicit occurrences of *father, dad* and equivalents are relatively rare (both alone and as part of *mum and dad* phrases). There are explicit mentions of father in only three of the childcare advice articles in *Parents*, two in *Baby Years* and five in *Parenting* (i.e. in around only one in three of the articles). (In contrast, *mum* and equivalents can be found in almost every article.) In the absence of a 'Part-time father' discourse (= Mother as main parent), this would be odd. Consider, for example: ' "If you wash the pacifier every time the baby drops it, you are going to be too tired to be a good mother," says Dr Margaret Byers Smith' [BY7]. This would presumably be true of fathers too. But, given the 'Part-time father' discourse, it does not read oddly.

The references to fathers (with one or more examples from each feature) are as follows:

Parents: PS1: 'Kids' health and safety: 'Daddy–baby bonding'
'Massage may help new fathers bond with their babies'

PS3: 'Discipline after divorce'
'That's just the way it is here. Dad and I just have different opinions about things'

PS8a: 'As they grow, 0–12 months: Pucker up!'
'Putting an open mouth on daddy's face shows just how scruffy his cheek is; placing it on mommy's reveals her skin's softness' [not a complimentary or constructive representation of daddy!]

PS8d: 'Hello, dolly!'
'your toddler will probably first be interested in playing mom or dad to his doll'

PS8f: 'I've got a secret'
'when her mother placed her [the child's] father's beauti-fully-wrapped present on the dining-room table ...'

Baby Years: BY2: 'Juggling act: do sibling bedtimes have to be a battle?'
'spend some good quality time with Mom and Dad'
'If you have a 4-, 5- and 8-year-old, the 8-year-old can stay up a little longer and hang out with Dad while Mom is bathing the younger ones ...'
'Sometimes, Mom and Abigail (4) might make lunches for the next day, while Dad and Ari (18 m.) read in the next other room'
+ the phrase *one parent ... and the other*

BY9b: 'A Guide to Baby's First Immunizations'
'Dr Humiston ... suggests that Dad or Grandma take the baby to that first appointment if Mom doesn't feel she can handle it'

Parenting: P2: 'Work and Family: How your working affects your child'
'As a society,' says Waldfogel [expert], 'we need to offer moms and dads more choices ...'

P5: 'Parenting as a team'
'when Martha explained that crying is a baby's only way of communicating that he needs mom or dad ...'

P8: 'Talking to kids about sex'
'moms and dads when they need to clean you'

P10: 'Money matters'
'Despite the best intentions, moms and dads sometimes give kids the wrong idea when it comes to finances'

P11: 'Involving your ex'
'Kids win when dads stay in touch'

Overall, however, the father is *not* interpellated, either with *you, dad* or equivalent – a 'missing trace' (but a clear one) characterizing the 'Part-time father' discourse.

There were several other manifestations of 'Part-time father' in the lexis – *step in, help out*, give mum a *break* and other less predictable lexi-calizations. Examples (emphasis added) include:

Parents: PS10: 'As they grow – 7–10 years – ewww, boys! Yuck, girls!'
'Avoid making statements such as "Guys never *help out*" '

Parenting: P5: 'Parenting as a team'
'That's why I'd [father] often *step in* and say, "I'll *comfort* the baby. You [mother] need a *break"* '
P9c: 'Ages and Stages: 1–2 years – "I want Mommy" ' '
'Include your partner. After you've performed your regular nighttime ritual, for instance, *he might give your child a massage or sing her a song*'

Baby Years: BY3: 'Feeding two at a time'
'Monroe … credits her husband, who works at home, for participating in childcare and *helping her* in difficult situations. But what happens if a tandem nurser doesn't have an understanding spouse?'

These can achieve propositional coherence (make sense) for a reader only within the context of a shared 'Mother as main parent/Part-time father' discourse (see Talbot, 1996).

In *Parents*, we also read that massage 'may help new fathers' in 'daddy–baby bonding' [PS1]. This linguistic trace of 'Part-time father' additionally seems to represent 'daddy–baby bonding' as something that may not be achieved without conscious intervention (imagine the sentence 'Massage may help new mothers bond with their babies'), and thus seems to represent fatherhood (beyond the biological) as something unnatural.

A father-friendly environment?

So, if the formal linguistic features in many of these magazine articles largely interpellate the mother, how about broader rhetorical stances? Can we find ways in which the father is indirectly addressed? Here I look at visuals, 'voices', the topic of breastfeeding and gender representations and stereotypes.

In each magazine dataset, three visuals include a father. These are

Parenting

- Baby with father in 'What every parent needs to know about why babies do what they do – newborn reflexes' [P7]
- Dad being reached out for by child with Mum behind, in '1–2 years – "I want Mommy!" ' [P9b]
- Father with child in 'Involving your ex' [P11]

Baby years

- Photo of mum, dad and three children sitting on a bench, in 'Have a safe and happy Halloween' [BY1]

- Mum and dad being disturbed by kids in pyjamas, with mum attempting to restore order, in 'Juggling act: do sibling bedtimes have to be a battle?' [BY2]
- Father with young twin boys in 'Healthy competition' [BY11]

Parents

- Father holding small child, in 'Kids' health and safety' [PS1]
- Line drawing of father listening for child breathing, in *'Parents* magazine emergency guide' [PS2]
- Father (with mother) on couch in front of protesting kids, in 'How to bratproof your child' [PS5]

While these visual representations cannot be said to be overwhelmingly stereotypical (they are, in fact, rather mixed), the *paucity* of visual representations of fathers is notable.

What perhaps contributes most to the mother-friendly environment of these magazines and thus to the indirect interpellation of the *mother*, however, is probably the array of different female 'voices' in the articles, which are noticeably heteroglossic. Embedding the 'individual voice' in this way may be an attempt to counterbalance the 'mass' nature of these articles, with their inevitable blandness (see also Sutton, 1999). The feature writer's own words constitute 'primary discourse' – the 'representing or reporting discourse' (Fairclough, 1995: 54, from Volosinov). Other explicit 'voices' constitute 'secondary discourse' – the 'discourse represented or reported'. 'Secondary discourse' voices include those of 'experts', who explain, and who are also often mothers: 'Dr Margaret Byers Smith, a mom and retired social psychologist from Fayetteville, Arizona', or are closely in touch with actual parental concerns: 'Sally Shaywitz, a paediatrician and neuroscientist.' However, more often, 'secondary discourse' voices are those of parents. With one exception, these are always mothers. Mums illustrate and exemplify. We read, for example, that ' "I got all choked up and teary when they had their first shots," says Heather M. Haapoja, a mom from Duluth, Minn.'

As with Dr Margaret Byers Smith, above, multiple roles and identities are often documented: in *Baby Years*, for example, we read that Carma Haley Shoemaker 'is a mother and contributing editor for *Baby Years* and *iParenting.com'*. This 'double role representation' happens frequently and looks like editorial policy. We are always told where the mums and experts come from, perhaps to lend interest, credibility and authenticity. Perhaps for the same reasons, their ('secondary discourse') words are in turn always reported using 'Direct Discourse' (using speech marks) rather than

'Indirect [reported] Discourse' (Fairclough, 1995). This is a case of apparent 'manifest intertextuality' (see Chapter 2), although we do not know how the mothers' and experts' words were 'acquired', or indeed how they have been edited and changed.

This multitude of voices means that a given article is unlikely to present a homogeneous representation of motherhood/fatherhood. In particular, writers tend to use *parents* throughout, and the cited 'experts' *mom*. However, the importance of these essentially *formal* features should not be overstated. The use of *parents* does not, as we have seen, in itself constitute a challenge to the 'Part-time father' discourse.

The mother-friendly environment is also achieved through fleeting, but reiterated references to breastfeeding, mentioned in three features in *Parenting*, five in *Baby Years* and one in *Parents*. Examples include:

> 'Drue Ramirez...found that nursing was an excellent distraction ...' [BY9b]
>
> 'Don't smoke or allow your children to spend time around smokers. And, just as importantly, breastfeed as long as possible ...' [BY9c]
>
> 'Breastfeed, if you can.' [P1a, on 'Early Signs of Obesity']

Injunctions to breastfeed clearly directly interpellate *mothers* and make clear that *you*, here, does not have a plural referent. While no one would wish to discourage articles on breastfeeding, it is perhaps surprising that fathers are not explicitly included. Fathers can provide support (for example, by burping the baby after the feed). They can also feed the baby *expressed* milk (at no cost to nutritional value). The father does not *need* to be textually absent here – but he is.

Lastly, there are some progressive representations of masculinity in general and fatherhood in particular, sometimes in surprising places. In 'Talking to kids about sex' [P8], for example, we read: 'If your little boy feels cheated [at not being able to have a baby], that's a cue to sit him down and tell him all the way a father helps take care of an infant.' While we are back with the predictable *help*, it is interesting that this problem and 'solution' were chosen. In 'As they grow – 2 years: Hello, dolly!' [PS8c] we read:

> 'there's nothing wrong with – and plenty right about – letting boys play with dolls. "It's not a sign of effeminacy," Dr Brody reassures.'

This, of course, presupposes that letting boys play with dolls *might* be wrong. However, more positively, the writer tells us that 'your toddler will probably first be interested in playing mom or dad to his doll'.

Many traditional gender stereotypes can however be found, and these recycle traces of familiar, traditionally gendered discourses. Interestingly, these are usually in the examples provided by the 'experts', by whom they are perhaps seen as a way of communicating some 'general truth'. One example is:

> 'I sometimes wish *parents* would ask themselves, "Would my *mother* have called the doctor about this?"' [P1g; emphasis added]

While this articulation may be attributable to a view that times have changed, others cannot be thus explained. For example:

> 'At some point, if you're a mom to a toddler, you must face the inevitable tantrum in the supermarket, in the restaurant, or wherever you'd least like it to happen ...' [BY4]

One might hope that in a 'parenting' magazine the reference would have been to a mum *or dad* to a toddler. And we have already seen the part-time father stereotype, articulated by a father:

> 'That's why I'd often step in and say, "I'll comfort the baby. You need a break"' [P5]

A similar example is:

> 'Include your partner. After you've performed *your regular* nighttime ritual, for instance, he might give your child a massage or sing her a song' [P9c; emphasis added]

In an already 'mother-friendly' magazine, *your regular* indexes 'mother', and *he*, I suggest, indexes a male partner (even for those who believe that *he* can be fully generic) in a heterosexual context. (Alternatively, *he* retrospectively indexes *your regular* as mother.) This leaves father interpellated only very indirectly, in contrast with mother. Note also the traces of both the 'Mother as full-time parent' *and* the 'Father as baby entertainer' discourses here.

Then there are the predictable female stereotypes:

> ' "Most of us at some point in life have been either the toddler or the *frustrated mom*," says Douglas [expert]. "We just have to hope that we don't end up turning into the *annoyed little old lady* down the road ..."' [BY4; emphasis added]

which provides support for the use of one gendered stereotype by adding another and would seem to multiply interpellate a mother 'we' rather than a father 'we'. Another (familiar) example:

> Dr. Humiston ... suggests that Dad or Grandma take the baby to that first appointment [for an inoculation] if Mom doesn't feel like she can handle it [BY9b]

stereotypes the mother as the 'default' carer *and* a potentially overemotional one, and stereotypes dad as someone who will 'step in' and be rational, not emotional!

Finally, the extended 'As they grow' section in *Parents* (PS7) has a whole cluster of parenting stereotypes. We have already seen one from '0–12 months: Pucker up!' (p. 110). Additionally, in '1 year – make No mean No', the advice that the child should be told 'No biting mommy' interpellates 'mommy' as the person responsible for the essential 'socialization' of the child, as does the suggestion for helping a child overcome shyness: saying 'No sitting on Mommy's lap at the party' ('3–4 years, why so shy?'). In '1–2: Hello, dolly!', we read ' "Early in life, a child doesn't think of herself as distinct from Mom", explains Kurt Fischer, PhD.' The intended point of substance is presumably that the very young child doesn't think of herself as distinct *from the main carer*, and the fact that this may *usually* be mum doesn't warrant the exclusive nature of Fischer's reported claim.

The 'dominant reading' of these texts can, then, be seen as one in which the main addressee is the mother, who is represented as the 'real' parent. In only one small feature (in *Parents*, on 'Daddy–baby bonding') are fathers the focus (P1). As Mills notes, although dominant readings may be unstable, most readers can nevertheless 'recognize the "obvious" role/s, positions and interpretations which the text maps out for them' (1992: 191). I suggest that the 'Part-time father' discourse is clearly being drawn on and (re-)produced here, and that fathers and mothers alike will recognize the rather different roles mapped out for them in these 'parenting' magazines.

Shared parenting?

As indicated, the dataset includes some occurrences of explicit 'shared parenting' lexis, for example *Mum or Dad, mums and dads,* and references to childcare tasks (not) 'being performed by the same person' together with a claim that not being the preferred parent 'can be painful for the one who's out of favor to hear' [both P9c]. A limited 'shared parenting' discourse may be being produced by the *writers* of the articles – if not by the reported voices of mums or experts – and this may be magazine policy.

A 'Shared parenting' discourse was never *explicitly* articulated, however, in the sense that, somewhat bizarrely (given the titles of these three magazines), shared parenting itself is neither actively encouraged nor discussed. The only article to come close to doing so is 'Parenting as a team' [P5]. And 'Parenting as a team' is particularly disappointing. Written by the father, 'Dr Sears', at first sight it apparently endorses shared parenting. There are frequent occurrences of *parents* and *mum and dad*, and sentences such as:

'[Hayden] helped us discover how necessary it is to share parenting responsibilities – from changing diapers to telling bedtime stories – both for our sanity and for the good of our children.

However, the word *share* here is less impressive than it might have been given that, in reality, the couple do not share the parenting at all! The article includes the sentence: 'That's why I'd often step in and say, "I'll comfort the baby. You need a break."' *Step in* and *break* both index *atypical* parts of any childcare regime and, with 'comfort the baby' (a non-survival-oriented, fun-related activity), are 'classic' traces of the 'Part-time father' discourse.

Shared parenting could also have been talked about in *Parenting*, in 'Work and family: how your working affects your child' [P2]. However, not only does *you* refer only to the child's *mother*, there is no discussion of how paid work and childcare might be shared between two (working) parents, to the advantage of all. There is fudging (at best) and disingenuity (at worst) in the article's conclusion:

The burden of juggling both a job and a family shouldn't rest on working parents' shoulders. 'As a society,' says Waldfogel [expert], 'we need to offer moms and dads more choices ...'

This 'works' because, as a statement, few would disagree with it (choices are normally seen as a good thing for everyone); at the same time, since the idea of the mother as the default carer in the body of the article is so naturalized, the disjuncture is barely noticeable. Gender relations around parenting are thus simply not problematized in these 'parenting' magazines.

Back to mothering ...

The main fatherhood discourse running through these 'parenting' magazines is therefore *still* that of 'Part-time father' (or Marshall's ironic 'Sharing the caring'), in the traces of which the father is referred to, but always in an auxiliary role. There is no evidence of the specific, 'supporting' discourse of 'Father as bumbling assistant' and little of 'Father as baby entertainer' (Sunderland, 2000a, 2002) – fathers here are not bumbling and do not just 'play' with their young children. What they *do* do, however, is nevertheless little more than 'step in' and 'help'. That 'Mother as main parent' remains the dominant discourse is suggested by all indexes of represented fatherhood here – pronouns, representations of shared parenting, visuals and the overall mother-friendly 'environment'. The person being interpellated is, overall, not father.

That these texts directly and indirectly interpellate the mother in a range of ways suggests that these 'parenting' magazines *are* women's magazines: 'attractive to women because they are about being female and the problems of being female' (Caldas-Coulthard, 1996: 252). With occasional exceptions, not problematizing gender relations (and hence parenting relations) is characteristic of women's 'lifestyle' magazines (Caldas-Coulthard, 1996); similarly, comments on the absence of discussion of gender politics and power relations here) just as 'advice' *is* a characteristic of women's magazines.

Mills (1992: 191) sees a dominant reading as one 'offered' by the text to the reader 'within a particular historical moment'; it is 'dominant' because of the *range* of ideological positions available at that moment which make that text coherent. The reading 'offered' here would seem remarkable if traditionally gendered parenting and other discourses were not already circulating. The most relevant ideological position is the 'naturalness' of the practices associated with the 'Mother as main parent' discourse. Althusser (1984) refers to such 'naturalness' as an 'obviousness' – something imposed, but without the appearance of imposition. For Althusser, 'obviousnesses' and interpellation *together* position the reader (Mills, 1992: 187) – in this case, as a mother who 'mothers' full-time and as a father who looks after their child(ren) on a part-time basis.

A text which constructs femininity in a particular way will then be made understandable 'because it is reinforced by a range of other texts and discourses on femininity' (Mills, 1992: 191). The gendered *fatherhood* discourses we have seen in these 'parenting' magazines, together with the absent 'Shared parenting' and 'Full-time father' discourses, are understandable – recognizable – because they are members of, and have intertextual links within, a wider 'order of discourse', which includes the traditional and normative fatherhood (and motherhood) discourses identified elsewhere (Marshall, 1991; Sunderland, 2000a, 2002).

The contribution of the reader

The above discussion hints at, but does not directly address, the different positions (future) fathers and mothers might adopt when reading such texts. I therefore conclude this chapter by looking briefly at possible readings of the same 'parenting' text. This is to consider *reception* (or *consumption*) of written texts (but see Stephens, 1992: 59, on the disparateness of 'reader response criticism').

Readers are positioned in a range of ways by texts, and indirect interpellation will include that of the discourses flowing through a given text. Clearly, readers cannot negotiate their positions *vis-à-vis* the text with the text producers, but they can do this by themselves in the process of reading and cognitively engaging with the text. Textual positioning can then, in principle, be accepted *or* resisted. Acceptance, say by a father, may contribute to him simply not continuing to read a given article (or not reading it in the first place) because he sees it as not 'for' him. One way interpellation can be *resisted*, however, is by having access to oppositional discourses (Talbot, 1996) as well as alternative reading strategies, and continuing to read *despite* not being interpellated, or interpellated in ways contradicting one's own position.

Mills (1992) examines what it is like to be a heterosexual female reader of a particular poem (John Fuller's 'Valentine') about the sexual feelings of a man for a woman, and suggests that one option is to read the poem as if it were addressed to her, i.e. the 'dominant reading'. The problem with this is that it then 'constitutes her within the dominant male view of femininity' (1992: 198), which she may not enjoy. Another option is for her to be a critical 'resisting reader'. Though dealing with a completely different genre and topic, the male reader of these parenting advice texts is in a not dissimilar situation. Let us assume he is a full-time, 'shared parenting' or at least 'hands-on' father, or plans to be so, and is genuinely interested in any advice these magazines may have to offer. Since there is considerable 'social difference' between him and the interpellated or implied female reader (see Talbot, 1995), he may recognize but negatively evaluate the 'Part-time father' discourse – resisting the female-friendly presuppositions and contesting the limited 'part-time father' positioning – but then continue to read, though 'against the grain'.[7] (A mother who is the *partner* of a full-time father, or even as an equal partner in 'shared parenting' may have to adopt a similar strategy.)

Alternatively, this father (to-be) may position himself as an 'overhearer' of a text addressed to women. For the 'overhearing' female reader of 'Valentine', Mills observes that

> even in this slightly distanced form of reading, the ideological messages of indirect address have to be agreed in order to understand the poem. Thus even here the reader will be interpellated by the poem. (1992: 202)

To make sense of these advice texts, the distanced male 'overhearer' will similarly need to be interpellated – as a part-time father.

All this, of course, assumes that a reader (any reader) looks at advice texts in parenting magazines actually seeking advice. This may not be the case: Cameron quotes research suggesting that readers of self-help books do so not for advice (they forgot the details of the advice offered), but rather 'for the pleasure of "recognizing" themselves' (2003: 464). If this is the case also with would-be full-time or shared-parenting fathers, they may need to read against the grain even more! More basically, we have been assuming that people do *read* these magazines (we can safely assume that they buy them). Caldas-Coulthard (1996) sees lifestyle-magazine reading as highly pleasurable for many women (see also Eggins and Iedema, 1997). Santhakumaran (2002), however, identifies at least a sector of women's magazine readers as 'reluctant readers' who rhetorically distance themselves from the magazines in various ways; given the similarity between 'parenting' and other 'women's' magazines, this again raises the question of how seriously advice is taken by readers.

Conclusion

Motherhood as an institution is changing. A leaflet produced by the Toxoplasmosis Trust includes the reminder that: 'It is important for pregnant farmers to be aware that toxoplasmosis can be caught from sheep at lambing time' – this cited by Talbot (1998: 127), who notes that 'Being married and a housewife no longer seems to be central to the definition of a good mother in medical discourse' (1998: 127). This is to be welcomed – especially since, if motherhood is changing, presumably fatherhood is too. From a CDA perspective in which there is a dialectical relationship between the discursive and the material, legislative changes relating to parental (including paternity) leave, together with changes in gendered employment patterns, may prompt discoursal change. Legislation may in turn be shaped *by* discourse. These 'Western', 'parenting' magazines nevertheless still include numerous textual traces of the 'conservative discourse of separate spheres between men and women' (Caldas-Coulthard, 1996: 253). And, perhaps because magazine sponsorship is likely to be related to *readership*, and because of sponsors' cautious approach to that readership, evidenced by the continuing promotion of 'consumer maternity', the traditional interpellation of mother as the main parent is still compelling. It is to be hoped, though, that interpellation of the *father* as part-time, supporting parent rather than co-parent in these magazines may in these times of flux and changing gender relations be 'partial and indirect rather than the successful and complete hailing which Althusser described' (Mills, 1992: 191).

6
Celebrity Fatherhood: The 'Blair Baby'

Before continuing with the topic of contemporary fatherhood discourses, it is worth looking at what fatherhood has *traditionally* meant, since new discourses develop interdiscursively out of older ones, and are thus likely to manifest discoursal links with these. In many cultures, fatherhood has traditionally been an indication of men's fertility, virility and manhood. *To father* has no female equivalent. Adrienne Rich writes 'To "father" a child suggests above all to beget, to provide the sperm which fertilizes the ovum .... A man may beget a child in passion or by rape, and then disappear...' (1976: 12). A child can thus be 'fathered' without any attendant pain of childbirth or risk of death, and certainly without child*care*. Genealogically, fatherhood has also provided a guarantee that the paternal 'line' will be continued and has meant the existence of a future beneficiary of any inheritance. It has thus been *important* as well as socially significant for men. Consider the language surrounding it: there still exist phrasings along the lines of a woman 'having' a man's child or baby. The importance of *paternity* has resulted in traditional restrictions on women's extramarital sexuality (recall Rich's exemplification of the chastity belt in Chapter 3). Continuing the line and being a beneficiary of inheritance were, however, often compromised in the event of the birth of a girl, who (if she survived) would probably change her name on marriage and/or relocate (geographically and socially) to her husband's family and thus disqualify herself from continuing 'the line'; women have also at times and places been legally ineligible to inherit (the motivating theme in Jane Austen's *Pride and Prejudice*).

Just as *to father* normally has no female equivalent, *to mother* (to care for, protect and raise children) normally has no male equivalent. What fatherhood has not meant, traditionally, is involvement with child*care*.

Times may have changed, though not radically, if the 'parenting' magazine representations we saw in Chapter 5 are anything to go by, and practices vary immensely, within and across cultures. But current discourses of fatherhood must be seen against this traditional backdrop – even though the backdrop may be far away and its linguistic traces very faint.

In Chapter 5 we saw overwhelming evidence of the 'Part-time father' discourse. What we saw little of was the specific discourse of 'Father as baby entertainer', and there were apparently no traces at all of 'Father as mother's bumbling assistant' or 'Father as line manager of the mother' (Sunderland, 2000a, 2002). In this chapter, however, I show *other* fatherhood discourses, as evidenced in British newspaper texts surrounding the birth of Leo on Saturday, 20 May 2000 to Cherie Booth (also referred to as Blair), a barrister, and her husband Tony Blair, the British Prime Minister since 1997.

National newspapers have more 'general' audiences than glossy magazines, and any news item will be reported with that general audience in mind. A measure of shared experiences and 'common-sense' attitudes are 'givens' (Talbot, 1995; Sutton, 1999). If the topic is fatherhood, the audience will include those who are not parents and those who have no interest in parenting (or, indeed, in the domestic lives of prominent politicians). But do newspapers constitute good materials for the study of media representation of fatherhood?

Newspapers represent and reflect social practices (cf. the *Mirror*) – though not straightforwardly – and discoursally and potentially reinforce particular social practices. Fairclough (1995) sees media language in general as important for *studying* social and cultural change. Laurel Sutton, however, claims that mainstream media 'are the product of the many, not the one, and are therefore too linguistically diluted to reveal much to the researcher of language and identity' (1999: 165)

Newspaper texts are indeed produced collectively, by reporters, journalists and editors, and are sequentially transformed and modified (Caldas-Coulthard, 1996). Sutton's argument is constructive – rather than mass media texts, she advocates the study of the alternative ' 'zines', which 'represent the words and thoughts of an individual who is solely responsible for their expression' and whose publishers are usually 'individuals who see little of their lives reflected in the pages of *Time* and *Newsweek*' (1999: 165). 'Zines are thus potentially valuable channels for feminism and for the study of new gender identities. However, although mass media texts may tell us little about cognitive processes or identity, as *representational* texts *in their own right* they are surely important for the study of *inter alia* their associated discursive practices, 'mass-ness' *and* popular appeal (why?).

Newspapers have in fact long provided valuable sources of data for the study of gender and language, in part because of their frequent and telling exemplification of sexist language, along with wider stereotypical and normative representations of gender. Caldas-Coulthard, for example, has shown that even in British broadsheet ('quality') newspapers: 'Women are more frequently labelled in their roles as wives and widows than men are as husbands and widowers' (1995: 231). Fowler (1991) found British newspapers categorizing women and men using different sets of noun phrases – men in terms of their occupational roles, women as wives and mothers (see also West et al., 1997). These can all be seen as linguistic traces of traditional gendered discourses. Jean Ward (1984; cited in Lee, 1992), identified several journalistic 'practices' which realize sexist ideology, two of which were 'After marriage, a man remains a man and a woman becomes a wife' and 'Homemaking and parenting are not work'. (We might now refer to these as 'discursive practices' or simply as 'discourses'.) There was, of course, contestation of all such practices, for example by the National Union of Journalists' 'Equality Council', which produced a booklet entitled 'Images of Women: Guidelines for Promoting Equality through Journalism'. Originally published in 1975, this was followed by at least three new editions (1977, 1984 and 1986). This booklet notes that 'Journalists [also] have a responsibility to publicise information which refutes myths about women and corrects popular stereotypes' (1986: 12).

Other studies have focused on the wider gendered discourses evident in newspaper texts. Kate Clark (1998), for example, takes issue with the UK tabloid *Sun*'s representations of women when reporting sexual violence, noting subtle and less subtle manifestations of the sexist 'Blame the victim discourse'. In some contrast, Litosseliti (2002) looks at gendered discourse practices and strategies in moral argumentation in the (broadsheet) *Guardian*'s weekly 'Head to Head' feature, in which opposing views were expressed in a series of letters between two (often male and female) individuals.

Much of the media nowadays are concerned to *appear* non-sexist and to promote the interests of women. This suggests a need for particularly delicate linguistic analysis. As Lazar's study of Singaporean 'governmental doubletalk' shows, texts 'can appear to promote equality between women and men while simultaneously conveying sexist messages' (West et al., 1997: 137; see also Lazar, 2002). Talbot (1997) cites a report in the *Sun* ('£6000 bill puts randy fish boss in his plaice!'), which demonstrates both a 'dominant sexist discourse', including Hollway's (1984) 'Male sexual drive' discourse, *and* a feminist 'Sexual harassment' discourse – the industrial tribunal in question is invoked and not ridiculed. The *Sun* is clearly responding to social changes brought about by feminism, but, as Talbot points out, though these changes may threaten male dominance in, say, the workplace, they do not undermine it.

Celebrity fatherhood

One argument for newspapers as potentially fruitful materials for the epistemological site of fatherhood (as for other institutions) is that they can cast into relief a *diversity* of current discourses, in part because of the range of newspaper genres (for example, 'hard news', Editorials, essays and letters). Of course, it is the 'celebrity' of a celebrity father that is responsible for the media representation of his fatherhood, but this has to be taken on board: celebrity fatherhood is newsworthy, often at a national and even international level, since it provides an insight into the private and personal life of a public figure; the footballer David Beckham is a good example here. 'Non-celebrity' fatherhood, being ubiquitous and *private* (and therefore uninteresting in a non-public figure), usually does not.

Celebrity fatherhood newspaper texts are also newsworthy for the coinciding of a lifestyle most of us do not share with experiences which many of us do, and for their novelty, since men in the news tend to be represented as speaking in public or professional roles (Caldas-Coulthard, 1995). Relatedly, as Fairclough points out, news reports tend to be 'ideational and conceptual', dealing with statements and claims, rather than 'feelings, circumstances, qualities of social and interpersonal relationships, and so forth' (1995: 64). If what is in the news is about a famous person and in part *personal*, about feelings and interpersonal relationships, there is always a curiosity (for some, a hope) about whether that prominent, perhaps powerful individual will remain so under changes in his or her personal life, and whether the principles he or she publicly espouses will founder in everyday practice. This sort of news thus has more than novelty value. Media representation of the birth of Leo is interesting epistemologically since Tony Blair was elected as a potentially dynamic and *modern* leader, the family man who already had three children, and no shortage of convictions and principles, who might be expected to promote (if not practise) 'shared parenting' more than most prime ministers.[1] Additional interest comes from the fact that

Cherie Booth had no intention of renouncing her professional career for full-time motherhood.

Celebrity fatherhood often creates plenty of data, since much mileage is extracted by the media from such events (consider magazines such as *Hello!* and *OK*). The 'Blair baby' was no exception. Data for the study come from almost all British national newspapers – the *Guardian, Times, Independent, Daily Telegraph, Sunday Telegraph, Observer* (broadsheets) and the *Express, Express on Sunday, Mirror, Sunday Mirror, Mail, Sunday Mail, Mail on Sunday, Sunday Post, Sun, News of the World, Sunday People* and *Sport* (tabloids),[2] as well as from one regional paper, the *Daily Mail North West Edition*. Most newspapers carried 'Blair baby' features on several pages, just after the birth and the days following. (There had already been extensive coverage surrounding the announcement of the pregnancy.)

The timing of the birth was relevant to the various newspaper features that followed. Cherie Booth went into hospital on Friday, 19 May 2000, and this was covered in the press. Leo was born at 12.25 a.m. on Saturday, and after a surprisingly short two to three hours was driven back to Downing Street, still in the small hours of Saturday – too late for the Saturday papers to report the birth (they were still reporting that Cherie had gone into hospital), but in plenty of time for the Sunday papers. As the (Sunday paper) *Observer* Editorial jocularly observed on 21 May: 'Welcome, Leo! We had feared you might be born a few hours earlier and give the Saturday papers the fun of reporting on your arrival and speculating on the coming upheavals to the lives of your illustrious parents. But your timing was perfect...' (p. 30). This meant that while some papers could report the birth as 'newsbreaking', others – those that appeared Monday to Friday/Saturday – could not. Monday papers had to be content with reporting the family's first two days with the new member of the family.

The birth of a prime minister's baby prompts not just 'hard news' reports but also 'spin-off' features on a wide range of related topics, such as children born to serving prime ministers, birth choices, older mothers (Cherie was 45 when Leo was born), mothers with careers and paternity leave. *The Times* of Monday, 22 May, for example, included features with the following titles:

I am tired but full of joy (p. 1)
Getting to grips with the first nappy change (p. 6)
'Tip-off' led to cut in odds on name (p. 6)
The Labour way is not for everyone (p. 6)

£1m bids fail for Leo's first photo call (p. 7)
Choice of parish church or cathedral (p. 7)
From Wembley to No 10, the new culture of Dadaism is born (p. 18)

As a prime minister, Tony Blair was considered to be a little left of cen-tre,[3] which creates expectations around (among other issues) childcare. Presumably non-coincidentally, another *Times* feature was 'Struggle to find affordable childcare' – in which the only reference to Blair was 'the warning...that he faces an exodus of women MPs unless the House of Commons adopts more family-friendly hours'. The Editorial (p. 19) was entitled 'Baby Blair: Best politics is making the world a better place for babies'. There was also a cartoon, two letters, and, in *Times 2*, three fea-tures (only very loosely related to the event) entitled 'A hard act to fol-low', 'New baby, new problems' and 'No love at first sight'.

Rather than using individual, pre-selected texts for analysis (though see Bell, 1999), I selected two (rather different) genres to examine from the newspapers – the main reports on Sunday, 21 May and Monday, 22 May (mostly on page 1), and the Editorials. These constitute two datasets (or small corpora).

Fatherhood discourses in the news reports

Here I examine the first reports of Leo's birth and of the events shortly after it. I look first at 'primary discourse' references to Blair as a father, i.e. 'representing or reporting discourse', as seen in Chapter 5 (Fairclough, 1995), excluding indirect as well as direct reported speech. I then look at 'discourse representation' in the form of the reported version of Blair's own words ('secondary discourse', i.e. the 'discourse represented or reported'), making a distinction between that written as direct speech, indicated by speech marks (which I am interested in) and that written in the various forms of indirect speech (Fairclough, 1995; Semino et al., 1999) (which I am not). I regard indirect speech as a further step away from what Blair actually said (i.e. from how he actually constructed himself) and, because of space constraints, I have deselected indirect speech from consideration.

Why is all this of interest? Fairclough writes that 'Semiosis in the representation or self-representation of social practices constitutes discourses' (2001: 235). In these reports we can see both self-representation by Blair and representation of him by the 'newsgivers'. As well as representing, media texts may also *construct* – Litosseliti (2002: 136) for example claims that newspapers are 'a prime public site...for *constructing* values and ideologies' (emphasis added). We can thus argue that in addition to the representation of Blair, *subject positioning* and *construction* of Blair (and construction of fatherhood) are going on too, in part through these discourses (see Chapter 8 on discoursal construction).

(a) Construction by the 'newsgivers'

To what extent and how is Blair represented *as an active father* by the news-givers' 'primary discourse' in these Sunday and Monday front-page reports? Blair is represented here as by no means distant or non-contribut-ing, but yet again we can see traces of the 'Part-time father' discourse. Consider, for example, 'Yesterday it was clear that Mr Blair had been *called on* to help out during Leo's first night at Number 10', and the phrases 'expected to do his share' with its classically agentless passive, and '*help out with* nappy-changing [diaper] duties' (all *Daily Mail*; emphasis added).

This discourse is also evident in the recurring themes of *tiredness* and *nappy-changing. The Times* reported that Blair *looked tired,* the *Daily Mail* (North West edition) that he was *looking tired,* the *Daily Telegraph* described him as *tired looking.* (There are also indirect speech examples of Blair *confessing* to feeling a little tired (*Guardian*), and *admitting* that he was feeling the effects of lack of sleep (*Independent*).) It is possible to speculate on reasons for (and thus readings of) the recurring media selection of Blair's tiredness for inclusion – to show that he has been pos-itively involved with Leo? That he (and, by extension, men) is not cut out to be a hands-on parent? That the country needs a prime minister who is not tired (and especially not tired for this reason)? A shortage of more newsworthy quotes? We cannot be sure – as Mills (1992) notes, writers' intentions are unrecoverable.

Nappy-changing is a focus in four papers shown in the following words:

Sunday Times: Blair, who has already helped change the new arrival's nappy…

Observer: … after a long night which Blair and the press shared awake, he changing nappies while Cherie slept.

Daily Mail: Mrs Blair will use both traditional and 'Green' dis-posable nappies for Leo, and her husband is expected to do his share of the changing. Instead [of taking paternity leave] for the next few weeks or so, [Blair] will spend more time with Cherie and help out with nappy-changing duties.

Sunday People: The chuffed PM put his world responsibilities on hold to perform one of life's less fragrant tasks as wife Cherie enjoyed a well-earned lie-in.

And on page 6 of *The Times* of Monday, 22 May:

> [Blair] and Cherie had agreed that they would take it in turns when the baby woke up in the newly converted nursery in Gordon Brown's former apartment above 10 Downing Street, but with Mrs Blair exhausted after being in labour for 12 hours, it appears that it was the Prime Minister who rediscovered the joys of changing a nappy to the backdrop of the dawn chorus.
>
> As Mrs Blair dozed – the Prime Minister said last week that even a nuclear bomb would not wake her in the middle of the night – he set about the task in hand.

Nappy-changing appears to be the prototypical activity for the 'hands-on' father within these reports' representation of Blair's new fatherhood, and perhaps seen as the prototypical activity outside it. I have heard more than one ask 'And are you changing nappies?' – something that would sound bizarre if asked of a new mother. The *Observer* example is telling here: if Cherie was sleeping (unlikely for long, if, as reported, she had chosen to breastfeed), it is impossible to believe that Blair *only* changed nappies. A new baby does not fall asleep immediately after being changed. Yet it is not the walking up and down with the baby or the rocking to sleep which is focused on here. Nor is it the 'sorting out' of wipes, used nappies and wet baby clothes (and indeed wet parents' clothes). I suggest that this is because nappy-changing lends itself nicely to various 'undisturbing' discourses of fatherhood – what we might call a 'Modern, hands-on father discourse', but also 'Part-time father discourse' (you can change a nappy without taking full responsibility for the child). Hence the *helped change, help out with, is expected to, do his share, while Cherie slept* and *as wife Cherie enjoyed a well-earned lie in* (a reminder of who the full-time parent really is).

Nappy-changing lends itself well too (too well!) to the 'Father as mother's bumbling assistant' discourse (Sunderland, 2000a, 2002). In various inside-page reports, there are indications of Blair's alleged initial trouble with Leo's nappies. For example, the report on page 6 of *The Times* included this (presumably speculative) information:

> For a man who has so much power at his fingertips, he found that he was all fingers and thumbs.

> After a few awkward moments with the nappy, Mr Blair re-acquired
> the knack.

These claims may or may not be accurate (and would be equally likely to
apply to new and out-of-practice mothers) – the point is that nappy-
changing (and awkwardness) has been selected for inclusion. Nappy-
changing seems to be one way the media are able to present Blair as an
acceptable 'new father' without running the risk of showing him as one
who might be fully responsible for (or even fully competent in) baby
care, something that would 'disturb' contemporary heterosexual gender
relations. This can be seen as *legitimizing and reproducing* existing asymmetrical gender relations as if these were a matter of common sense. The
'newsgivers' may have been hoping to establish or maintain important
rapport with the reader (see Fairclough, 1995: 62), rather than risk jeop-
ardizing this.

There are several mentions of Blair's eschewing of paternity leave:

Express on Sunday	For the next few weeks the Prime Minister will go into what he has called 'holiday mode'. But despite Cherie's attempts to persuade him to take paternity leave, he will attend Prime Minister's Question Time on Wednesday and keep in touch with developments in Northern Ireland.
Express	The Prime Minister has promised to scale down work commitments to enable him to spend as much time as possible with the new baby – but has ruled out taking paternity leave.
Daily Mail	Although his wife, in a speech to fellow lawyers, cited 'The fine example' of Finland's Prime Minister Paavo Lipponen who has twice taken full paternity leave, the British Premier has no inten- tion of relinquishing power in the same way.
Sun	[Cherie's] PM husband has ruled out taking paternity leave.

The *Daily Telegraph* does not mention paternity leave *per se*. However,
after noting Blair's 'scaled-back' commitments for the week, it quotes an
aide as saying, 'Obviously with British forces deployed in Sierra Leone,
he wants to stay focused on key areas.' That *obviously* is telling.

While no approval or disapproval is explicitly expressed here, again it
seems that the newspapers have selected the 'undisturbing'. Expressing

surprise at the Prime Minister not taking paternity leave would be just too much! It is also possible that the *Daily Mail* and the *Express on Sunday* welcomed the opportunity to hint at a spot of marital discord in high places (a subject of perennial interest to the tabloid press).

In such 'primary discourse', there is plenty of room for rhetorical manoeuvre on the part of newsgivers, and these representations cannot be separated from what Blair actually said. What I have looked at might also include some 'unsignalled' secondary discourse (Fairclough, 1995, gives the newspaper headline example of 'Mrs Thatcher will not stand for any backsliding'). The conclusion, however, has to be that just as the 'parenting' magazines in Chapter 5 drew hugely on a 'Part-time father discourse' in relation to fatherhood in general, these news reports textually represent/construct Blair as an *individual* father (not part of an institution of fatherhood), in part through a 'Modern, hands-on father discourse', but mainly through that same 'Part-time father discourse'.

I will conclude this section with the *Observer*'s unique front-page report of Sunday, 21 May. The relevant section (which continues on page 2) is:

> Briefly, then, a rumour swept the gates that Blair would be going to the FA [Football Association] cup final. Men were incredulous. 'He wouldn't, would he? That's much too Old Labour,' said eastender David Longman. 'Rubbish,' countered his wife. 'It's just what she would want, after something like that … get the bloody man out of the way.' Blair did not, of course, go to the game. He was probably asleep.

This ironic little text is interesting (and amusing) on three counts. First, there is the implication that if the reason Blair would not go to the Cup Final was that this would appear too 'Old Labour', then his family- and baby-oriented actions at home might equally be seen as being done in part to make sure he appeared suitably 'New Labour'. Second, there is a trace here of what I see as a traditional 'Useless new father discourse' (with a 'Strong woman who holds the family together despite all' discourse – seen in the 'strong working-class woman' of British soap operas – as the other side of that coin). This discourse has not surfaced hitherto – though it can be seen as having intertextual links with the weaker 'Father as mother's bumbling assistant'. Here, the 'Strong woman' discourse is being parodied (we don't know if the 'wife' actually said this or, if she did, whether she meant it seriously). But it has to be said that for some women paternity leave may actually be dis-preferred – either because the new father would indeed be in the way or perhaps because he would only abuse it (by going to a football match, for example). Third, the suggestion that Blair might have chosen to sleep at the time of the cup final is, I believe, ultimately a sympathetic one.

(b) Blair's self-construction

Fairclough comments that the representation of discourse in news media can be seen as 'an ideological process of considerable social importance' (1995: 65; see Fairclough's chapter for an examination of the various forms of discourse representation, with possible reasons for these). Compare, for example, the TV news by-line 'Blair says we will find weapons of mass destruction' with Blair's actual words to a press conference: 'I am confident that we will find weapons of mass destruction' (both reconstructed). The by-line is shocking in its arrogance; the words controversial, but considerably less arrogant.

In looking at the 'secondary discourse' of Blair's *actual words* as *reported*, I am conceptualizing Blair as *constructing himself* (in some sense) in part by drawing on and producing certain discourses of fatherhood – possibly with the prior assistance of members of his publicity machine (see Chapter 8 on *construction*). I am not, of course, assuming that Blair's reported words were his exact ones or (in any report) the totality of what he said: his words have by definition been mediated (and certainly 'tidied up').

The similarities in Blair's represented direct speech suggest that all newspapers had the same to go on (and not much of it). The minor differences illustrate how the newspapers were not concerned with *complete* accuracy – and, more widely, how bits of actual speech can be manipulated (or deselected) and recontextualized to give different impressions, in conjunction with the potentially legitimating primary discourse.

From the similarities in different reports, Blair probably did indeed say something much like what he is reported to have said. (What we do not know is how much of this was in response to journalists' questions: this means that he may have elected to construct himself in these ways, or may rather have responded to journalists' prior constructions of him.) It is therefore possible to see in these linguistic traces vestiges of the discourses he did produce. Similar rich linguistic traces may be evident in his speech as *indirectly* reported ('Tony Blair confessed yesterday that becoming at dad again at 47 was ALREADY taking its toll' – the *Sun*).

Most obviously, indeed self-evidently, with his references to the baby and his other children, Blair is constructing himself textually as a *father* – and, from all the positive adjectives (*gorgeous, lovely, delighted, thrilled, absolutely fine*), a happy father of a newborn. When he mentions Cherie, he is also constructing himself as a *husband*.

More interpretively (and see Chapter 8) in the *Express on Sunday*, these mentions combine with the positive mention of his own father to construct Blair as a 'real family man'. There are possible traces of a 'Traditional family fatherhood discourse' here, but Blair is also constructing himself as a *modern, hands-on* father by providing broad details of the birth (*natural, a long labour*), the fact that he was present and being positive about the experience. From the *Sunday Mail*: 'I feel like any father who sees their baby being born. It's very moving really and if any of you have been through it you'll know', and 'It's quite an experience' (*Sunday Times*). Then there is: '[Leo's] been really good through the night. The thing is, you forget how tiny they are, and also changing nappies in the middle of the night' (several papers, on both the Sunday and Monday), and, on Monday, 'I didn't get much sleep last night' and 'I'm feeling more than a little tired' (the *Sun*) – implying that he had been very closely involved with caring for the baby since the family returned home. Interestingly, in the *Express on Sunday*, *Sunday Mail* and *Observer*, Blair explains why he was not present at the birth of his other three children. We can speculate that this was both to imply the regret of a modern father *and* to deflect criticism (e.g. that being and talking about being present only at *this* birth was an electoral ploy). While this may sound cynical, his explanation nevertheless comes across (to this reader, at least) as just slightly 'marked' as part of his first (reported) words following Leo's birth.

Related to Blair's construction of himself as a modern father is the construction of himself as a *concerned and sympathetic husband*. Again from the *Sunday Mail*: 'It was quite a long labour, it went on for quite a few hours, but it was quite a struggle in the end for Cherie and I think she is very relieved it's all over. She is just resting now with the baby which is really good.' The *News of the World* included a reported similar utterance.

Blair can thus be seen as constructing himself as a modern, caring, hands-on father and husband, in part by producing what can be called a 'Modern, hands-on father discourse' (and by extension a closely related 'Modern husband discourse'). Whether he succeeds in constructing himself this way *for the reader* will (as always) depend on that reader herself.

'Success' may also be influenced by the contribution of the primary discourse of the co-text, which can ascribe legitimacy ('cumulatively but implicitly') to such secondary discourse (see Fairclough, 1995: 61).

Lastly, the *Sunday Mail* reported Blair as saying: 'They [doctors and nurses at the National Health Service hospital] were absolutely fantastic. The birth was straightforward, and Cherie and I were very, very grateful.' (The *Sunday Mail* on page 3 reported a similar utterance.) While public expression of thanks to medical staff involved in a birth is not unusual, when the thanks come from a Labour Prime Minister they have to be seen a little differently – as (in part) an indirect plug for the NHS. Here, then, are what we might describe as left-of-centre and pro-nationalized healthcare discourses. This caring husband, father and family man is therefore not *just* constructing himself here.

These news reports are more similar than different. The dominant discourse appears to be again 'Part-time father', with elements of 'Modern father' (who can potentially be full- or part-time, but is definitely 'hands-on', even if this only extends to nappy-changing). We can add to these the tentative, provisional but *related* discourses of 'Useless new father' and 'Strong woman who holds the family together', which potentially compete with the 'Modern father discourse'. 'Useless new father' and 'Strong woman' are, at least to me, recognizable discourses – but these were used humorously, and in just one report. Their traces thus did not seriously compete with traces of 'Modern father' in other news reports.

Fatherhood discourses in the Editorials

Editorials (also known as 'Comments' or 'Leaders') can be distinguished from other newspaper features since they normally occur in groups of around three, are not credited with a named writer, and are relatively brief – no more than a few paragraphs, and occasionally (in the tabloids) just a couple of sentences.

Caldas-Coulthard claims that 'In media discourse in general, evaluation is a crucial entrance point to the hidden discourse' (1996: 268). Newspaper Editorials are thus particularly appropriate epistemological sites for the study of discourses, since evaluation and opinion are the purpose of the genre. Evaluation and opinion can also be 'read off' in a relatively straightforward way – though with allowance for irony and humour. Though the ostensible focus of these Editorials was Leo's birth, this event was used as a springboard for non-impartial discussion of many other topics. In the process, a variety of discourses of fatherhood discourses were produced.

Almost all the papers included an Editorial relating to the birth of Leo. Most were warm, positive and congratulatory in tone – sharing the pleasure of the Blair/Booth family. There was a frequent focus on the importance of privacy. In some Editorials there seemed to be *no* obvious, recognizable discourse of fatherhood. The *Daily Mail*, for example, focused on Cherie as a role model (having a baby at 45 and through a natural birth; 'balancing' a profession and family life). (This can, however, imply the existence of a fatherhood discourse in which combining being a dad and a having a profession is *not* seen as difficult in any way, i.e. the 'Part-time father discourse'.) The *Express* took the opportunity to get at the Office of Trading Standards and their 'metric tyranny' by welcoming the fact that Leo's birth weight had been announced in pounds and ounces. The *Express on Sunday* talked about links to the past, hope for the future and how births unite families. The *Sunday Mail* welcomed the name 'Leo', but facetiously suggested alternatives. And the *Sun* celebrated the life of Leo Blair Senior (Tony Blair's father), who 'has seen his family transformed from poverty to the most powerful in the land'.

Linguistic traces of several interesting fatherhood discourses were, however, evident. Returning to the sketch of 'traditional' fatherhood at the start of this chapter, this traditional backdrop is faintly visible in what we might refer to as the 'Triumphant father discourse'. Traces are evident in two Editorials. The *Sunday People* refers to Blair as 'a proud and delighted new father who wanted to share his joy with the world'. And the *Sunday Telegraph* focuses on the role of 'any new father', i.e. announcing the birth (jocularly making the point that whereas 'most men … can use the traditional route for such announcements – a series of telephone calls to relations, followed by a notice in the *Daily Telegraph*', Tony Blair did it facing a battery of cameras).

Other newspapers used Leo's birth to address a more Political (capital P) agenda. Several produced a recognizably conservative, provisionally named 'Traditional family fatherhood discourse'. The *Mail on Sunday* Editorial is headed 'Blair as the family man we elected'. This refers to Blair as 'a man for whom the family was of fundamental importance', claims that ' "married with children" is still, overwhelmingly, the lifestyle to which Britons aspire' and expresses disappointment about

> why the Prime Minister has allowed the Chancellor to skew the tax and benefits system even further against marriage by scrapping the Married Couple's Allowance. And why the Cabinet as a whole has

seemed so strangely determined to advance a social agenda whose outcome, if not avowed objective, would be to put homosexual relationships on a legal and moral par with marriage.

The *Mail on Sunday* also appears to be trying to use Blair's apparent principles against him, to suggest that he has sold out ideologically. Its Editorial concludes:

> it would be nice to think, as Mr Blair enjoys a well-earned two weeks with his expanded family, that when he again picks up the reins of power, he will be inspired to use them to advance the values he so clearly espouses himself.

A 'Traditional family fatherhood discourse' is evident too in the *Sunday Times*, though the linguistic traces are 'weaker'. This Editorial rather oddly wishes Cherie 'a speedy recovery', very traditionally refers to Leo as being 'born to a serving prime minister and his wife' and notes 'the prime minister's position as the head of a conventional family – and, despite increasing rates of family breakdown, 70% of children are still brought up by their natural, married parents'. It critically raises the issue of 'benefit-dependent' couples with children and single parents whose income has been rising proportionately more than that of couples (one or both of whom are working) with children. It suggests that 'the pendulum may have swung far enough in the direction of greater liberalism and that society's conventional defences need shoring up' and concludes:

> Leo Blair is indeed fortunate to have been born into a happy, traditional family. His father should not hesitate to ensure that such families do not become a minority, and that they are encouraged as the best means of bringing up children.

Political in a more progressive direction were the Editorials in the *Guardian* and the *Observer*, both broadly drawing on what we can call a 'Shared parenting discourse'. The *Guardian* commented:

> Now, it is going to be very hard not to look to Blair family circumstances for evidence on a number of hot policy topics, especially the protection and support offered by the state to mothers and the obligations of employers to female (*and male*) staff with children. (emphasis added)

It also refers positively to the European Union parental leave directive.

The *Observer* Editorial refers to babies' uncompromising demands and how 'sometimes their yells reverberate through their *parents'* offices, factories, county courts or schools' (my italics). The second paragraph reads:

> If, Leo, you one day read today's issue of this paper, you will find that we had barely begun to sort out how parents should raise children while earning money for their needs: the 'life-work balance' it was called. You may learn that as your mother went into hospital to give birth, another 'Blair babe', Tess Kingham, was forced to concede that she could no longer represent her constituents and answer the demands of her family within today's archaic parliamentary system.

This is presumably not intended to read that Kingham was incompetent, disorganized or poor in her time-management, or that she should not have tried to be a Member of Parliament in the first place (or that mothers should not thus try) – though it *could* be read as any of these. It *is* presumably intended to identify the *parliamentary system* (and, by extension, other organizational systems and places of work), described as *archaic*, as causative and at fault in leading Kingham to make this decision. This can be seen as drawing on an implicit discourse of 'Positive state intervention' in relation to parenthood (and indeed beyond), intervention which is needed if women like Kingham are to remain as MPs. However, there also seems to be a trace of a *traditional* parenthood (and thus fatherhood) discourse here in that 'Positive state intervention' seems to start from the position that women are the 'main carers' and that it is this 'given' and the problems it causes which need to be addressed institutionally (e.g. with 'family-friendly' hours of work, allowing breastfeeding in the House of Commons, and so on). It does not seem to start with a recognition of the possibility and value of 'shared parenting' (which would, after all, considerably reduce the onus on women, and bring demands for change from all MPs).

An explicit 'New fatherhood discourse' (named by me; see below) was most apparent in *The Times*:

> Tony Blair is now going to be woken by hungry cries. Old-fashioned fathers quickly learn to simulate sleep throughout the crying. But the Prime Minister takes pride in being a new man as well as New Labour.

And he has gone on record with the statement that it takes a nuclear explosion to wake his wife after she has gone to sleep. So for at least half the night alarms, he is going to be the stumbler around in the dark.

The washing machine has sanitised some of the smelly drudgery that a baby brings into a house, even in Downing Street. But Mr Blair is going to have to relearn other old parenting skills of testing bottles and baths for warmth, rocking the baby in his arms to bring up wind or stop him screaming, and keeping his voice down when Leo is asleep.

Unlike several of the newspaper reports, this goes well beyond nappy-changing as the prototypical practice of the new father. And the Editorial is paying Blair the compliment of saying he will have to *re*learn these old parenting skills – implying he became competent at them well before the days when everything he does risks being seen as a publicity stunt. At first sight, this construction of Blair as a father who shares the childcare is surprising, since *The Times* is not by any means a left-wing paper. The Editorial can, however, be read as mischievously trying to hoist Blair by his own petard and setting him up to fail – i.e. he believes in all the above, but will he do them in practice? I refer to this discourse somewhat ironically as 'New fatherhood' since I suspect that *The Times* has its tongue at least partly in its cheek (and is satirizing New Labour). I intentionally do not refer to it as a 'Shared parenting discourse' – not only because of its teasing nature, but also because of its individual, asocial focus, and because there is no *explicit* mention of either shared childcare or parental leave.

The Times is the only newspaper whose Editorial draws substantially (though ironically) on this 'New fatherhood' discourse. (The *Sunday Mirror* does so to an extent with a reference to how '[Tony Blair] spoke movingly of, for the first time, being at the birth of one of his children from beginning to end'.) *The Times* may be anticipating evidence of hypocrisy (or at least of Blair not living up to his principles in his lifestyle and personal practice); this is, however, a much weaker critique than that in the *Mail on Sunday*, which implied that Blair had already sold out by inadequately supporting the traditional nuclear family.

The *Independent* does not draw on a specific fatherhood discourse. It does, however, draw on what might be seen as a liberal discourse of (late) modernity, and – to the extent that this is most definitely not a 'Traditional family discourse' – a wider 'Progressive discourse', which extends to fatherhood. The Editorial (in its entirety) reads as follows:

It is not very significant for the destiny of the nation that Tony Blair is the first serving prime minister to have a baby for 151 years.

But it is a little, because politicians will keep pontificating on 'the family'.

There is something unmistakably modern about the balance between Mr Blair's tolerance of the forms families take and his insistence on the moral responsibilities they require.

As for form: his wife has kept her name; his press secretary, chief of staff and secretary of state for health have young children and are not married; and his is the first Cabinet to contain ministers who are open about being homosexual. As for responsibility: Mr Blair keeps the state out of it except to try to make fathers play a part in bringing up their children, and to increase child benefit, which rightly puts the child's welfare at the centre of public policy.

Of course, the new baby's privacy must be respected. But, to the extent that he strengthens Mr Blair's authority to speak on these matters, and prompts us to question the authority of the childless ideologues who demand that the state decree what kinds of family people ought to have, Leo Blair should be welcomed to the public stage.

This 'Discourse of diversity', implicit in the latter traces of in paragraph 4 – in contrast to that of 'Traditional fatherhood' in the *Sunday Times*, whose traces included expressions of approval of the 'conventional family' – clearly embraces unmarried (presumably responsible) fatherhood, as well as adoption by gay male (and female) partners.

The newspaper Editorial has proved here to be a fruitful genre and epistemological site for the investigation of fatherhood discourses, having enabled the interpretive identification of a 'Triumphant father discourse', an ironic 'New fatherhood discourse', a 'Traditional family discourse', a 'Shared parenting discourse' and a 'Progressive discourse'. To have been thus recognizable (at least to this analyst) and, indeed, produced, these discourses must also (by definition) be circulating and their traces evident *outside* these Editorials. The first and third we can see as being part of the same 'order of discourse', the fourth and fifth part of another, and we can see the two pairs as competing. 'New fatherhood' on the surface shares the same order as the 'Shared parenting' and the 'Progressive' discourses. Wider discursive practices (e.g. the political stance normally adopted in *The Times* Editorials), however, enable us to read the discourse being produced here largely ironically, so that 'New fatherhood' may not 'comfortably' share this order of discourse with the 'Shared parenting' and 'Progressive fatherhood' discourses at all. However, for the irony to work, *The Times* Editorial must be seen to be appropriating traces of these discourses and, in so doing, it intertextually acknowledges them.

Conclusion

Weiss and Wodak's observation that texts 'are often sites of struggle in that they show traces of differing discourses and ideologies contending and struggling for dominance' (2003: 15) may be particularly true of media texts. This is in part because their production is complex and often lengthy, usually involving more than one person, and in part because they may have conflicting goals – a commercial imperative to establish rapport with their readership, and a professional obligation to report what may in the event 'disturb' and alienate. And though the many different discourses in, say, a single issue of a newspaper, may not 'contend and struggle for dominance', they may sit together less than comfortably.

If there were intratextual contradictions between discourses in individual texts in the 'parenting' magazines, newspaper reports or Editorials, these were not salient. Nor do the parenting magazines and newspaper *reports* as a whole vary significantly in the fatherhood discourses they draw on and (re-)produce. The parenting magazines draw largely on the 'Part-time father' discourse, and the news reports on the 'Part-time father' and 'Modern hands-on father' discourses. Blair's self-construction and his representation by the 'newsgivers' are achieved very similarly, discoursally, in the newspaper reports. Fatherhood itself is presented as experience, not institution.

The set of newspaper Editorials in contrast did draw on very different, competing discourses of fatherhood. Only the *Guardian* and the *Observer* directly problematized fatherhood as institution, by raising the social and political question of how best to facilitate the combining of paid work and parenthood.

The next chapter is the last empirically focused chapter and the last on written texts. It looks at award-winning children's literature, which poses particular questions for the interpretive identification of gendered discourses.

7
Gendered Discourses in Children's Literature

Children's literature has been a focus of the modern Women's Movement since its inception, with 'sexist' children's stories being critiqued,[1] advice provided for teachers and librarians (see Moss, 1989) and alternatives identified, welcomed, written and published. The academic study of gender in children's books has often taken the form of *content* analysis (e.g. Nilsen, 1977; Peterson and Lach, 1990; Berman, 1998). Content analysis provides important background on what a text is broadly about, including potentially useful quantitative information, for example the number of female and male characters (protagonists and subordinate characters), and male and female characters' involvement in different activities.[2] *Linguistic* analyses are rarer – though see Baker and Freebody's (1989) study of early reading books, which included analysis of *boy, girl* and the verbs used to represent their actions; and Luke (1988, 1991) on different versions of *Dick and Jane* books. Linguistic analyses can provide a more nuanced understanding of the less visible (and perhaps more pernicious) workings of texts – it is also possible to consider, for example, transactivization (see Talbot, below) and verb types (for example, cognitive and material (Halliday, 1994), and who is associated with which). This linguistic 'research space' suggests a range of possibilities for future studies. However, although it is possible to do linguistic analyses of entire books for very young (pre-school and infant) children, since these usually contain relatively few words, linguistic analyses of entire full-length books for older children (or adults) requires computer analysis of an electronically-scanned text, 'manual' analysis of just one or two features, or analysis of exemplary, perhaps 'telling' sections.

The focus in this chapter is critical discourse analysis of gender in children's literature (mainly but not exclusively fiction). As before,

I interpretively identify a range of (recognizable) discourses, in part through linguistic traces. These traces include particular *extracts*. The extracts are intentionally not representative of a whole book, but like the 'Boy-as-OK/Girl-as-not-OK' discourse we encountered in Chapter 4 can be seen as 'telling cases' (Mitchell, 1984). As before, I acknowledge the value and indeed necessity of researcher subjectivity, inference and experience of the world.

Discourse analysis in linguistics is usually carried out on non-fictional texts, fictional texts being more the province of stylistics. It is relatively unusual for *critical* discourse analysis to treat a work of fiction as a suitable epistemological site. There are, however, exceptions – for example, Talbot's (1998) analysis of gender representation in Harlequin Mills and Boon (popular light romance) stories, in which she critiques asymmetrical social representation. Talbot cites the following extract from a story called *No Guarantees*, by Robyn Donald (1990):

> Her glance fell to his hands. Lean-fingered, tanned, they were more than capable of physically silencing her. She had a momentary vision of them, dark and strong against the transparent pallor of her skin, and swallowed, appalled at the flicker of forbidden excitement it aroused in her.

What is selected for inclusion from the paradigmatic pool of available choices is important, and Talbot notes 'the eroticised power ... located in the character's hands', pointing to the lexical items *transparent pallor* (of the woman's skin) and the man's *tanned* hands. While this is not about actual violence (the woman and man are at an auction and the man has jokingly told the woman he will clap his hand over her mouth if she bids), it *is* about strength and power as well as eroticism, which in these books depends on the 'maximization of gender difference' (Talbot, 1998: 199) – through particular lexical traces of the pervasive 'Gender differences discourse'.

Talbot (1995) also uses CDA in a study of verbal transitivity in the science fiction novel *Lair*, by James Herbert. She selects a scene to show how the distribution of transitive and intransitive verbs establishes one person rather than another as 'making things happen', and does so in a gendered way. The hero's actions are most often represented by transitive verbs (e.g. *reach, grab, shield, take*), the female character's by intransitive verbs (e.g. *stand, lean back, watch*). Fiction, then, is not a stranger to CDA[3] – but does carry its own complexities (discussed below) for analysis of social asymmetry and for social critique (Stephens, 1992).

First, conceptual 'point of view' in fiction is not self-evident. Unlike, say, a newspaper Editorial (as seen in Chapter 6), which expresses a particular political perspective, a fictional text cannot be assumed to have an 'axe to grind', and certainly there is no 'mechanical' way of recognizing any such 'axe'. The narrator may clearly not be the author, or there may be several narrators. But even when there is just one, omniscient narrator, she cannot be *neatly* equated with the author, or as straightforwardly representing in fictional form some 'argument' on the author's behalf.

The various characters who populate the story also have voices and different points of view. Each character may 'focalize' ('show their perspective'; see Mills, 1995; Benwell, 2002) at different points in the book, or some characters may not focalize at all. Again, however, it makes little (perhaps even less) sense to 'read off' from the characters what the author thinks – though we might *speculate* whether the author sees herself in some relation to a particular character. Any sentiment expressed by a character cannot be taken as indexing *approval* by the author (Bakhtin, 1981: 324, refers to the 'refracted' intention of the author in this connection). Traces of a sexist discourse in a character's words may, for example, have been included precisely so that the discourse can be contested, through one character arguing with another. Fiction has a special status here, given that it is almost always dialogic. Dialogue allows for a range of alternative and perhaps oppositional discourses, as well as dominant ones, and for the former to constitute an implicit or explicit challenge to the latter. And, of course, aside from the characters and the narrator, a range of other 'voices' carrying ideas and discourses will intertextually 'populate' the work (see Talbot, 1995).[4] Formally, characters' words and thoughts will be 'represented' in a range of ways, in combinations of different forms of direct and indirect speech (Stephens, 1992; Fairclough, 1995; Semino et al., 1997; Semino et al., 1999), presenting further layers of meaning.

A second question for discourse analysis of a fictional text is the roles of irony, satire and humour. While these may be present in any text (written or spoken), they are commonplace in fiction – and meaning can never be 'read off' an ironical, satirical or humorous text in any straightforward way. Arguably, claims made about 'meaning' in fiction, perhaps especially about 'significance' (Stevens, 1992), should be particularly tentative.

A third issue is fantasy, common in children's fiction in more than just fairytales. What happens in a work of fantasy is in a different dimension to what happens in 'realistic' fiction (which limits comparison of the two). In particular, fantasy gives the writer special scope for extension and broadening of female and male characters' practices.

Fourth, visuals are very important in much children's fiction. Analysis thus needs to be multi-modal, considering different readings of the text and visuals *as a totality*, and the relationship between the visuals and the written text (see Kress and van Leeuwen, 1996; Johnston, 2000). Do the visuals provide complementary, different or even intentionally contradictory details? This raises questions about the fictional representation of animals, which are often given human characteristics. Since the sex of many animals is not obvious visually, there is a tendency and temptation for illustrators to give animals stereotypically anthropomorphic gendered accessories, such as bowler hats for males, aprons and head scarves for females (see Stevens, 1992).

The fictional children's genre which has been the recipient of most feminist scholarly work to date is probably the fairytale (e.g. Zipes, 1986; Cosslett, 1996; Levorato, 2003), a 'narrative predicated upon magic' (Knowles and Malmkjaer, 1996). Since the same fairytales are part of many societies' collective consciousness, commonalities can be identified, along with linguistic traces of several gendered discourses. These discourses may vary from version to version, and the versions Western children are now most familiar with have undergone processes not only of selection but also of sanitization (Zipes, 1986). Having said this, consider: Rapunzel imprisoned in her tower, Sleeping Beauty in her castle and Snow White in her glass coffin; Snow White's and Cinderella's domestic responsibilities;[5] the passivity of the Sleeping Beauty and Snow White, awakened only by a rescuing prince's kiss; the cruel stepmothers in *Hansel and Gretel*, *Snow White* and *Cinderella*, the Wicked Fairy in *Sleeping Beauty* and the *Snow Queen*, and the Wicked Witch in *Hansel and Gretel*; the beauty attributed to Cinderella, the Sleeping Beauty, Snow White, the miller's daughter in *Rumpelstiltskin*, the Twelve Dancing Princesses and many more; the transformations of 'beasts' into princes in *Beauty and the Beast* and *The Frog Prince*; and the inevitable wedding after a period of brief acquaintance. It is not difficult provisionally and interpretively to identify a range of linked gendered discourses here. Drawing on the commonalities, I suggest:

'Some day my prince will come'
'Women as domestic'
'Active man/Passive woman'
'Women as beautiful *or* ugly' (recall the 'Privileging of appearance – in women' discourse in Chapter 4)

---

continued

'Women as jealous of other women' (recall 'Women beware women'
also in Chapter 4)
'Blissful heterosexuality 5 they lived happily ever after' (recall Marshall's
ironic 'Ultimate fulfilment' discourse in Chapter 5).

Heterosexuality and marriage are the overarching themes that shape and drive the fairytale; these are perhaps expressed most extremely in Hans Christian Anderson's *Little Mermaid*, in which the mermaid sacrifices her voice and tail for an opportunity to meet the prince (consider one of the interpretations of the *Have/hold* discourse, discussed in Chapter 3, as it positions women here!).

These discourses circulate outside fiction, but they also resonate with those in other tales such as the British classic *Peter Pan* by J.M. Barrie (about a boy who never grows up – though this is not presented ironically), at the end of which it is arranged that Wendy will return to Peter once a year to do his spring cleaning. I should make clear at this point that I do not consider that these books have nothing to offer young readers; on the contrary. But these gendered discourses suggest that they are not *just* imaginative books which provide pleasure for children.

Traditional fairytales have prompted feminist rewrites, such as Babette Cole's *Prince Cinders*, and 'new' feminist fairytales such as *The Paperbag Princess* by R. Munsch and M. Marchenko. Feminist discourses are evident here. *Prince Cinders* contains traces of the 'traditional' gendered discourses manifested in *Cinderella* (Stevens, 1992, observes that it inverts the original almost point by point). In the 'new' feminist fairytales there are princes and princesses, knights and ladies, dragons and rescues, but the humour (and indeed feminism) of these texts relies on the intertextuality and interplay between intentionally conflicted discourses.[6]

Of course, feminist fairytales may not be *read* in a feminist way (Davies, 1989). However, traditional fairytales do not have to be read in a traditional way either. Cosslett refers to the possibility of 'reading against the grain' (1996: 84) (seen in Chapter 5) and cites Gilbert and Gubar's (1979) reinterpretation of Snow White's stepmother as

a powerful, inventive, active, creative woman, constrained by demands of patriarchy. Her seeming vanity in front of the mirror is explained by [Gilbert and Gubar's] interpretation of the voice of the mirror as the voice of the absent King, representing patriarchy, judging women by their appearance.[7]

This is, of course, 'consumption' – how a text is used. Even without reading 'against the grain', readers (or listeners), however interpellated, are in principle able to 'negotiate' their own position in relation to a text – a girl may adopt the subject position of the evil but powerful stepmother in *Sleeping Beauty*, or the prince, perhaps aided by 'androgynous' visuals. An actively 'resistant reader' may construct alternative gendered discourses. Readers and listeners may be assisted here by interventions of primary/elementary school teachers, who these days are unlikely to draw only on traditional gendered discourses when teaching a fairytale. Teachers' voices, comments from parents reading fairytales aloud and, indeed, the reader's own voice (audibly articulated or not) can all be seen as contributing to the intertextuality of a work of fiction (see Talbot, 1995) and to the co-construction of discourses therein.

To return to contemporary children's fiction, Sue Adler (1993) makes a three-way distinction between non-sexist, anti-sexist and feminist children's books. This is somewhat problematic. Not only are there questions of satisfactory definitions and different readings, but also different parts of a book can warrant different classification (consider main and embedded narratives; or the voice of the narrator and those of different characters). Feminist discourses may be seen in 'realistic' children's stories featuring strong, independent female protagonists, struggles against traditional constraints or boys engaged in non-traditionally gendered activities. However, feminist discourses may also be apparent in largely unfeminist books, including those manifesting traces of traditional or even sexist discourses. And *topic* and *plot* can always be misleading, since the oppression of women and girls can be fictionalized by the feminist (exposing and challenging it) and the sexist (celebrating it) alike.

Many modern children's books (fiction and non-fiction) are set in the recent or distant past. In non-fiction, as in any history, the writer must make particular choices about representation. In 'realistic' historical fiction (as opposed to fantasy tales), we would expect to find traces of gendered discourses broadly corresponding to contemporary social and discursive practices, with women and men, boys and girls involved in traditionally gendered practices. This might mean a large measure of gender differentiation, with opportunities and restrictions relevant only to men/boys or to women/girls. And we might also expect traces of different discourses of patriarchy in, if not the words of the narrator, the represented words or thoughts of the characters. However, many modern historical stories for children are, I suggest, thoroughly heterogeneous in terms of gendered (and other) discourses. Traces of traditional gendered discourses do not *preclude* traces of different emancipatory or feminist discourses in the same book – *even though such discourses might not have been circulating at the time in which the book is set.* Such traces are particularly interesting if the 'plot' could have proceded in almost the same way without the details they carry, suggesting that the author has made a conscious, perhaps ideological choice to include them.

Gendered discourses in American award-winning children's books

The data for this study are a principled selection of recent award-winning children's books published in the US, where there are two main annual 'medal' awards for children's books: Newbery and Caldecott (the latter for picture books).[8] There is no distinction between fiction and non-fiction. The Newbery criteria include 'distinguished writing' in interpretation of the theme or concept, presentation of information, development of a plot, delineation of characters and setting, and appropriateness of style; the Caldecott criteria include excellence of execution in artistic technique and appropriateness of style of illustration. The awards are 'not for didactic intent or for popularity'. 'Children' go up to the age of fourteen. The judges are members of the Children's Librarians Section of the American Library Association.

In deciding to study recent award-winners, I had not seen the texts prior to conducting the study. Perhaps because I am not American, I was not familiar with the authors. Working from a critical feminist standpoint, I was hoping to find evidence of feminist discourses, but I had no idea whether this would actually be the case. The point is worth making since one of the criticisms levelled at CDA – which in my search for linguistic traces of feminist (and other gendered) discourses (present and absent) I was drawing on here – is that a particular text may be chosen for its capacity to allow the analyst to make a particular (ideological) point (see e.g. Widdowson, 2000).

I decided to look at eight recent books (four Newbery and four Caldecott winners) in order to arrive at some sort of overall picture of gendered discourses. Those which won awards between 1999 and 2002, with a (woefully inadequate!) summary of each 'plot', are as in the table that follows.[9] The non-fiction works are two Caldecott winners: *So You Want To be President?* and *Snowflake Bentley. So You Want To Be President?* is largely descriptive, but *Snowflake Bentley* bears a close generic resemblance to much children's fiction in that it is the story of one individual, narrated in chronological sequence. Both books raise issues of gender

Prize	Book	Year of award	Author	Publisher	'Plot'
Newbery	*A Single Shard*	2000	Linda Sue Parker	Clarion Books	A Korean boy learns to become a potter.
	A Year Down Yonder	2001	Richard Peck	Dial Books	A teenage girl goes to stay with her grandmother during the Depression.
	Bud, Not Buddy	2000	Christopher P. Curtis	Delacorte Press	A boy runs away from his unkind foster family to find his father.
	Holes	1999	Louis Sachar	Frances Foster Books/ Farrar, Strauss and Giroux	A boy sent to a Juvenile Detention Centre finds treasure and changes the life of another boy.
Caldecott	*The Three Pigs*	2002	David Wiesner	Clarion Books	The three pigs change the story in which they traditionally belong.
	So You Want to be President? (non-fiction)	2001	David Small (text – Judith St. Giles)	Philomel Books	Characteristics of American presidents from George Washington to Bill Clinton.
	Joseph Had a Little Overcoat	2000	Simms Taback	Viking/ Penguin	Joseph turns his overcoat into smaller and smaller garments.
	Snowflake Bentley (non-fiction)	1999	Mary Azarian (text – Jacqueline Briggs Martin)	Houghton Mifflin	The story of Willie Bentley, who took photographs of snowflakes.

representation similar to those raised by fiction, as well as issues particular to non-fiction (see below).

I read each book at least twice, looking for linguistic traces of gendered discourses. I noted such traces in the voices of the narrators and the characters, in the representation of the latters' thought or speech. I was broadly assuming that the writers' purposes would *not* be primarily feminist ones, but similarly that writers working in the last ten years would be aware of and sensitive to feminist issues (one understanding of 'post-feminism') and thus might produce linguistic traces of these in their own work. I considered not only my first 'intuitions' about gendered discourses but also *presence* in terms of topic, linguistic items and embedded narratives, which might index gendered discourses. Similarly, what was notably *absent* that might logically have been present? It was again also important to look at both linguistic traces and at resonances with gendered discourses outside the particular book, and indeed outside books in general. My assumption was that different books would manifest different ways of deploying gendered discourses, i.e. no *single* 'analytical framework' could be applied across the board. This will I hope become clear in what follows, and will enable other discourse analysts to co-construct or provisionally identify gendered and other discourses in children's books.

I interpretively identified four sets of gendered discourses in these books. Evident in most of the books were traces of more than one such discourse – from more than one of these sets. I was open to the possibility of contradictions and competing discourses, for example, if a discourse evident in the words of one character is contested in the words of another.

Traditionally gendered discourses

The first set of gendered discourses I refer to as 'Traditionally gendered'. Traces of traditionally gendered discourses are perhaps most evident in Linda Sue Park's *A Single Shard* (Newbery, 2002), set in twelfth-century Korea, whose protagonist is a young orphan boy, Tree-ear. If child characters in historical fiction are 'other' in relation to modern child readers from the 'same' culture, Tree-ear is *doubly* 'othered' for Anglo-Saxon readers (see Stephens, 1992). Also important are Tree-ear's friend, *de facto* guardian and mentor, Crane-man, and the potter, Min, to whom Tree-ear informally apprentices himself. The only real female character is Min's archetypal serene and supportive wife (whose name we never learn). From the characters' domestic and economic practices, it is not hard (partly since this book is set in very patriarchal times) to identify a gendered 'Division of labour discourse' in this book, with men as household heads and, accordingly, women as 'inside-the-house people' (corresponding to the expression 'her indoors', still current in some British English dialects). Of course, it would have been inappropriate for Park to show things otherwise, given her intention to re-create realistically the events surrounding the creation of ceramics in the Korea of the time.

'Division of labour' is evident too in the non-fictional *Snowflake Bentley* (Caldecott, 1999), by Jacqueline Briggs Martin and illustrated by Mary Azarian. Wilson ('Willie') Bentley, born in 1865 in Vermont, as a teenager examined snowflakes under the microscope and drew the snow crystals. He developed a way to photograph snowflakes, and eventually became famous. Willie's mother is prominent in the story, but is almost always pictured in a domestic setting, carrying out some domestic task. The family herd of ten cows is described as '[Willie's] father's'. We can thus also see traces of a traditional 'Guardian of the hearth' or 'Woman behind the man (or 'men'!)' discourse here.

Constituting 'Division of labour' are thus those linguistic and visual traces indexing what men and boys (only) actually *do*, occupationally and in terms of other activities, and the importance attributed to this. In these books, not only is Min a potter and Willie's father a farmer, Joseph in *Joseph Had a Little Overcoat* (Caldecott, 2000) appears to be a farmer *and* an amateur tailor and writer, and Bud's grandfather Hermann Calloway in *Bud, Not Buddy* (Newbery, 2000) plays in and leads a jazz band. (In *Bud, Not Buddy*, women do have jobs, but only in the contemporary *Holes* (Newbery, 1999) are occupations evenly distributed between women and men in terms of professional status.) Interestingly, Min, Willie, Joseph and Hermann Calloway are also all artists of sorts and this is crucial to each narrative. It is possible to see a 'Men as artists discourse' here, one that has echoes outside these books. Consider the familiar question 'Why have there been so few really famous female playwrights/composers/sculptors...?'

But let us take just one of these artists: Joseph, who lives in a small, rural, Jewish community sometime in the nineteenth century. Joseph's artistry lies in his sewing of one new garment after (and out of) another (jacket, vest, scarf, necktie, handkerchief, button), the resultant garments getting smaller and smaller. The book is aimed at younger children, presumably with the idea that this story will be read to (and talked about with) them. There is repetition and opportunity for interaction, with cut-out shapes to enable the child to work out what Joseph's garment will have turned into on the next page. There is just one line of text on the top of each page. The words follow the pattern of:

> Joseph had a little overcoat. It was old and worn.
> So he made a jacket out of it and went to the fair.
> Joseph had a little jacket. It got old and worn.
> So ...
> [several pages]
> Now he had nothing.
> So Joseph made a book about it. Which shows ... you can always
> make something out of nothing.

'Garment' words are thus frequent, as is the preceding adjective *little* – not conventionally associated with the wardrobe of male farmers. The dénouement of a story can retrospectively change the meaning of what has gone before, and Joseph could have been made to look ridiculous after all his (feminine?) creative work with textiles, or incompetent if he had failed. However, his sewing is presented very creatively (partly perhaps because of the association of tailoring with masculinity in nineteenth-century Jewish communities).

Paralleling 'Men as artists', we can also identify a 'Boy as adventurer' discourse. Knowles and Malmkjær (1996) identify 'the young (male) hero' as central to the 'adventure story sub-genre' in traditional juvenile fiction. Tree-ear in *A Single Shard*, Bud in *Bud, Not Buddy*, and Stanley in *Holes* are not 'physical' types who are presented with straightforward 'right or wrong' choices, as were the heroes of nineteenth-century fiction. Tree-ear, Bud and Stanley however all travel, independently and under their own steam, exposing themselves to considerable danger.[10] To take Christopher Paul Curtis's *Bud, Not Buddy* as an example: Bud is a ten-year-old Black boy living on the fringes of American society in 1936. His (single) mother died when Bud was six, and when he is placed in yet another foster home, where he is ill-treated, he runs away to find his father, who he thinks is a famous band leader and musician. The man he meets turns out to be his grandfather and the story ends happily, with Bud learning the saxophone. In contrast, Mary Alice in Richard Peck's *A Year Down Yonder* (Newbery, 2001), though she undergoes a similar psychological journey of maturation to Bud, Stanley and Tree-ear, travels only to her grandmother's small-town house by train from Chicago. (All four Newbery award-winners can be considered as a *bildungsroman*.)

However, things are often not quite as they seem, or at least not as simple. I will take the example of the mother of Willie Bentley (the snowflake photographer) here. Mary Azarian's illustrations, attractive hand-coloured woodcuts, show a range of scenes from Bentley's life, and there are as many female as male characters among Bentley's illustrated family members, friends and neighbours. Bentley's mother is more prominent than his father in many of these woodcuts. *Snowflake Bentley* also includes extra textual information (factual, sometimes scientific) in the margins, and his mother is textually foregrounded. Examples (from the main text, margin texts and illustrations) follow:

p. 5   Text:
He could pick apple blossoms and take them to his mother. But he could not share snowflakes because he could not save them.
Text in margin:
Willie's mother was his teacher until he was fourteen years old. He attended school for only a few years. '*She* had a set of encyclopedias,' Willie said. 'I read them all.' [emphasis added]
Illustration:
Willie giving his mother (who is holding a feather duster) a bunch of apple blossoms.

p. 6   Text:
When his mother gave him an old microscope, he used it to look at flowers, raindrops and blades of grass. Best of all, he used it to look at snow.

p. 10   Text:
When he was sixteen, Willie read of a camera with its own microscope. 'If I had that camera I could photograph snowflakes,' he told his mother.
Illustration:
Willie talking to his mother (who is sitting in a rocking chair, knitting). He is showing her a document.

p. 11   Text:
Willie's mother knew he would not be happy until he could share what he had seen. 'Fussing with snow is just foolishness,' his father said. Still, he loved his son. When Willie was seventeen, his parents spent their savings and bought the camera.
Illustration:
Willie's mother showing Willie's father a document (presumably intended to be the same one, providing information about the camera).

The representation of Willie's mother can be read as traditional. Linguistically, *gave* (p. 6) is the only material verb (Halliday, 1994) in the above examples which represents the 'processes' with which she is associated; she is the subject of the first sentence in the margin text on p. 5 and the text on p. 11, but not the agent; and in the page 6 example is the agent of the transitive verb *gave*, but not the subject. Nevertheless, Willie's mother *is* represented otherwise as agentive in terms of being a shaping, influential force. She may be 'other-centred' (Lazar, 2002) in relation to her son, but she is also represented as playing a major role in his achievements – she teaches him, provides the encyclopedias and persuades his father to purchase Willie's special camera.

A work of non-fiction, perhaps especially one that is presented as a narrative, raises special questions for analysts. In general, what is the relationship between what is known of the actual facts and their chosen representation here? Did Willie's mother perhaps do much more for him intellectually than indicated in *Snowflake Bentley*? Did she do less, but have her contribution exaggerated by Briggs Martin's text and Azarian's woodcuts? This may represent something of a new research space.

Whether we are reading traces of traditionally gendered discourses or of something else is arguable also in *A Year Down Yonder*. This book has two female protagonists – fifteen-year-old Mary Alice, the narrator of the story, and Grandma Dowdel, with whom she is sent to stay during the Depression. Since it is 'woman/girl-centred', providing a female perspective, this work could almost be described, in Adler's (1993) terms, as a 'feminist' book. Mary Alice is depicted as a quiet, pleasant, observant girl who does not wish to make enemies and who always tries to be co-operative. Grandma Dowdel, in contrast, is a large, hardy, feisty, unpredictable, distinctly 'unfeminine' woman, who keeps a shotgun behind her woodbox, is intimidated by no one and nothing, who might be described as a 'rough diamond'. One of her neighbours, a 'Legion Auxiliary Lady', observes, 'you're not everybody's cup of tea. But it's common knowledge, isn't it?' When Grandma Dowdel meets Mary Alice at the station:

> You couldn't call her a welcoming woman, and there wasn't a hug in her. She didn't put out her arms, so I had nothing to run into .... The picnic hamper quivered, and she noticed. 'What's in there?'
>
> 'Bootsie,' I said. 'My cat.'
>
> 'Hoo-boy,' Grandma said. 'Another mouth to feed.'

A Year Down Yonder is, however, a rather 'traditional' book in its discourses. Grandma Dowdel, who supports the wider family by 'taking in', feeding and clothing her grand-daughter as best she can, may echo representations of actual pioneer American women, but is also not an unfamiliar figure in fictional representation (she is like those 'strong women' in UK soap operas – referred to in Chapter 6 – who are the centre of their working-class communities). There might be just a trace of a proto-feminist discourse in her response to the question, 'Did your late husband go to war?', which is 'Only with me... and he lost every time'. However, this also sounds like a trace of a (provisionally named) 'Battle-axe wife' discourse – though because of the focalization (Grandma Dowdel's perspective), must be a trace of a rather different discourse from this derogatory, misogynist one. And although Mary Alice becomes a journalist in Chicago (after having written, anonymously, 'Newsy Notes' for the town's newspaper), the book ends with her marrying the boy she quietly 'set her cap at' while at school – with Grandma Dowdel 'giving her away'. The last two lines of *A Year Down Yonder* are 'Then I married Royce McNabb. We lived happily ever after.' While it is impossible not to see any irony in this (given the phrase's dominant association with fantasy and fairytales), it remains a less than satisfying ending even in the book's rather traditional own terms.

Feminist discourses

Several of the books contain traces of what I would call feminist discourses, manifesting these in interesting ways. By a 'feminist discourse', I mean that there is evidence of struggle against patriarchal practices, and/or that these practices are critically presented, and/or that an individual girl or woman is represented in a particularly progressive way. Three of the books here, *Holes, A Single Shard*, and the non-fiction work *So You Want To Be President?*, can be seen as deploying a feminist discourse. The ways in which they do this, as I show, include, variously, the explicit inclusion of women where this is not necessary to the plot, counter-stereotypical characterization of women, the use of propositional language which could be read as 'feminist' and embedded narratives in conjunction with 'achronological intertextuality' (Stephens, 1992).

So You Want To Be President? (Caldecott 2001), written by Judith St. George, has as illustrations the award-winning watercolour drawings by David Small of Presidents from George Washington to Bill Clinton. *So You Want To Be President?* is a humorous but factual account of frequently shared presidential characteristics, such as the first names James, John or William, being born in a log cabin, having several siblings, having pets and having been in the army – as well as of ways US presidents have differed. It also points to the importance of being honest to keep the job – one picture is of a guilty-looking Richard Nixon and Bill Clinton slinking together down the steps of the Capitol. An index matches faces with names, and there is also a (largely positive) 2–3-line summary of each president, their years of office and the main concerns of their presidencies.

Relative to men, few women are illustrated. Gender representation is of course a challenge here, since all US presidents to date have been men, and it is interesting to see how David Small has responded to this. Several recognizable female characters (wives, a daughter, a reporter and a vice-presidential candidate) are pictured and named in the index. They are:

p. 7	Eleanor Roosevelt (drinking tea in the White House garden with Franklin Roosevelt)
p. 8	Pat Nixon (standing in the background with Henry Kissinger and Gerald Ford while Richard Nixon plays ten pin bowling in the White House)
p. 26	Ethel Roosevelt (daughter of Eleanor and Franklin) with her four brothers and some of the animals in their White House 'zoo'
p. 31	a 'woman reporter' (unnamed) who snatched John Quincy's clothes while he was skinny-dipping in the Potomac River, and sat on them until he gave her an interview
p. 32	Andrew Johnson's wife/teacher who taught him to write (which he did not learn to do until after he was married)
p. 43	Geraldine Ferraro standing (with Jesse Jackson) in a cordoned-off area at a gathering of all (white, male) US presidents

On page 43, the text reads:

Every President was different from every other and yet no woman has been President. No person of color has been President. No person who wasn't a Protestant or Roman Catholic has been President. But if you care enough, anything is possible. Thirty-four Presidents came and went before a Roman Catholic – John Kennedy – was elected. Almost two hundred years passed before a woman – Geraldine Ferraro – ran for Vice President.

The illustrator and writer of *So You Want To Be President?* appear to have worked hard together to create a children's book which tries to interpellate both girls and boys, despite the obvious historical constraints – and to make the interpellated addressee of *You* in the title female or male. Gender in the above paragraph can be seen to take precedence over ethnicity: Ferraro is mentioned by name; Jackson is not (though he was a presidential candidate). The propositions in the sentence 'Every President was different from every other *and yet* no woman has been President' (emphasis added) constitute, I suggest, traces of a feminist discourse: an elegant way of saying 'Why not? Surely this is surprising.' The sentence 'But if you care enough, anything is possible' is optimistic and constructive. The cordoning off of Ferraro (and Jackson) can be read as a semiotic trace of this discourse, one that represents barriers, not inability.

The darkly humorous *Holes* (Newbery, 1999) by Louis Sachar is set (apparently) in the time in which it was written – the late 1990s. In this it is the only 'contemporary' book in the dataset. The protagonist of *Holes*, Stanley Yelnats, is a quiet, overweight fourteen-year-old White boy who is sent to the Green Lake Juvenile Detention Center for stealing a pair of sneakers (his actual crime is of a lesser demeanour). A male counsellor who keeps reminding the boys that they are not at a Girl Scouts camp is represented unfavourably. An important female character is the powerful and sadistic Warden (Stanley was expecting a man, as I imagine are most readers).

However, a more important female character is the feisty outlaw 'Kissin' Kate Barlow', who robbed Stanley's great-grandfather, and for whose accumulated loot the Warden is making the boys dig the holes. Katherine Barlow was the schoolteacher in Green Lake 110 years before Stanley's story starts. Her story is embedded at intervals in the 'present-day' one. Katherine fell in love with 'Onion Sam', the Black man who 'turned the old run-down schoolhouse into a well-crafted, freshly painted jewel of a building that the whole town was proud of' (p. 110). (Sam 'wasn't allowed to attend classes because he was a Negro, but they let him fix the building'.) Their first and only kiss is observed and Sam (and his donkey) are shot. The schoolhouse is destroyed while the sheriff sits back and says to Katherine, 'You're sure pretty.... You kissed the onion picker. Why won't you kiss me?' Chapter 26 concludes:

> Three days after Sam's death, Miss Katherine shot the sheriff while he was sitting in his chair drinking a cup of coffee. Then she carefully applied a fresh coat of red lipstick and gave him the kiss he had asked for.
>
> For the next twenty years Kissin' Kate Barlow was one of the most feared outlaws in all the West.

Kate dies laughing twenty years later, as a result of having been bitten by a poisonous yellow-spotted lizard in the presence of a rejected suitor

Figure 7.1 Martha Jane Concurray (Calamity Jane)

from Green Lake who is trying to get her to reveal where her loot is buried.

The representation of this female outlaw, I suggest, constitutes traces of a feminist discourse: the traces contain an implicit critique of the sheriff's sexist (and racist) assumptions. I also suggest that this representation would not have taken the form it did, nor have been enjoyed by and recognizable to readers, before the advent of the second wave of the Women's Movement (nearly a century after these fictionalized events). Importantly, Kissin' Kate Barlow is not ridiculed, but rather admired by Stanley:

> Actually, Stanley had been impressed when he first found out that his great-grandfather was robbed by Kissin' Kate Barlow. True, he would have preferred living on the beach in California, but it was still kind of cool to have someone in your family robbed by a famous outlaw.
>
> Kate Barlow didn't actually kiss Stanley's great-grandfather. That would have been really cool, but she only kissed the men she killed. Instead she robbed him and left him stranded in the middle of the desert.
>
> 'He was *lucky* to have survived,' Stanley's mother was quick to point out. (p. 10)

And, of course, 'Kissin' Kate Barlow' has a real-life historical counterpart in Martha Jane Canarray, the nineteenth-century 'Calamity Jane' of Arizona and Dakota who wore men's clothing and was no stranger to a gun. Texts about and broad knowledge of Calamity Jane, entailing her implicit countering of traditional feminine discourses, constitute important intertextual links, which I suggest contribute to the production and recognition of feminist discourse apparent here.

Gender at times cannot be analysed separately from ethnicity/race, and in *Holes* traces of anti-racist discourses are evident *in addition* to those indexed by the relationship between Katherine and Sam, and its consequences (for example, in the relations between the boys, and the boys and the counsellors). Discourses, as we have seen, take their identity in part from *accumulations* of intratextually-related traces. Here, anti-racist discourses can be seen as intertextually linked with feminist discourses, and their co-occurrence and mutual support not only 'multiply position' and interpellate readers as open to these discourses, but also constitute a discourse of equality and anti-discrimination more broadly.

The third example of feminist discourse (or discourses) comes, in some ways surprisingly, from the historical *A Single Shard* – set in twelfth-century Korea. Feminist discourses are apparent in several passages which simultaneously critique prevalent patriarchal practices and point to women's agency and resistance.

The first passage concerns 'Min's wife', whose subordinate status is gently problematized. First, Tree-ear, who has received a continuous supply of food for himself and Crane-man from her,

> wished he could think of a way to show his gratitude for her kindness. What was it she wanted? She seemed to have no desires of her own ... or perhaps her wishes were those of her husband's. (p. 90)

This last sentence, with its particular 'focalization', is, I think, capable of being read ironically, as a critique of the gender relations of the time. I am suggesting this not only on the grounds that this sentence *could* have been omitted (but was not), but also because of related, accumulating discoursal traces. On the following page, Min's wife agrees to ask her husband if Tree-ear can be his emissary to the court on the condition that 'from now on, you will call me *Ajima*' [auntie] (p. 91). There is no suggestion that this request originated with Min or had even been discussed with him; this wish appears to be hers (i.e. she *does* have desires of her own and will articulate them). Relatedly, Min's wife is, I think we are expected to assume, quietly agentive in bringing about Min's full acceptance of Tree-ear.

A further trace of this critical feminist discourse is Tree-ear's persuasion of Crane-man to accept Min's wife's offer of work while he (Tree-ear) is away. Crane-man says:

> 'Are you thinking of me, my friend? Do not worry. I fed myself – and you, for that matter – for many years before you worked for Min. I can do so again. Do you think me so helpless now?'
>
> 'Not you!' Tree-ear shouted, flapping his arms in frustration like a giant bird. 'I am not talking of you! It is Min's wife I am thinking of! She is an old woman now – would you have her poor back ache from pulling weeds? And those long walks into the mountains, for mushrooms or berries – she should long ago have earned rest from such tasks! From her husband she gets no help at all. He thinks of nothing but his work!' (p. 102)

Another set of linguistic traces which can be seen as indexing contestation of traditional gendered discourses consists of references to an alleged historical event. Crane-man has advised Tree-ear to stop on his journey to the court at the 'Rock of the Falling Flowers', just before the city of Puyo, an old capital city. Five hundred years previously, the T'ang Chinese had invaded. Crane-man tells Tree-ear:

> 'The King and his party were forced to retreat to the very highest point of Puyo – a cliff overlooking the Kum River. There was no escape. Bravely, the King's guards placed themselves a little way down

the path between the enemy and their sovereign. They were overrun in moments.

'All of the King's concubines and ladies-in-waiting crowded round him, determined to protect him to the last. The women knew well that the T'ang would not kill them; no, they would be taken prisoner, probably to be tortured. Their terror can hardly be imagined ...

'The T'ang army charged up the hill. All at once, as if their minds had become one, the women began jumping off the cliff. Every one of them preferred death to becoming a prisoner.

'Can you see it, my friend? The women jumping one after another from the cliff, their beautiful silk dresses billowing in the air – pink, red, green, blue ... indeed, like flowers falling.'

Tree-ear gasped, his eyes round. What courage it must have taken!

'The T'ang were victorious that day, but the women's efforts were not in vain, for they have since been an inspiration to all who have need of courage. Their memory will live for a thousand years, I am sure of it.' (p. 116)

This is significant on two counts. First, the interpretation of this mass suicide as an act of *courage* (the word is repeated) – focalized again as Tree-ear's own perspective, through his 'represented thought'. The story is also returned to later in the narrative (p. 121). Second, in the extract quoted, the women's action can be seen as actively *choosing* suicide over both protecting the king (now left defenceless) and submission to torture (interpretable by an adult reader as sexual abuse in all forms). Though the representation of the act as 'flowers falling' may be seen as sentimental, it is significant that the word *sacrifice* (often a trace, I would argue, of a very traditionally gendered discourse) is notably absent. The (muted) feminist discourse can be seen as evidenced by the description of these women's agency, and their resistance to a particular set of patriarchal social practices – and, indeed, in the reference to these patriarchal practices themselves.

Accumulations of intratextually-related traces in *A Single Shard* thus facilitate the production of a feminist discourse – and its co-construction by the reader. And while the focus of *A Single Shard* is the maturing of Tree-ear, within a historical setting, it is possible also to see this as a 'carrier' of 'an ideological position [which] ... includes a desire to promote social change in the modern world' (Stephens, 1992: 238).[11]

Like Louis Sachar in *Holes*, Linda Sue Park in *A Single Shard* has produced a feminist discourse through embedding a narrative within the main story. Both sets of narratives refer to periods of time considerably *before* the main stories (several generations before in *Holes*, several centuries before in *A Single Shard*). More interestingly, using 'achronological intertextuality' (Stephens, 1992: 85), these embedded feminist narratives refer (successfully) to a time well before even the first wave of the modern Women's Movement.

Non-androcentric discourses

Five of the eight books have human male protagonists and in a sixth (*So You Want to be President?*) men outnumber women. The focus is thus largely on *masculine* experience.[12] *Bud, Not Buddy* is narrated by Bud, and in *Holes* and *A Single Shard* events are frequently focalized through Stanley and Tree-ear. It could thus be said that a 'Male-as-norm', androcentric discourse is pervasive in this small corpus. However, in *none* of the books is the discourse entirely androcentric. We have already seen how *Snowflake Bentley, So You Want To Be President?, Holes* and *A Single Shard* avoid this. I will now look at how the question of limited gender representation in books with male protagonists is addressed in *Joseph Had A Little Overcoat* and *Bud, Not Buddy*.

Joseph Had a Little Overcoat (Caldecott, 2000) is illustrated as well as written by Simms Taback. The page-size illustrations include (quasi-) photographs, portrait-style, on the walls of Joseph's house. There are 'texts' within the visuals – posters and mottoes on the walls, newspapers on the floor ('Fiddler on the roof falls off roof'). The illustrations include many other human characters, who provide a backdrop to the different things Joseph does with what was once an overcoat. Taback seems to have addressed the question of wider gender representation by including large numbers of women in these illustrations. There are male and female adults at the fair, women and men at his nephew's wedding, his married sister and family in the city, and women and men in his house watching him make a button out of the last remnant of cloth. (It has to be said, though, that there are slightly more men than women represented, even without counting an illustration of the men's chorus in which Joseph sings.)

In *Bud, Not Buddy* (Newbery, 2000), there are important female characters: Bud's most recent foster mother, Mrs Amos – abusive, but no more so than his foster father; the librarian Miss Hill who had helped him with books in the past and another librarian who (unintentionally) helps Bud plan his journey; Miss Thomas, the singer in his grandfather's band, who looks after him properly; and of course Bud's dead mother,

Angela Janet Caldwell, who told him that his name was 'Bud, not Buddy', by whom he has been greatly (and positively) influenced. These women are all instrumental to the plot, as well as highly relevant to the way Bud sees the world, and together combat the absolute dominance of androcentric discourse here.

A subversive discourse?

The Three Pigs (Caldecott, 2002), written and illustrated by David Wiesner, is a very different sort of book from the others, being fantasy and an animal story. It is in fact a reworking of the traditional *The Three Little Pigs* ('Who's in charge of this story? Who gets to decide? Has anyone asked the pigs?') The absence of *Little* from the title may be telling!

In Wiesner's watercolour illustrations, the pigs do not wear clothes. They are all, however, referred to as *he* (as is the wolf). The story starts off in traditional mode, with the wolf watching the first pig build a house out of straw. When he huffs and puffs, however, the first pig is pictured falling backwards off the page, saying (in a speech bubble), 'Hey! He blew me right out of the story!' The same happens to the second pig, encouraged by the first (who puts his snout round the traditional picture, dislodging it) and the third. They are then pictured walking on top of the pages of the traditional 'Three Little Pigs' story: they turn this into a paper aeroplane which takes them to a world of children's pictures and story books. The pigs find themselves in a fairytale with a dragon about to be slain by a prince – and rescue the dragon. They then come across a picture of the third pig's house (made of bricks) and go home, taking the picture. When the wolf tries to blow their new brick house down, he is repulsed by the dragon. They 'all lived happily ever after' – with the wolf having to settle for sitting on the hill outside.

In the 'multi-modal' illustrations, one text is laid upon another in a very post-modernist, inter- and hypertextual way (see also Johnston, 2000). Wiesner has, however, creatively shaken up and indeed 'disturbed' the *narrative* of both *The Three Little Pigs* and a traditional 'dragon-slaying' fairytale, in what Barthes might call a very 'writerly' way. The 'dragon-slaying' tale recasts the dragon as victim *and* the hypothetical princess – here there is no need for rescue, since there is no princess (other than a tiny line drawing of a (possible) one in association with a possible other story). At a higher level of abstraction it is possible to see a relation between these 'reworkings' and that of feminist fairytales, since both challenge the traditional, the familiar and the patriarchal. A *general* subversive discourse in relation to fairytales (at least) can thus be seen here.

Gendered literacies

I will conclude this chapter by commenting briefly on gendered *literacies*. Mary Alice in *A Year Down Yonder* becomes a journalist, but literacy practices also play an important functional role for the male protagonists. In *Holes*, Stanley teaches the clever but illiterate Zero to read and write – at Zero's request – and Zero's success saves Stanley from trouble. Bud in *Bud, Not Buddy* is an avid reader of library books about the Civil War, and with the help of a librarian plans his trip to Grand Rapids using an atlas. Joseph in *Joseph Had a Little Overcoat* writes a book and Willie Bentley in *Snowflake Bentley* reads about his coveted new camera.

This raises questions of gendered literacies outside children's literature and of concerns about boys (at least on both sides of the Atlantic) tending to have a harder time with reading and writing than do girls (see Chapter 4). Girls and boys tend to choose different genres as well as different forms of fiction (at times perhaps encouraged by teachers), and girls also read *more* (Christian-Smith, 1989; Swann, 1992; Millard, 1997; Nichols, 2002). Given that most characters in children's fiction are male (Swann, 1992), an asymmetry which may now be intentional, even institutionalized, in response to apparent gendered asymmetries in reading *practices* – as indeed may be the literacy practices as represented in these award-winning books – this almost inevitably means that girls are more likely to read 'boys' books' than boys to read 'girls' books'.

Are girls *disadvantaged or disempowered* by reading 'boys' books', in that they are not accessing 'self-affirming' representations of themselves, but are rather accessing representations of themselves as 'other'? (*Are* they, though, accessing 'non-self-affirming' representations of themselves? 'Boys' books' may be about boys, but – as this study shows – this does not mean that the gendered discourses therein are misogynist or even sexist ones. Further, girls may at times *identify* with male characters.) It may also be that in accessing a wider *range* of books (with a wider range of characters), girls are advantaging themselves in their understanding not just of literature but of a range of both discourses and epistemologies. As Moss suggests in relation to boys and girls at secondary school, the 'diversity of discourses' can work 'to the advantage of those who are marginalised by dominant discourses' (1989: 124). At the same time, though, boys may be maintaining the boundaries of masculinity and indeed masculine power by not engaging with what they perceive as 'girls' books'; this may have implications for the wider perceived value of those 'girls' books'.

Conclusion

Using related traces within the texts, relationships between these books and other texts, and a measure of inference, I have interpretively identified a range of gendered discourses, often in the same book. By extension, a range of gendered discourses is likely to be evident in other works of children's literature. Feminist discourses have to an extent been mainstreamed, and hence now circulate widely. They may therefore be evident in books without an explicit feminist *stance*, their traces popping up in unlikely places.

Other gendered discourses could I am sure be co-constructed in these eight books (though I suspect that other feminist analyses would not co-construct a completely different set). I say *co-construction* since, ultimately, recognizing a gendered discourse must be a matter of negotiation between text and reader (normally, one who is reading for pleasure, not primarily for the purpose of discourse analysis). The extent to which readers do co-construct gendered discourses is an avenue for further research.

I hope I have shown that the gendered discourses apparent in children's books may be of more interest and concern to the critical text analyst than the simple distribution of female and male characters and what they do. I hope also to have pointed a way for others to identify gendered discourses in children's literature, bearing in mind that different books often suggest different approaches to analysis.

Part III

Theorizing Gendered Discourses and Linguistic Intervention

Introduction

Part II of *Gendered Discourses* focused on empirical work on gendered discourses from the classroom, parenting magazines, newspapers and children's books. Part III does not leave this work behind, but concentrates on more theoretical issues, using these examples as illustrations. Chapter 8 looks at the issues of discourse(s) and the *construction* of gender: namely, what do different researchers and writers working within different theoretical paradigms mean by *construction*? In particular, does it refer to construction 'beyond words spoken and written'? What is the role of *discourse* in construction? Here I would like to acknowledge the Lancaster University 'Gender and Language Research Group', which, one way or another, regularly returns to such questions. I also look at the concept of *performance*, acknowledging the relationship between the two concepts and suggesting that, at times, construction *is* performance.

Chapter 9 looks at the question of 'damaging discourses' – damaging from a feminist perspective – and the related question of '(feminist) intervention in discourse'. To my knowledge, the phrase *damaging discourse* has not been widely inscribed in reports of discourse analyses. For some post-structuralist discourse analysts, this may be because of the theoretical difficulty of evaluating a discourse and characterizing it with something as judgemental as *damaging* – this difficulty conflicting with the feminist imperative of doing precisely this. Many of the discourses identified in this book have, however, been discussed – and named – *critically*, with writers implying they have the potential to damage women and girls, or men and boys, or gender relations, or human beings in general, in some sense. This could be immediate and material – as in the finding that 'generic' masculine items in job advertisements kept female high school students from applying (Bem and Bem, 1973) – or 'symbolic', as in Bourdieu's (1991) idea of 'symbolic violence'. If discourses *are* somehow damaging, then there is a role for discoursal intervention; I explore different documented forms of this, together with a consideration of the place of discoursal intervention in different approaches to discourse analysis.

The rationale behind these two chapters is that I am frequently aware not only in my reading of others' work, but also in my own writing and thinking, that a theoretical concept is often invoked without making the particular concept clear – for example, the writer not saying how she and/or others understand it, or using it in different ways *without comment.* While I am not requesting rhetorical closure of meaning, since this would restrict any project which is always seeking 'possibilities', or fetishistic absolute consistency here, I would welcome more reflexivity and meta-discourse from discourse analysts on the theorization within their own written academic texts.

8
The Discoursal Construction of Gender

In this chapter I address some issues of gender and discourse which I feel receive insufficient attention in the literature. I look mainly at the notion of *construction* in relation to discourse and gender, assuming that discourse *constructs* gender *in some sense*. I also consider *performance*, assuming that discourse can be actively used, and discourses *produced*, to perform gender. A third assumption is that the concepts of *construction* and *performance* are related, but not the same thing. A fourth is that both can be achieved in speech and in writing. I also consider how claims of construction and performance might be empirically supported.

Construction and discourse

The notion of *construction* can be used to mean that accounts are 'constructed' in the sense that they are not, and cannot be, full or objective reports. A description of a political event, for example, is a *construction* in the sense that it is partial, produced by a human being who is fallible, experiences things subjectively and may have a particular point of view she wishes to express. However, *construction* can also mean that words put together in some coherent form *themselves* have the capacity to construct. Language use can thus be seen as *a construction* and as *constructive* (Potter, 1996: 98).

Using *construction* in the second sense, it is commonplace nowadays to read that *gender* can be constructed by *language* (in text, in discourse) – that is, is not only linguistically reflected or represented – and accordingly that the language which constitutes a given stretch of data does just this. We have already looked at the discoursal construction of fatherhood in Chapter 6. After the birth of his son Leo, Tony Blair constructed himself not just as a father *in his reported words* in a range of

British newspapers, but also as a modern, hands-on father. Newspaper journalists too constructed him as hands-on (if part-time) father in their words, and all this was done in part by Blair and the journalists drawing on and producing certain discourses of fatherhood. In the wider sense, gender itself was also being constructed 'in' these texts in that allegedly gendered characteristics (associated with the 'Part-time father discourse') were being drawn on and the discourse was being maintained and reproduced.

Much work has been done within a framework not just of *the social construction of gender* (a somewhat redundant phrase, if gender *is* social), but also of the *discoursal* construction of gender. Marshall, for example, in her analysis of motherhood discourses (see Chapter 5), refers to accounts 'construct[ing] an essentially consistent medical/psychological discourse which presents one version of the meaning of motherhood', the various accounts then working together 'to construct motherhood as a wholly positive experience' (1991: 82, 83). The focus on discoursal/linguistic construction as a form of social construction has represented a sea change in gender and language study, and beyond. The 'traditional', paradigmatic research question (still asked, of course) came to be 'How do women and men speak differently?' The paradigmatic research question is now variations of 'How is gender (including the (re-)production of gender relations) constructed in the talk and written texts of women and men, boys and girls, and institutions?' This means a shift away from the importance of 'sexed, language-using individuals' – men, women, boys and girls – towards gender as an *idea* or construct.

In Chapter 6, in discussing textual constructions of fatherhood, I said that I was using *construction* to mean achieved by and *as evidenced in the words used*. And so far, in this chapter, we have been concerned with construction *in discourse* – which is not unlike representation. But can construction go beyond 'the words spoken or written' – as social constructionism sees it as doing? Can it extend to 'construction of the person'? Might an individual's identity, or 'inner workings', be constructed (variously: maintained, created or contested) by a given language event? Might people's (gendered) understandings be shaped (created, confirmed, disturbed) by the talk (or written text)? What might constitute linguistic evidence of such construction? One problem here is that a writer's or researcher's use of *construction* is often not explained, perhaps because *construction* has become something of a given. As Deborah Cameron writes in her review essay of books on gender, language and discourse in *Signs*, 'it is more likely [than in the early years of gender and language study] to be assumed, now, that the role of language is a strongly constitutive one' (1998: 962). This is partly due to the wider late twentieth-century 'linguistic turn' in the humanities and social sciences, in which language (actually, discourse) has assumed a new importance, and after which language has been newly seen as constitutive across the disciplines.

Lack of explanation may be appropriate when *construction* is used in a general sense ('the construction of gender in the classroom'). However, it is less satisfactory when it is used in a particular one ('X constructs himself as a heterosexual when he says ...'). Let us take as an example a paper by Scott Kiesling, 'Power and the Language of Men' (1997). Kiesling uses *construct[ion]* in the following ways:

1. 'In particular, I will demonstrate how sequentiality and activity type must be taken into account when exploring *the construction of men's identities through language.*' (p. 65)
2. 'In this section, I will explore how four men employ different discursive means *in order to construct* powerful identities.' (p. 72)
3. '*His identity construction in the second statement therefore shows* the situated, sequence-dependent nature of identity.' (p. 80)
4. 'I have thus shown how four men employ both similar and varied discursive devices *in order to construct a particular kind of identity.*' (p. 81)
5. 'We can still say that, in some general sense, many men in the United States *construct powerful, competitively oriented identities.* Moreover, due to the ideology of difference in US society, *the motivation for men to construct these identities* is of a different nature than for women.... *Men who construct the 'preferred' gender identity* are rewarded with power...' (p. 83; emphasis added)

Kiesling uses *construction* in a general sense in example 1, and first and third sentences of example 5, though the example 5 sentences do seem to assume that construction can be straightforwardly recognized. In example 3, construction is seen as self-evidently *there* – evidenced by the words in question – and is *itself* used to show something about identity. Kiesling also attributes an important role to *intentionality* (examples 2, 4 and the middle sentence of example 5). This is problematic, in part because intention is notoriously difficult to establish or even investigate ('perceived intention' is not the same thing).

Kiesling is not alone in not problematizing *construction* itself and I am *not* singling this paper out as a bad example: the above statements are representative of a lack of explicitness more generally. Other cognate terms (*cast, present, enact, accomplish*) are also widely used with similar lack of articulated reflexivity.[1] Lack of explicitness may sometimes index a particular theoretical position – however, when that is the case, clarification would be welcome.

Further, claims of construction (at least 'beyond the words') are often not supported empirically, and thus remain rhetorical, requiring an act of faith on the part of both writer and reader. Related concerns have been raised in relation to *discourse*. (Baxter, who identified several 'competing discourses' in the classroom in relation to girls' and boys' speech (see Chapter 4) critiques studies of discourses which do not focus on the actual language used (2002b; see also Widdicombe, 1995).) Work on both *construction* and *discourse*, carried out within a post-structuralist framework, in particular, has tended to be stronger theoretically than on details of actual workings.

I will shortly return to the important question of construction 'beyond words spoken or written'. First, however, six questions surrounding the notion of 'construction' *in the words spoken or written*, and its relationship to gender:

- How do we know that *gender* is being constructed? On what linguistic (or other) basis can we claim gender construction (what 'warrants' can we – and do we – draw on)?
- How do we know *when* gender is being constructed, as opposed to ethnicity, or sexuality or another identity?
- Can an individual construct their own gender identity simply in their own utterances, even if this is entirely monologic, for example in writing? Or can identity construction occur only in interaction (and hence with negotiation)?
- What are people constructing themselves and others *as*, in relation to gender? How do we know?
- Does it make sense to talk about intentionality in construction?
- What is the relationship between particular discourse(s) being drawn on and the construction of gender?

The first two of these questions are addressed by Joan Swann (2002), in an article entitled 'Yes, but is it gender?' Swann is concerned with *operationalizing* gender, not so much to define what it *is*, but rather to enable us to claim when 'something to do with gender is going on'. 'The danger is,' she observes, 'that researchers may make such assumptions [about the relevance of gender] without an appropriate warrant to support them' (2002: 60). Researchers do, however, *use* warrants. As Swann points out:

> Across a whole range of empirical studies, it is possible to identify a series of warrants for gender; that is, a series of decision procedures

adopted by analysts that justify interpreting data (an utterance, or a linguistic construction, or a set of linguistic features) as, in some way, gendered. (2002: 49)

The 'warrants' which have been used to say 'Yes, it *is* gender' Swann identifies as:

1. quantitative and/or general patterns (derived from correlational studies of language use, large (computerized) corpora or other systematic comparison between the language of divergent social groups);
2. indirect reliance on quantitative/general patterns;
3. 'participants' orientations' as evident in the text (the traditional 'CA' perspective);
4. speakers'/participants' solicited interpretations (e.g. in interviews or questionnaires);
5. analysts' theoretical positions (e.g. CDA);
6. analysts' intuitions;
7. speakers/participants are female, male (or whatever).

Swann identifies the limitations of each warrant, and argues for 'a sort of pragmatic eclecticism' (2002: 60). I refer readers to her article for further explanation and exemplification.

In their turn, the remaining four questions could (but do not) come from an article entitled 'Yes, but is it construction?' One answer, of course, to all four is 'It depends on the analyst's theoretical position.' As I have said, though, this position is not always provided. I will therefore attempt to relate ways of understanding *construction* to various theoretical positions.

I address the four questions in three sections: 'Self-construction', 'Negotiating construction in interaction' and 'Construction "beyond words spoken or written" '. Frustrating as this may be for the reader, I do not address each question in a separate section, since the three headings cut across the four questions. I do, however, indicate what questions are being addressed in each section.

Self-construction

I will start with the questions of self-construction in an individual's own talk (or written text) and of what (we can claim) she is constructing herself *as*. This section also addresses the question of intentionality.

As with the Blair example, an individual can construct herself linguistically *in her talk*. At times, this construction may *intentionally* be striven for. This assumes something of a liberal humanist approach to discourse and to construction – what Butler (1999) refers to as 'voluntarism'. Self-construction can also be seen in a more constrained way as unintentionally producing or even accommodating to established (or emerging) *pre-existing* discourses (a post-structuralist perspective).

We have all probably approached certain events by asking 'How shall I play this?' (= what shall I construct myself as here?) If someone in a job interview says, in response to the question 'Do you consider yourself a social scientist', 'Yes, I consider myself a social scientist' (an actual, reconstructed example), self-construction seems intentional. Other genres in which intentional self-construction as likely can be argued for are those in which we are not known: typically focus group introductions and personal columns. In all these, speakers/writers conventionally talk/write about themselves for the benefit of others – who they are, what they look like, what they like, what they do, have done and are able to do, what they think, and so on – in a particular way. These genres lend themselves to intentional construction in a salient, even theatrical way: we can see this sort of construction as *performance* (see later). There are also opportunities for intentional self-construction in less 'performance-friendly' genres like routine committee meetings, going out for a social drink or taking a telephone message for a friend, for example, through the particular performance of certain 'dispreferred' speech acts (e.g. advancing an unpopular argument in a committee meeting, warning an unwanted caller that a friend wants no more telephone calls). Purpose-oriented genres and speech acts dovetail here: an ad in the personal column is aimed at finding a partner, as are the speech acts articulated in that ad.

People can construct themselves (intentionally and otherwise) in a range of linguistic ways. In addition to speech acts and genres (see also Liang, 1999, on pragmatic implicature), the analyst can look at *topic* – what is selected for the telling and what is not (that could have been)? A woman who has a career and a family can be seen as constructing herself differently when she talks about one than when she talks about the other. Here different discourses come into play. Topics entail ideational meaning and ideology (even if this is only 'Topic A is important', and, implicitly, 'Topic A is more important in this context than Topic B'). They also entail interpersonal meaning: 'Topic A is something I talk about with you.' And the *way* a topic is talked about will constitute a trace of one or more discourses.

It is also possible to speculate about linguistic items that can constitute self-construction. Candidates include (but by no means stop with)

I am phrases, verbs such as *have, like, want, do, think,* and first-person possessive pronouns (if you refer to 'your something' you are arguably constructing yourself as the owner or at least associate of that something – *my car, our university*).

To see how self-construction in one's words might work, let us return to the focus group introduction and its associated speech acts. Focus group members have typically not met each other before. If asked to introduce themselves, they have virtually free rein over what they can select to say (including what may not be true), and can thus *intentionally* self-construct. In one focus group of which I was a member, a man included in his introduction the information (reconstructed) 'I have two children – that I know of', thereby constructing himself not only as fertile and heterosexual, but also as something of a Lothario – a 'lad' rather than a 'new man'. He could be said to have been drawing on a 'discourse of laddism' – gloriously untrammelled. Introductions may be influenced by the topic of the meeting (or what members perceive as the topic), motivated by members' desire to find out what they have in common (Myers, 2000), shaped by how the facilitator introduces herself, or what she requests (in the focus group above, we were asked to say something interesting about ourselves) and may become more patterned with each introduction. The prototypical speech act nevertheless essentially remains the broad *describing oneself* – broken down *into describing one's interests/family/place of origin/profession* ..., etc. First-person pronouns are predictable here (though these may be sentence-initial elided, as in the focus group data below).

Juliane Schwarz's focus groups discussed non-sexist language items. Members of one group (mature women students, 49–59 years old) seemed to feel that they had to explain in their introductions why they were mature students. The identities they could be seen as constructing were frequently gendered in terms of domestic roles and relations. After giving her name and where she has lived, Michelle says:

> I went to university at the right time (.) when I was 18 (.) did half a degree and dropped out (.) became a nurse (.) got married (.) had a baby (.) been a nurse ever since (.) got my little baby (.) got a divorce (.) got married again (.) and now I'm back (.) [laughs] back at university (.) at the tender age of 49 [she goes on to talk about becoming a research student]. (Schwarz, 2003)

It may have been possible for Michelle to construct her mature student identity for the group without recourse to this 'family discourse', but my guess is that this would have been difficult for her. We can make the claim that she constructs her identity (what she did and does) through this discourse in the words she uses. What we *cannot* claim is that she is also constructing herself as a person – for example, developing or 'reinforcing' a sense of who she is. This stretch of talk may shape such 'inner workings', but we do not know.

At some level, in some form and *in some sense*, intentional self-construction may be a part of much talk. However, intentional self-construction cannot even be striven for (at least not at the same level of intensity) all the time. Rather, we go through the day with other agendas, interacting with people for whom we have *already* constructed ourselves. And though most people do care what most others think about them, and therefore are never *un*concerned about how they are constructing themselves, just as in the slogan 'First impressions are so important', the emphasis is clearly on *First*. 'Reconstruction' is arguably harder to achieve with each interaction with a given other person, and any attempted self-construction may thus lose impact with length of acquaintance.

But what is a speaker constructing herself *as*? In Chapter 6 we saw how we can safely say that Tony Blair constructed himself as an involved father and as a husband – but as a 'good father', and a 'good husband'? Similarly, a woman might say, on a Saturday afternoon, in response to the question 'What have you been doing today?', 'I took my children to dancing class this morning.' It seems safe to say that she is constructing/has constructed herself as a mother ('my children'). But is she also in effect constructing herself as a *good* mother, using a 'Good parents provide extra-curricular opportunities for their children' discourse? She may or may not have been intending this; depending on her interlocutor, she may or may not have achieved it (the utterance's 'perlocutionary effect'). Similarly, if this woman is also an academic, who then starts to talk about how later that day she will be marking assignments and the importance she places on her students' ability to analyse data, is she constructing herself as an academic? Presumably, yes. But as a good, rigorous academic? A good, rigorous and caring academic? Does the fact that she will be doing this on a Saturday evening make a difference? Is she constructing herself as diligent or as lacking in time-management skills? It is not obvious how these questions should be addressed.

If we can talk about 'attempted' construction, can we also entertain the notion of construction as 'successful' in terms of communicating, say, 'good motherhood' to an interlocutor? This may only be ascertainable in interaction. Success here will depend in part on the *value* placed by the interlocutor on (a) the time parents/mothers spend with their children, and (b) dancing classes. If the children are girls and the class is ballet and the interlocutor is a feminist opposed to such traditionally feminine performing arts as helpful extracurricular activities for girls, any such a construction may not be 'successful' at all.

Negotiating construction in interaction

In this section I look mainly at the question of negotiated interaction and construction, but also at the construction (in one's talk) of others, and the question of *when* gender is being constructed. Again, the stance may appear somewhat 'voluntarist', but less so if discoursal interaction is seen as speakers variously taking up, accommodating to or, importantly, resisting particular subject positions made available by already existing discourses.

The possibility of self-construction in talk (and writing) implies the possibility of also constructing others (present and absent) in that talk. That academic and mother might be said to be (or be read as) implicitly constructing parents who do not take their children to dancing class, or academics who do not concern themselves with their professional work at the weekend, or do not rate their students' ability to analyse data quite so highly – and perhaps to be doing so negatively. Accordingly, social structures may also be constructed in talk. As we saw in Chapter 6, for example, Tony Blair constructed the National Health Service positively in his talk to the press about the birth of his son in an NHS hospital.

However, this is still to look at construction in a virtually *monologic* way. Alternatively, *construction* of an individual is achieved not in the talk of that individual, but is socially negotiated in interaction (Wheeler, 2002), and perhaps shaped by associated power considerations. Certainly, the idea of construction in interaction may be *more* convincing: coming from discursive psychology, Antaki et al. refer to speakers in interaction not only as 'invoking social identities' but also 'negotiating what the features or boundaries of those identities are' (1996: 488). If the interlocutor in the previous section perceives that she is being negatively constructed and critiqued, she may contest what she hears – with, for example, 'I think it's better all round not to do academic work at all at the weekend', thus *negotiating* the construction of a good academic and parent. Such ongoing interaction allows work to be done on the particular construction, including work of contestation, thus grounding the construction further and refining in the talk. Antaki et al. refer to speakers in interaction 'accumulating a record of having [social] identities' (1996: 488). Not every single word or utterance will 'index' gender, of course (see below), and 'gender construction' will always need to be 'worked at', sometimes through a 'long conversation'.[2]

The most obvious linguistic 'way in' to the construction of gender *in and as evidenced by* talk in interaction (and even monologue) is when a speaker uses a social category such as 'women' as part of a claim, thereby (probably) drawing on and producing traces of the 'Gender differences' discourse, and perhaps additional gendered discourses (e.g. 'Women as emotional/Men as rational'). Here, the speaker can be seen as linguistically constructing women (and implicitly men, and indeed her/himself), in those words. This corresponds to Schegloff's (problematic) conversation analytic privileging of participants' *own* orientations in a text – without which a particular category (gender, in this case) cannot be said to be relevant to the analysis (e.g. 1997, 1998; see also Wetherell, 1998, for a critique; and Kitzinger, 2000). A second linguistic 'way in' or 'warrant' is to see construction of gender in a speaker or writer's reference to a male or female individual, or group of individuals, *in a way that draws on a recognizable gendered discourse.* For example, stories of men who defrost their fridges by simply switching them off, put still frozen steaks under the grill and can monitor only one saucepan on the hob at a time, can be seen as drawing on and reproducing what we might call a 'Men as domestically incompetent discourse'[3] and at the same time as constructing (some) men as domestically incompetent.

These questions were examined by Kay Wheeler, in an MA dissertation (2002) entitled 'How Do We Know Gender is Being Constructed?' Wheeler's twin focus was how construction can be theorized and the empirical question of what (sort of) language in what data entitles the analyst to identify and claim gender construction. Using an audiorecorded, transcribed, hour-long conversation between two male and two female undergraduates (three British and one American, Annie, James, Romeo and May (all pseudonyms)) – but explicitly *not* looking at 'gender differences' in their talk – Wheeler looked for evidence of where gender in some form *seemed salient*, and thus might be seen as, in some sense being constructed.

Most of the conversation showed no apparent evidence of gender in the *content* of the talk. At times the participants arguably *did* 'orient' to gender – though Wheeler needed different 'warrants' to claim this. She accepted as the strongest Schegloff's (1998) 'orientation' requirement that speakers themselves invoke the social categories of *women, men* or their equivalents. This happened in just one segment of the hour-long conversation. Part of the relevant extract follows:

1. Romeo: can I say and this might not apply to you two [proba-
             bly addressing Annie and May] but

             (.) in my experience (.) when you're out with a bunch
             of people (.) people most likely to get you into trouble
             are women hh
2. James: [really?] (.) I've not seen that happen
3. Annie: [hh]
4. May: [***] witnessed that before?
5. Romeo: I I I've been out like in a sort of group yeah (.) like
             someone's come up to you in the street and started
             mouthing off (.) and you're like oh fair enough they're
             pissed and then the women start saying oh but you're
             not [well we're like no no we] won't we just want to go
6. James: [really? **************]
7. Annie: [hh]
8. Romeo: to the pub ************
9. James: I sorry I I do not agree sorry yeah I've never had that
             happen (.) it's [always from the guys who are]
10. Annie: [***************start it]
11. Romeo: I must hang around with some really bad women then
12. All: (laughter)
13. May: trust you (.) your choice of friends
14. James: I don't know maybe it's just my experience but I've
             never had (.) never had that happen
15. Romeo: I suppose the other thing is if you're around with a
             group of women (.) you're more likely to act macho
             than you would be with just [***]
16. James: [yeah] but there's certainly an argument for that (.)
             although I did have a friend it
             was quite humorous his girlfriend was talking all this
             trash to this other girl about my boyfriend will beat up
             your boyfriend
17. All: (laughter)
18. James: you know and seriously she was (.) and he's sit he's
             sitting there right behind her going
             (makes gesture?)
19. All: (laughter)

20. James: no I'm not gonna beat that guy up I don't even know
                 him he (.) he hasn't done anything to me (.) he was
                 just basically and finally and finally the only way he
                 could resolve it (.) he couldn't think of any other way
                 to resolve it it's not the best way but it (.) was all he
                 could think of at the time he said look (.) if you two
                 girls wanna fight
21. All: (laughter)
22. James: you can fight (long pause) that's the only time I've
                 ever really seen that happening (.)
                 and I was quite amused by that to be honest hh (long
                 pause) um
23. Romeo: I can't (?) really remember mates getting me into fights
                 um

In invoking the social category of gender (*women, the women*), Romeo
can be seen as linguistically constructing femininity in conversational
interaction by making generalizations about women. He does this by
suggesting that it is women who provoke fights – at the start of the
extract, more indirectly, in utterance 15, and at the end (the implication
being that if it is not 'mates' (coded male) who get him into fights, it
must be women). Romeo thus, Wheeler suggests, 'appears to draw on an
explicit gendered discourse that has echoes of Greek mythology, in
which Sirens (women) lead ships (of men) onto the rocks to "meet their
doom" because of their sexually manipulative nature' (2002: 26).

There is, however, conversational *negotiation* of Romeo's construction
of (heterosexual) femininity, and therefore of the nature of this. Annie
does nothing to endorse Romeo's construction. May and James *contest*
Romeo's construction of women: May puts it down to Romeo's particular set of friends, and James claims that he has not seen evidence of
women provoking men to fight. Though James does give an example of
when he has seen this, he mitigates this with *that's the only time I've ever
really seen that happening* (utterance 22). Wheeler thus claims that in his
attempted construction of women, Romeo has in a sense failed.

In the course of attempting to construct femininity, Romeo can also
be seen as indirectly constructing his own masculinity as a rational,
non-fight-provoking human being, and only a *potentially* macho one
(utterance 15), but not an atypical male (note the frequency of *you*
(= one, i.e. *we men*)). Wheeler suggests that Romeo constructs himself as
having a 'new sexist' identity. Although he makes a clear distinction
between women and men, generalizing about women in what would

probably be to many an offensive way, he mitigates his claim with *in my experience*, and excludes Annie and May from his generalization. Wheeler relates this to a wider view of men as the rational thinkers in society. She also claims that Romeo's self-construction additionally shores up a masculine/feminine binary opposition, which entails hegemonic masculinity. Romeo's linguistic self-construction, however, again remains open to interpretation as to *what* is being constructed: 'some may see Romeo as constructing a sexist identity...others may interpret his utterances as constructing a "passive male" who is averse to fighting' (Wheeler, 2002: 29).

To return to the second way of identifying gender construction in talk, i.e. indirect reference to gender through producing certain gendered discourses, Wheeler draws on the warrant of the *analyst's intuition* to identify a second extract in which gender can be seen as being constructed. This is to go beyond conventional CA and into the realm of post-structuralism and CDA. The topic is slugs and insects in the kitchen.

1.	Romeo:	our house was a complete shithole (.) we had like um a family of slugs (.) and we used to sort of like
2.	Annie:	ahh that's gross (sneeze) I heard stories about that but I never ever met anyone that (anyone?) actually had slugs*
3.	Romeo:	well you didn't ever see them but you just saw the trails on the lino
4.	May:	yeah
5.	Romeo:	you know (?) as they were going round
6.	James:	yeah yeah yeah
7.	May:	my sister had that as well in her house in Exeter they h in their kitchen (.) when they first moved in all the snail (.) tracks everywhere
8.	Romeo:	yeah
9.	Annie:	** there's ants in our kitchen it's horrible
10.	James:	um you know you know you don't want to go anywhere tropical Annie you think ants are (.) a problem (.) don't go anywhere south of maybe France
11.	Annie:	hh
12.	Romeo:	cockroaches I can't be doing with cockroaches
13.	Annie:	I hate them they're scary ***
14.	James:	er yeah it's (.) I mean their their their way of life * you CANnot get rid of them
15.	Romeo:	um

16.	James:	(.) you can have the exterminator out to your house everyDAY (.) you'll still have cockroaches
17.	Romeo:	especially the flying ones
18.	James:	yeah *** bugs those (.) nasty *
19.	Annie:	err
20.	May:	that's disgusting
21.	James:	about that big and they fly hh
22.	Romeo:	yeah
23.	Annie:	I don't like Daddy Long Legs cos they fly
24.	May:	yeah ** flying? and it really gets hot
25.	James:	the moment you flip on the lights wuh ***

Wheeler suggests that Annie's use of phrases such as *that's gross* and *they're scary* might constitute linguistic evidence to support the claim that she draws upon a discourse that indexes a particular kind of femininity. It is a specific discourse that represents insects as disgusting and the cause of much angst that 'shores up' a dominant discourse (Sunderland, 2000a: 249), that of an irrational female who is governed by her emotions and, as a result, is frightened by small things that cannot harm her (2002: 38).

The (gendered?) contributions of the other participants in the conversation may not matter here. For Romeo and James, emotion is backgrounded, and May uses the word *disgusting* just once, to refer to cockroaches. The point is that Annie produces linguistic traces of a discourse that is arguably recognizably gendered. Wheeler's conclusion is that gender – and not just personality – *is* relevant here and *is* being constructed, since 'these discourses index an emotional feminine identity and an unemotional masculine identity', an indexing which again 'represent[s], produce[s] and reproduce[s] the ideological binary of irrational female versus rational male, used to assert a hegemonic masculinity' (2002: 42). This is to see gender as *discursively constructed* difference.

When Wheeler found relatively few references to gender in the hour-long conversation, she noted: 'It may well be the case that gender construction occurs continuously, but this aspect of identity is not foregrounded in every interaction' and that 'gender may be a salient category for analysis at one point, but not in another' (2002: 20, 49). Rhetorically, of course, it can be claimed that, *in principle*, gender construction *is* ongoing in an individual's (waking?) social practices, including their talk. However, it may be difficult to find convincing linguistic *evidence* of this, and such evidence will vary with genre and research methodology. Naturally occurring talk, and even arranged but unguided talk sessions such as this, can be compared with focus groups and interviews on gender, for example (e.g. Wetherell et al., 1987; Edley, 2001), which may yield richer data, simply because the topic has been pre-set.

I conclude this section with the CA idea of 'orientation'. Here Jonathan Potter is critical of post-structuralism's (traditional) general claims about familiarity and habitual forms of understanding. For him, CA can show better how construction is '*achieved* using some devices or techniques' (1996: 102; emphasis in original), of which orientation is one. Speakers 'orient to' each others' utterances (Potter, 1996; Schegloff, 1998), as part of negotiation, and conversational, interactional data show speakers doing this. Hopper and LeBaron (1998) apply 'orientation' to gender through identification of an interactional *series*: 'gendered noticing', which follows 'peripheral gendered activity', and is itself followed by 'extending of gender's relevance'. As an example they give the case of two birdwatchers talking about a singing bird (the layout using their category labels is mine):

Cissy:	He was- (0.2) he was so pla:in, hh wasn't he	[PERIPHERAL GENDERED
	(1.8)	ACTIVITY]
	I'm saying he, it might be a she, huh huh huh =	[GENDERED NOTICING]
Mary:	= If it sings it's a he	[EXTENDING
	[conversation continues]	OF GENDER'S RELEVANCE]

Hopper and LeBaron write:

> As Cissy calls explicit attention to her use of a masculine pronoun to refer to the singing bird when she does not know its sex, she indicates something about her own gender politics. She notices that uncritical use of the pronoun *he* may be problematic. (1998: 62)

One reading of Cissy's words is that her (intentional?) construction of herself, if not as a feminist, is as someone aware of and sympathetic to issues of feminist linguistics. Alternatively, she may simply be (unintentionally? self-consciously?) accommodating to the subject position made popular by a 'Critical feminist linguistics discourse' in resistance to the default androcentric discourse, traces of which she has just produced. The notions of 'orientation' and 'gendered noticing' may not be relevant to construction outside the text, but are useful and interesting ways to look at construction as evident *in the words spoken or written.*

Construction 'beyond words spoken or written'

The discussion in the previous sections suggests that:

(a) constructions of gender may be *explicit* in talk (and, by implication, written text);
(b) other gender constructions can be *inferred*;
(c) these constructions may be relevant not only to the speaker (or writer), but also her interlocutor(s) (or reader(s)); and
(d) constructions can be seen in monologue (including writing) and in interaction.

These, however, are essentially *linguistic* constructions: constructions *in the words used*, but not necessarily beyond. As Potter observes, the 'metaphor of construction' (from a *construction yard*) suggests that 'descriptions and accounts construct the world, or at least versions of the world' (1996: 97). These are, of course, two rather different things.

However, 'beyond the words spoken or written' claims are often made. In Wheeler's study of construction, for example, she observes, 'Annie's consistent and repeated performances of drawing on this [gendered] discourse to represent insects may constitute a warrant on which to claim the construction *of her gender identity*' (2002: 38; emphasis added), though note Wheeler's cautious *may*. Others express their claims with more conviction. Pavlenko and Piller observe that 'gender identities are...constructed *by* discourse' (2001: 34; emphasis in original). Bucholtz refers to the 'geek feminist' as a 'discursively constructed identity' which 'reworks normative gender arrangements' (1999: 303). This is a bold claim, which goes beyond the linguistic, the personal and the interpersonal. And Peterson refers to 'the range of discourses available for students to construct their gender and literate identities', discourses which 'constrained or opened up' students' writing choices (2002: 363).

Let us look from different theoretical perspectives at the question of *whether construction takes place 'beyond words spoken or written'*, for example in the speaker, his or her interlocutors, 'legitimate overhearers of talk' and/or societal/institutional structures.

From the point of view of 'linguistic construction', writes Potter, the answer is 'No':

> The story of linguistic construction left little to explain; whenever words are uttered construction gets done. There is some value in this, as it is certainly the case that using descriptive language produces versions of the world. Yet it does not engage with the question of why some versions 'work' and some do not ... (1996: 102)

Answering *that* question requires notions of both ideology and discourse.

From the point of view of conventional CA, one blunt answer at least must be 'Not interesting, and we can't tell anyway.' Construction *in the talk* is sufficient – indeed, is all that *can* be identified (but see Kitzinger, 2000a).

From a feminist theory/gender and language study perspective, the answer is 'Yes'. Mary Bucholtz identifies the principle that speakers' identities emerge from discourse as 'the fundamental observation of discourse analysis', noting that discourse analysis is thus 'highly compatible with the social-constructivist bent of much current feminist research' (1999: 4). Current feminist research draws interdisciplinarily on the social constructivist 'discourse' approaches of post-structuralism, discursive psychology and critical discourse analysis (CDA). Conversation analysis (CA) (see Wetherell et al., 1987; Gill, 1995), however, on which current feminist research also draws, does not come under this bracket.

Social constructionism is the key here. For social constructionism, 'language and discourse are the meaning systems that produce ... gender as an important and salient social category' (Weatherall, 2002: 85). And social constructionism is embraced (to various extents) by CDA and post-structuralism alike, as well as some discursive psychology (see below). For post-structuralism, and in the Foucauldian understanding of discourse, the answer to the question of whether construction takes place 'beyond words spoken or written' is thus also, resoundingly, 'Yes'. CDA and/or post-structuralism inform much current discourse theory here, though this is not always acknowledged in research papers. The distinction between constructions of gender 'in' and 'beyond' words spoken or written is not really relevant to post-structuralism, since discourse is the semiotic means by which ideology is constituted and maintained, and pervades all semiotic forms – talk, writing, social actions and institutional arrangements. *Discourse* is by definition constitutive (the adjective used in post-structuralism, rather than, say, 'constructing') *beyond the spoken or written text* (as well as 'within' it). Bronwyn Davies thus writes: 'the individual is...constituted and reconstituted through a variety of discursive practices' (1989a: xi). And Foucault (1978), as we saw in Chapter 3, argues from a broad post-structuralist perspective that sex was actively produced in discourses of sexuality.

The Foucauldian/post-structuralist concept of discourse inspired not only the notion of 'discourses', but also *discursive* social psychology (introduced in Chapter 1). From a discursive psychological perspective, asking whether, for example, talking about oneself in a particular way can bring about changes in one's attitude, sense of identity or understandings is to assume a very traditional (indeed, unworkable) paradigm. Discursive psychology rather looks at construction in a principled *anti-cognitivist* way, and instead of considering such things as schemata and memory stores, looks at how accounts relate to particular interactions, in social human practices. Discursive social psychology is thus of considerable interest to linguists, to discourse analysts in particular.

McIlvenny (2002) makes a distinction between the post-structuralist branch of discursive psychology and what he calls 'CA-inspired discursive psychology', which has been drawn on by feminist linguists as well as psychologists (see Wilkinson and Kitzinger, 1995; Kitzinger, 2000a). Wetherell et al., working within the post-structuralist approach, write:

> many of the problems with traditional psychological analyses might be resolved if the emphasis shifted from the fixed characteristics and traits of the person or gender group to the systems of making sense available in their society. (1987: 59)

And Potter (1996), working within the CA 'branch', critiques de Saussure's structuralist semiotics for its individualistic emphasis on cognitive processes at the expense of participants' practices, 'the way language is orientated to activities' (1996: 72). Potter does not say that there are *no* 'in-the-head' representations or perceptions, rather that a study of 'fact construction'[4] is better served by 'selectively combining elements from the constructionism in linguistics, conversation analysis and post-structuralism' (1997: 120). Potter's view of CA thus goes beyond 'orientation' to 'construction' in discursive interaction (see also Stokoe and Smithson, 2001). For both psychologies, 'emotions, beliefs and opinions are *not* private things hiding inside the person: they are created by the language used to describe or account for them' (McIlvenny, 2002: 17);

again, the 'within' or 'beyond' language distinction thus does not really obtain for discursive psychology.

For CDA, discoursal construction extends to 'situations, objects of knowledge, and the social identities of and relationships between people and groups of people' (Fairclough and Wodak, 1997: 258), and by institutions.[5] Fairclough and Wodak also claim that discursive practices 'can help produce and reproduce unequal power relations between (for instance) ... women and men' (1997: 258), and can in principle also help produce (and reproduce) more *progressive* arrangements than currently exist (see Chapter 9). Although both post-structuralism and CDA see discourses as shaping material conditions and structures, CDA differs importantly from post-structuralism and explicitly Foucauldian approaches in that it sees discourses as also *being shaped by* those material conditions and structures in a dialectical process. In this, certain conditions and structures for CDA are *extra-discursive*. Fairclough makes an explicit distinction between 'construction' and 'construal', i.e. 'we may textually construe (represent, imagine, etc.) the social world in particular ways, but whether our representations or construals have the effect of changing its construction depends on various contextual factors – including the way social reality already is, who is construing it, and so forth' (2003: 8).

For all theoretical approaches, whether a speaker constructs *others'* 'selves' (certainly beyond discourse) must be related to whether the construction (of those others) is 'taken up', and how. The 'success' of Romeo's attempted construction of masculinity, for example, will be related to the 'effect' of his utterances (Wheeler, 2002). 'Uptake' of an intended discoursal construction presumably requires that the discourse in question be recognized – an issue addressed by discursive psychology. Potter points out that

> the use of a particular descriptive term, or even a familiar discourse, may not be enough to construct a version of events which will be *treated* as real or factual .... [T]hese techniques ... can be deployed effectively or badly, and they can be undermined vigorously or accepted credulously. (1996: 102; emphasis added)

A person trying to construct herself, or others, in a certain way for the benefit of her conversational interactants (who may *be* those others), in that she hopes the intended construction will have a certain effect, may fail as far as the interactants are concerned because of her inadequate efforts or because of the resistance or scepticism of the interactants. Conversely, however incompetent that person's efforts, a given construction may 'succeed' for a gullible (inexperienced, young, drunk, etc.) interactant. These are important reminders of the very *relative* and indeterminate nature of construction.

Performance

We have already come across the idea of performance as 'intentional self-construction' which I suggested earlier may happen in, for example, job interviews, focus group introductions and personal columns. To these we can add Web chatrooms. 'Constructing oneself' in talk or writing can thus at times be seen as linguistic performance. 'Performance' is not an unfamiliar idea to lay people: 'What a perform-ance!' we say of a particular theatrical episode of real-life interaction between relations, colleagues or friends. Many people will admit (if only to themselves) to having 'performed' a particular identity for another or group of others through the use of a rhetorical style, or introduction of a particular topic or point of view.

A more *specific* concept than construction, performance is thus done *by* oneself, *for* the benefit of particular others (whereas we may attempt to construct someone's identity, it would seem hard to perform it for them). Performance is also I suggest less likely than *construction* to con-note a close relationship with 'in the head' understandings. The notion of performance has been theoretically developed (as 'performativity') in relation to gender by Judith Butler (for example in *Gender Trouble*, 1990, 1999). It is a *practice*, or set of practices: 'performativity is not a singular act, but a repetition and a ritual, which achieves its effects through its naturalisation in the context of a body ...' (1999: xv). Though Butler does refer to discourses (for example, 'the reigning discourses of law, pol-itics and language' (1999: xxvi), which hinder recognition of the status of sexual minority groups), her main concern is not discourse analysis *per se*. Rather, she shows how the notion of performativity contributes to the understanding and deconstruction of 'common-sense' binary notions of gender and sexuality. *Gender Trouble* asks: 'how do non-nor-mative sexual practices call into question the stability of gender as a cat-egory of analysis?' (1999: xi). A drag queen, for example, 'performs' gender in a subversive way which 'disturbs' the gender 'binary': 'the pur-pose of the example [drag] is to expose the tenuousness of gender "real-ity" in order to countenance the violence performed by gender norms' (Butler, 1999: xxiv; see also Hall, 1995; Barrett, 1999). To see gender as performance can accordingly 'open up the field of possibility for gender without dictating what kinds of possibilities ought to be realized' (Butler, 1999: viii).

Performance in the job interview, focus group introduction, Web chatroom and personal column may be primarily verbal. However, Butler's reference to the body entails non-linguistic performance. Butler refers here to *theatricality* (the drag queen), linguistic *or* non-linguistic. In her revised 'Introduction' to *Gender Trouble*, she notes that 'my theory sometimes waffles between understanding performativity as linguistic and casting it as theatrical' (1999: xxv). This may not be problematic: performance in the job interview may not be theatrical, and the drag queen need not speak. Butler continues:

> I have come to think that the two are invariably related, chiasmically so, and that a reconsideration of the speech act as an instance of power invariably draws attention to both its theatrical and linguistic dimensions. (1999: xxv; see also Austin, 1962)

The implication that the locus of 'power' is not fixed, and indeed can (momentarily) reside in (the words of) anyone, is one we have seen exemplified in Baxter's (feminist) post-structuralist discourse analysis of gendered classroom (and other) discourse (2002a,b, 2003).

Gender Trouble had as one of its objectives to show how 'the substantive effect of gender is performatively produced', the book's subtitle being 'feminism and the subversion of identity'. (Butler, 1999: xv, does not deny 'the internal world of the psyche', but considers that it is a signifi-cant theoretical mistake to take this for granted.) Certainly other writers do not see performativity and identity as *oppositional*, as the papers enti-tled 'Performing gender identity' (Cameron, 1999) and 'Polyphonous identity and acts of performed identity' (Barrett, 1999) attest.

Other documented examples of gender 'performance' include trans-sexuals researching alleged male and female speech styles (Hall and Bucholtz, 1995) and telephone sex workers using a style of speaking which connotes female powerlessness, since this is what they think their customers want (Hall, 1995). Performativity thus challenges the whole notion of gender, which becomes 'something that is "done" in context, rather than a fixed attribute' (Swann, 2002: 47). Since this entails gender as something other than pre-existing, should it then never be an *a priori* category for researchers? We can, of course, make a distinction here between gender as 'men' and 'women', and gender as discourse *about* men and women. On a *political* level, Cameron argues not only that feminists still need to account for such dualisms' 'continuing power and pervasiveness' in the world's speech communities (1998: 955; see also Gill, 1995), but also that that gender dualisms should not be 'deconstructed out of existence'. At certain times and in certain places there may be very good reason to look differentially *inter alia* at the language used by, and the discourses available to, women and men (e.g. Hanong Thetela, 2002).

What is the relationship between discourse(s) and performance? Performance (like construction) can be achieved in part – or at least attempted – by producing particular discourses. Recall our discussion of the academic/mother after the dancing class. Traces of particular discourses may be produced in an intentional, even strategic way. Importantly, an intentional and explicit *affiliative* position may be taken in relation to a discourse, since, say, an 'Equal opportunities' discourse may be drawn on to contest it as well as to promote it. I recall a parliamentary debate on lowering the age of consent for gay men, in which an opponent of the bill argued that this was 'not an equal opportunities issue'.

Being able to 'select' discourses for affiliation or rejection does not, however, equate to a 'free choice' of how one performs one's identity. Not only is awareness of discourses limited, access to, wider recognition and acceptability of those discourses of which we *are* aware are circumscribed too. Although seeing gender as performance can help us avoid the idea that people are passively 'put together' by discourse (Talbot, 1998), we need to understand that performance and agency are always subject to constraints, in particular what Butler calls 'the regulatory practices of gender coherence' (1990: 24).

Conclusion

This chapter has addressed some theoretical issues in relation to the concept of discourse, in relation to the different possibilities of *construction*: 'in' and 'beyond' words spoken or written. While social constructionism (which entails construction beyond words) must be welcomed by feminists, not all feminists will *fully* embrace a social constructionism in which 'language and discourse ... produce gender as an important and salient social category' (Weatherall, 2002: 85). For many, gender and its associated problems are 'produced' by things material, and things material are often seen as extra-discursive. In the final chapter I continue this theoretical exploration by looking at whether, and within what paradigms, it makes sense to talk about 'damaging discourses'.

9
'Damaging Discourses' and Intervention in Discourse

This chapter is in two main sections. The first deals with the theoretical question of whether, and in what sense, discourse(s) can legitimately be characterized as 'damaging'. The second looks at the related question of feminist *intervention* in discourse – in particular, the different forms this has taken, and different theoretical approaches here.

Damaging discourses?

Damaging *language* was an important issue early in the second wave of the Women's Movement. The American feminist Robin Morgan claimed in *Going Too Far* that

> The very semantics of the language reflect [women's] condition. We do not even have our own names, but bear that of the father until we exchange it for that of the husband. We have no word for what we are unless it be an auxiliary term for the opposite: man/wo-man, male/fe-male. No one, including us, knows who we really are. (1969; cited from edition of 1977: 106)

Targets thus included what was linguistically *absent*. By 1970 Emily Toth was similarly railing against *one-man tents*, and Germaine Greer in *The Female Eunuch* (1972) noted how terms of 'endearment' for women are also terms for food (*honey, sweetie*).[1]

The damage in question was, however, not always specified and often left vague. Miller and Swift, in the *Handbook of Non-sexist Writing* (1989), referred to common gender terms used to refer to men, as in 'Any politician would have trouble running against a woman', for example, as 'particularly harmful' (1989: 4). The damage Morgan was citing can, however, be seen as in part *social* (note the frequency of *we*). Subsequent work had a similar thrust: lexical and grammatical items like *Mrs/Miss, son-of-a-bitch, manageress* and the 'generic' *he* in the English language were seen as defining, degrading and stereotyping women *as a group*, and as potentially rendering women invisible.

Together with the additional argument that sexist language impeded communication, much of the critique focused on the psychological and cognitive, and hence the individual. Wendy Martyna (1983), for example, in an article entitled 'Beyond the He/Man Approach: the case for non-sexist language', quotes Marge Piercy's and Mary Daly's understandings of the psychological damage done by sexist language. The assumption was that language could influence self-image and understandings, and that sexist language was damaging in that it influenced women's self-image, and women's and men's understandings of gender, both for the worse. Dale Spender boldly claimed:

> By promoting the symbol *man* at the expense of *woman* it is clear that the visibility and primacy of males is supported. We learn to see the male as the worthier, more comprehensive and superior sex and we divide and organise the world along these lines. (1980: 153)

There was in fact evidence for the ability of 'sexist language' to *bias* thought – at least in the short term. The 'generics' *he* and *man*, for example, were found to be interpreted in the specific, non-inclusive, masculine sense (Bem and Bem, 1973; Schneider and Hacker, 1973; Nilsen, 1977; Shimanoff, 1977; Silveira, 1980). In contrast to Spender's rather strong claims, a 'weak' form of the Whorfian hypothesis was broadly accepted, namely, that sexist language items did not determine, but could reflect and influence thought (including sexist thought).

A feminist approach to language *as discourse* can, however, no longer see a given word as straightforwardly 'sexist', since its *meaning* will always vary with context. The way it is used and its use through history will be unpredictable. 'Grammar defines meaning only very partially: it is in relation to a market that the complete determination of the signification of a discourse occurs' (Bourdieu, 1992: 38) – though note that Bourdieu's use of 'market' is very broad, including what he saw as 'cultural' and 'symbolic' capital). For this reason alone a given word cannot be seen as more than potentially damaging, in any sense. Even if a word is agreed to be sexist in a particular context – for example, a derogatory term intended to be abusive by a speaker and taken as abusive by a hearer – 'damage' may not be a result. (Though the feminist analyst, at least, will maintain an awareness that 'potential' damage may always become 'actual'.)

The 'radically contextual' nature of meaning is also one reason why 'sexist language' is now of less interest to feminist linguistics than previously. Cameron writes:

> '[D]iscourse' rather than language per se is [now] seen as the main locus for the construction (and contestation) of gendered and sexist meanings. As discourse has attracted more attention, 'sexist language' has attracted less. (1998: 962)

One thing that *discourse* as a locus can achieve that a 'sexist language' approach cannot is the critique of sexist texts which do not contain any sexist language items – for example, many pornographic written narratives, and constructions using common gender terms to refer to men, such as Miller and Swift's *politician* example.

If language can construct 'beyond words spoken and written' (a tenet of social constructionism; see Chapter 8), discourse(s) can presumably do so in damaging ways. And convincing claims are made about the potential for discourses to do *broad* damage – not directly, but rather through their mediation of social practices and understandings. Cameron, for example, suggests that discourse about women's superiority in (oral and written) communication may be 'intended to distract attention from factual evidence suggesting that in material reality, women are still "the second sex"' (2003: 457), and that representations of gender and language which stress differences (in essence, traces of the 'Gender differences discourse') 'are part of a society's apparatus for maintaining gender distinctions in general .... In many cases they also help naturalize gender hierarchies' (2003: 452). However, also important here is the innumerability of discourses and their diversity. As Moss (1989) suggests, this may work to the disadvantage of the powerful. The intermittent if unpredictable arrival of discourses newly in the ascendant means that authority and power are always vulnerable to discoursal undermining.

Discoursal diversity is one reason why discourses should not be considered in isolation when considering their impact, but should rather be considered as parts of orders or networks. Discourses 'articulate' with each other: operating alongside, converging with, jostling and temporarily mingling with other discourses, at times becoming absorbed in one, at times absorbing another, disappearing and reappearing. Discourses have strong and weak links with other discourses, support and oppose each other in different proportions and strengths, cluster under an overarching discourse and at the same time 'shelter' groups of others. 'Social actors' in any language event will simultaneously be positioned in different ways by the particular nexus of discourses the linguistic traces of which constitute that event. Any potential 'damage' from a given gendered discourse within the nexus must be seen in the light of these discoursal *relations*.

The idea of a given gendered discourse as 'damaging' is in any case now more complex than was characteristic in the feminist 1970s and 1980s. Critical gendered discourses which represent(ed) women as victims – for example, the '(Male) dominance discourse' as manifested and documented in the classroom – are now frequently critiqued from a feminist standpoint, and women's and girls' *agency* and *resistance* shown instead (Jones, 1993; Arnot et al., 1998). Judith Baxter in her classroom inter-action study notes:

> Anne's ability to withstand male interruptions, to develop her argument, and to complete her turn … may actually strengthen her aptitude as a public speaker in the world outside school, where interruptions, heckling and multiple or parallel conversations are often quite routine. (2002b: 838)

Whereas some individuals may be damaged by sexist discourse, others will recognize it for what it is, resist it, laugh at it and/or become empowered in the process. Any damage must be highly contingent. (A critical discursive psychology approach might explore this through interactions and articulated orientations; see Potter, 1996.)

I have not hitherto explicitly described any of the discourses identified in this book as 'damaging', and the phrase 'damaging discourses' is not widely used.[2] As a phrase, it is more emotionally loaded than early 'dominance' terms like *sexist* and *oppressive*. I see it as very wide-ranging, applicable to both individuals' 'identities' and 'inner workings' (hard as these are to explore) – and indeed phrases like *damaged child* and *damaged man* are sometimes encountered. I also see it as extending to personal relationships, social relations more widely, institutions and social structures. There is nothing in *damage* (alone) that entails *beyond repair* though, and this is important for activists. Repair, of course, often means that the repaired 'entity' may be as good as before the damage, but not necessarily the *same*.

Damage is often implied in descriptions of and names given to discourses. Adrienne Rich (1980), for example, is highly critical of

'Compulsory heterosexuality' (see Chapter 3), and Cammack and Kalmbach Phillips (2002) refer critically to a 'Discourse of patriarchy'. The phrase 'dominant discourse' also often signals a critical stance (e.g. Bourdieu, 1992; Baxter, 2002b). Many of the gendered discourses identified in this book are, from a feminist perspective, clearly problematic and deserving targets of critique precisely because they are seen as potentially damaging (we are not just talking niceties). In Chapter 4, I showed how even the 'Girls-as-neat' and 'Girls-as-good language learners' discourses are far from straightforwardly welcome. In Chapters 5 and 6, I referred critically to the 'Traditional family' and 'Triumphant father' discourses of fatherhood, as well as to the 'Part-time father discourse' and its supporting 'Father as mother's bumbling assistant' and 'Father as baby entertainer' discourses. Marshall's related 'Sharing the caring' (a discourse of motherhood) is critical in its ironic naming.

Whether such traditional discourses are actually damaging means considering not only types of damage (material, symbolic, psychological, social, communicational), but also to whom any 'damage' might apply. Here we can draw on both personal/social and theoretical perspectives. As an example of the former consider the correspondence in a workplace electronic newsletter concerning a publicly displayed poster in which a female employee's face had been superimposed onto a (possibly) naked woman's body. The poster, presumably largely visual, semiotically evidenced traces of discourses – but very different ones were co-constructed by different people. The gendered discourse co-constructed by a woman employee *protesting* about the poster, was one of degradation of women through objectification and exposure to the male gaze. Her letter included the claim that: 'there is absolutely no excuse for objectifying, degrading and embarrassing women in this way'. For her, the poster most definitely showed traces of a 'damaging discourse'. For the woman visually portrayed, though, it did not. *She* responded: 'I would like to take this opportunity to say thank you to all my friends and colleagues who made me feel very special on my 40th birthday' (see below; also Schegloff, 1998; Beach, 2000; Speer, 2002).

This episode allows us to address the question of *to whom* discourses might be damaging. The writer of the first letter was not objecting, I suggest, on behalf of either woman represented in the poster. Rather, she was protesting *socially* for women generally – including herself. This sort of complaint is often misunderstood, as when women who pose for pornographic magazines insist in response to feminist anti-pornography campaigns that they are not being exploited, they are doing what they want and being paid well for it – and they don't need 'help' from 'do-gooders', thank you very much. This writer was, however, I infer, producing what we might rather clumsily call an 'Objectification of one woman damages all women discourse', for which women are a social group with interests in common, as opposed to a collection of individuals. From both a feminist *and* a discourse perspective, the damaging potential of a given discourse must be relevant to more than just an individual. The last point here is that if discourse can damage the relatively powerless, it can, in principle, also damage the relatively powerful and dominant, if only by undermining their legitimacy. For this reason it can be used interventionally to progressive ends – the focus of the second section of this chapter.

From a broad feminist perspective, then, the notion of a 'damaging discourse' makes sense. But what of other linguistic and discourse approaches? Within what paradigms can a given gendered discourse be seen as potentially damaging, not just to an individual who 'encounters' and is positioned in a particular way by it, but to women, to men in a way which is in turn deleterious to women, or to gender relations based on principles of gender equality?

Bourdieu (1992) refers not to 'damaging discourse' but to 'symbolic power' and 'symbolic violence'. These concepts were developed with reference to gift exchange as a power mechanism, which can create a relationship of obligation and indebtedness; but the point is that power and domination can be invisible and unrecognized. Interestingly, in relation to the importance of ideology and indeed of the recognizability of discourses, Bourdieu writes that 'A symbolic power is a power which presupposes recognition, that is, misrecognition of the violence that is exercised through it.' Important related concepts are the 'oracle effect' achieved by 'delegates' (including politicians) who 'speak in the name of the masses', which he describes as 'a sort of usurpatory ventriloquism' (1992: 209, 210). Bourdieu's focus is class rather than gender, his concern being the correspondence between the social spaces (e.g. politics, religion) in which 'specialized discourses' are produced and 'the structure of the field of social classes within which the recipients are situated' (1992: 41). However, there are clear connections here with the way gendered discourses *position* women and men. For feminist purposes, a particular concern is the relationship between symbolic violence and real world consequences in the form of material violence or disadvantage.

Post-structuralism and, more particularly, post-modernism are sometimes characterized and critiqued by adherents of more 'committed' approaches as representing discourses as relative and value-free (see Gill, 1995, on Edwards et al., 1995, for example). A post-structuralism which represents discourses as relative and value-free cannot encompass ideas of 'undesirable' let alone 'damaging' discourses. While welcoming some of what post-structuralism has to offer, including the interrogation of the partiality of Enlightenment thought and the 'white Western male' who constitutes its unified subject, Gill writes that much post-structuralist thought

> has served to problematize the very language that we use to intervene politically, without yet offering us new and alternative languages with which to engage. (1995: 173)

She argues that 'a new, principled realm for discourse analysis would be one in which values come to the fore, are made explicit, placed in a realm where they can be argued about' (1995: 182). Much post-structuralism does *not* have a total commitment to relativism, however, and indeed both feminism and post-colonialism can be seen as integral to it (see e.g. Mills, 1997; Baxter, 2002a, 2003).

Several feminist discourse analysts have drawn on and used post-structuralism in ways that *do* allow for – or even facilitate – evaluation and critique. Bronwyn Davies, for example, in *Frogs and Snails and Feminist Tales* (1989a: xi) writes:

> I choose to take [post-structuralist theory] up here because it provides me with the conceptual tools to make sense of my data.... It is a radical discourse because it allows us to think beyond the male-female dualism as inevitable...

And adds:

> Poststructuralist theory ... provides a radical framework ... for conceptualising social change. *The structures and processes of the social world are recognised as having a material force, a capacity to constrain, to shape, to coerce* as well as to potentiate individual action. (1989a: xi; emphasis added)

Because of the prior feminist focus on education and the classroom, it is not surprising that feminist post-structuralist work has also come from this domain. We have seen in Chapter 4 Baxter's (2002a,b) development of *feminist post-structuralist discourse analysis* (FPDA) from her *post-structuralist discourse analysis* (PDA). Neither embraces political or epistemological relativism. Baxter refers critically to how speakers are 'variously positioned as powerful *or powerless* by competing social and institutional discourses' (2002b: 828; emphasis added), and to how dominant discourses can *disempower*. In particular relation to the discourse she names *gender differentiation*, but also in relation to other discourses in her data, Baxter notes critically that while girls are far from powerless in the classroom and should not be constituted as 'victims', they 'are none the less subject to a powerful web of institutional discourses that constitute boys more readily as speakers and girls more readily as an appreciative and supportive audience' (2002b: 839).[3] The post-structuralist notion of 'multiple identities' and multiple subject positions allows for someone being simultaneously put upon *and* resisting – a victim *and* a resistor. This may be the case with Anne (see p. 194), who may not have emerged completely unscathed from the 'male interruptions' she encountered.

For Baxter, certain 'dominant discourses' – those that 'seek a will to truth' and therefore 'a will to power' (these terms from Foucault) – are in effect damaging:

> In the spirit of Bakhtin (1981) and Derrida (1987), prevailing discourses such as these aim univocally to displace, suppress, overwhelm and overturn the interplay of minority or oppositional voices. A dominant discourse serves to inhibit the possibilities for a kinetic interplay of diverse voices, perspectives, accounts and narratives representing multiple social groups. (Baxter, 2002b: 831)

As an example, Baxter cites 'the institutionalization of school discursive practices that systematically privilege male over female speakers in the public space' (2002b: 840).

Discursive social psychology, one branch of which follows post-structuralism and emphasizes the importance of discourses, has as we have seen been drawn on considerably by feminist linguists, as attested by Wilkinson and Kitzinger's (1995) collection *Feminism and Discourse: Psychological Perspectives*. I think it can be safely assumed that all the contributors to this collection see discourse as having the potential to damage, symbolically or otherwise. Widdicombe (1995), for example, is concerned with discourse's *political significance* in the way power and resistance are played out, and social inequalities experienced, as evidenced in the detailed analysis of talk. Similarly, Edley describes his approach as 'this more critical form of discursive psychology', one of whose aims is 'to enquire about whose interests are best served by different discursive formulations' (2001: 190).

Lastly, CDA frequently indexes the potential for social and political damage in the lexical traces of its own discourse: 'power and domination', 'domination and exploitation' and *hegemony*, a term used to 'emphasize forms of power which depend on consent rather than coercion' (Fairclough, 2000: 232). CDA by definition eschews a position of political and moral relativism, and critical discourse analysts frequently identify their own political allegiances and the standpoint from where a given critique comes. CDA, like (F)PDA, can thus be assumed to see many gendered discourses as potentially or actually damaging to the relatively powerless. Baxter, however, argues that CDA is more likely than (F)PDA to see oppression as entailing powerlessness, and that (F)PDA is more likely than CDA to 'argue that females are multiply located and cannot be dichotomously cast as powerless, disadvantaged or as victims' (2002b: 840).

Intervention in discourse

Early linguistic intervention and social change

If gendered discourses can and do damage, the feminist project entails attempting to redress this. Feminism recognizes the possibility of change and strives for it, including through explicit contestation of the existing social order *through language*. For some, the goal of feminism may be to make gender categories redundant: requiring radical intervention in the dominant 'Gender differences discourse' (Cameron, 1998; see also Davies, 1989b). But how can intervention be achieved? To what extent can damaging discourses be negotiated in an emancipatory way or contested with counter-discourses?

Feminist intervention and activism in the first and second waves of the Women's Movement brought about major upheavals in the social order in terms of rights and opportunities for women, as well as perceptions of what girls and women can achieve and should expect. Women and men in many countries now officially have equal rights and opportunities enshrined in law. The analyses of 'sexist language' in the second wave of the Women's Movement in the 1970s and 1980s additionally enabled discursive intervention through creation of anti-sexist alternative linguistic items (for example, *Ms, manager* to refer to both women and men, *spokesperson, he or she, s/he*), the active *use* of these in campaigns and language practices of individuals, and contestation of sexist usages. This intervention in its early stages was entirely independent of any official *language policy* or *language planning* (see Pauwels, 1998).

These alternative linguistic items were, however, soon documented in institutional codes of practice (in universities and trade unions, for example), in Miller and Swift's *Handbook of Non-sexist Writing* (1982, 1989), and new lexicalizations and new meanings of familiar items appeared in grammars and dictionaries (Hennessy, 1994; Sunderland, 1994b). Hellinger and Bußmann (2001: 19) see such codification as instruments of language planning which 'reinforce tendencies of linguistic change by means of specific directions'; this may be overoptimistic, but it is indeed possible to see codification as one indicator of success.

One interesting example of feminist intervention has been the 'generic' *she, her* and *herself*, as in 'If the researcher checks her understandings with her respondents, she may find that …'. I have chosen to single out this rather radical item since it is probably the one that requires the greatest volition on the part of the writer (and, some would say, nerve). It is also probably the item that raises most objections (although *s/he* would be a close contender). In my experience, the typical objection is that it is not gender-inclusive and therefore not an advance as it does no more than exclude men rather than women. But that is precisely the point. 'Generic' *she* is a strategy, and a symbolic one:

> it draws attention to the way women are excluded and marginalised by the traditional convention; by undermining our normal expectations as readers and listeners, it forces us to ask why we take those expectations as natural, and therefore to acknowledge sexism for what it is. (Cameron, 1997: 31)

And it *is* used, certainly in spoken and written academic discourse, in reference to 'the researcher' (sometimes) and 'the teacher' (rather more often), for example.

Just how effective overall was this early intervention in sexist discourse, this attempt to replace sexist language with inclusive language in the hope that people might think in more gender-inclusive, less gender-stereotypical and less damaging ways? What were intended as replacements have succeeded in becoming *alternatives* (so that instead of *Mr* and *Ms*, we now have *Mr* and *Miss, Miss or Ms* (with *Ms* enjoying only feeble success), especially in the UK – *Ms* has been more successful in the US). The interventions were, however, effective *discursively* to the extent (as many will vouch) that people *talked* about them. A backlash became evident (revived later in ready accusations of 'political correctness'), and letters and commentaries appeared in the British tabloid and broadsheet press. This backlash was in turn resisted, notably in the academic sector by critical analyses of arguments against non-sexist language (Blaubergs, 1980; Henley, 1987). The growing awareness that there was a linguistic *issue* here also prompted a different sort of public awareness, that there was an important underlying *social* issue: something not just linguistic was going on. Tellingly, when the interventions were contested, the linguistic reforms being often ridiculed and charged with triviality, some of that ridicule was more extreme and extended than 'triviality' seemed to warrant (see Cameron, 1995). As Michael Swan wrote, on language change more generally, 'When people deplore changes in their language, they are in fact nearly always worried about something else' (1985: 7).

There is evidence of progressive change in a range of gender-related language practices (Adamsky, 1981; Cooper, 1984; Pauwels, 1989). Pauwels (1998) cites change in naming practices (names and titles), occupational nouns and professional titles, generic nouns and pronouns, and avoidance of gender stereotyping – though in public rather than private settings, and in writing rather than speech: employment advertising, educational administration, bureaucracy and publications, print media, dictionaries, grammars and religious texts. Non-sexist items are definitely *in use* and may even be increasing in some contexts. On the whole, however, the success of the non-sexist language project can be described as patchy. Women may be referred to in British tabloid newspapers as *blondes* less than they used to be, but this has not affected sexist journalistic practices more generally (see e.g. Talbot, 1997). Not only has *Ms* has became an alternative to *Mrs/Miss*, rather than a replacement, in the process it has acquired connotations of, variously, feminism, lesbianism, man-hating and divorce (see also Schwarz, 2003). In English, *chair* or *chairperson* are similarly *alternatives* to *chairman* (still preferred by some women); a *chairperson* is almost always female. Despite *he or she*, 'generic' *he* has not disappeared, and may even (now that the pressure has diminished) be enjoying something of a comeback. Hellinger and Bußmann observe that 'appropriation', i.e. alternatives being used in unintended ways, can be seen as 'redefining and depoliticising feminist meanings' (2001: 19). Discourse *always* allows for this possibility. On the other hand, in some continental European languages (German, Dutch, Norwegian), a universal title for women (originally indicating 'married' status) is increasingly being used. In Germany, for example, the 'title' for single and married women alike is now *Frau*.

For some – perhaps younger 'Western' women (Schwarz, 2003) – any patchiness of success of the non-sexist language project is at best an irrelevance since, as far as many are concerned, women now have equality with men, and the non-sexist language debate, like pay differentials for women and men doing the same jobs, is a thing of the past. Indeed, arrangements in responsibility for domestic work may be changing, largely because of the increase in women in full-time positions and high-powered positions in the workforce, and, in the US, the 11 per cent of marriages in which (in 2001) the woman earned more than the man (*Sunday Times*, 11 May 2003; the UK percentage may be even bigger).[4] In the US there has been a rise in the (still small) number of husbands staying at home to look after children – from 558,000 in 1990 to 795,000 in 2000 (*Ann Arbor News*, 5 January 2002, p. 1). The increase in the number of single fathers there has risen more sharply in the same period – from 1.9 to 3 million (although being a single father does not necessarily neatly equate with heavy involvement in childcare).

Sadly, however, Utopia is not with us yet. Feminist issues today may be more subtle and less obvious, but they are there. Worldwide, women and children make up the vast majority of refugees, and lack of literacy affects women far more than it does men. In Western countries, domestic violence may have been 'deprivatized' (it is no longer just a matter for the family concerned), but has not disappeared, and Internet pornography is rampant. Young women are besieged by often digitally altered representations of supermodels. There are still gender disparities in salaries, even between women and men with equal qualifications. Recent figures from the Office of National Statistics, for example, show that whereas men in their forties earned an average of £40.00 per week more than men in their thirties, women in their forties tended to earn £25.00 *less* than women in their thirties (and £171 per week less than men). A contributory (or explanatory) factor appears to be that 'women who take time out of their career to have a baby are offered a worse job when they go back to work' (*Daily Mail*, 3 January 2003, p. 41). *Within* the UK (*inter alia*), where for example it has been claimed that 'sharing' domestic work largely applies to middle-class women who 'are earning more and can tell their men to get stuffed' (psychologist Ruth Coppard, quoted in the *Sunday Times*, 11 May 2003). And though boys tend to have more problems than girls while at school (see Chapter 4), this does not disadvantage them in their later wages and salaries. Hence the need for *continuing* feminist intervention – including in discourse(s).

Six types and some examples

Intervention through the creation and use of single 'non-sexist language items' can be seen as limited in its success precisely because it was concerned with words rather than with social meanings and discourse.

(As Cameron (1992 [1985]: 102) observed nearly two decades ago, 'there is something absurd about the notion that language or words can be attacked independently of their users'.) Intervention in *discourse* (cf. Davies, 1989a; 1993) thus needs to be distinguished from the feminist 'non-sexist language' linguistic activism characteristic of the 1970s and 1980s.[5]

Discourses undergo change without any actual intention or interventional practice of a language user or campaign group, because of their unbounded, unstable, fluctuating nature, and the enduring potential for interdiscursivity. Peterson (2002: 352) refers to the 'dynamic nature of discourse production', which means that even dominant discourses can be 'interrupted'. (Other writers use words such as 'troubled' or 'disturbed'.) This is important since, however 'natural' or resilient or a matter of 'common sense' a discourse may appear to be (the 'Gender differences discourse', for example), even when progressive, human, agentive change seems impossible (both outside and within conditions of extreme repression), in a globalized world there is still *potential* for change. (Bakhtin, in *The Dialogic Imagination* (1981), refers to the role of *polyphony* and the ways in which alternative, perhaps oppositional voices always rise up to challenge dominant or hegemonic ones.) Here I use the phrases *discoursal intervention* and *intervention in discourse* to indicate grass roots and informal forces of change. I do not use the phrases entirely in contrast to official *language policy* and *language planning* (see Pauwels, 1998), since these may stem from and contribute to informal interventional discoursal change, but these are not my concern here.

I will now suggest six related ways in which intervention in gendered discourse (henceforth *intervention*), both spoken and written, may occur (though I am sure there are more than six). These are:

1. deconstruction of discourses through meta-discoursal critique;
2. principled *non-use* of discourses seen as damaging;
3. principled but non-confrontational *use* of discourses perceived as non-damaging;
4. principled, *confrontational* use of discourses perceived as non-damaging;
5. facilitated group discoursal intervention by people *other* than discourse analysts/feminists;
6. 'rediscursivization'.

These interventions I see as currently being conducted, variously, by discourse analysts, feminist researchers, activists, politicians and educational groups as well as members of the general public. These groupings may widen as discourses continue to flow, jostle and create new subject positionings.

First, intervention may involve deconstruction of discourses through meta-discoursal critique, by (critical) discourse analysts. This includes much of the work reviewed in this book, and this book itself. Other examples are Walsh's (2002) critique of 'Masculinism in the institutional discourse of the [UK] Parliamentary Labour Party' and the critique of the more salient and damaging discoursal 'masculinism' in the institution of the police system in southern Sotho, Lesotho, in which 'men's language', which women speakers of Sesotho need to use if claims of rape and sexual abuse are to be taken seriously, is in fact precisely what they are expected *not* to use (Hanong Thetela, 2002).

The remaining five forms of discoursal intervention go beyond *critique*. The second form is the principled, intentional, reiterated *non*-use of gendered discourses seen as damaging, such as a refusal to refer to single teenage mothers as 'scroungers' (i.e. having a baby to qualify for state support and/expecting state support as of right), or deliberate avoidance of the 'triumphant', reactionary, complex discourse of 'Anti so-called "Political correctness"', which has undergone such evident discursive drift (Cameron, 1995; Johnson et al., 2003; Suhr and Johnson, 2003). Feminists and others, at least in some communities of practice, are likely to do this as part of the normal course of events.

Third, and accordingly, intervention may involve principled deliberate and/or repeated *use* by feminists and others of discourses perceived as non-damaging (or less damaging), as alternatives or counter-discourses to those perceived as damaging, but without explicit or confrontational contestation. Those who are parents and teachers may see these discourses in turn being taken up by their children and students. An example might be 'quietly' abandoning the 'Teenage mothers as scroungers' discourse in favour of 'Teenage mothers as young women in need of support', or using *Ms* not only on forms, but when asked the question 'Is that *Mrs* or *Miss*?' Another example was provided in Chapter 3: the 'Feminist menopause discourse' represents menopause as a return to calm and the end of bodily transition, 'an attempt to reject the postmodern obsession with the body in favour of emphasis on the spiritual, inner life' (Coupland and Williams, 2002: 439). Coupland and Williams see this as *implicitly* challenging dominant constructions of the menopause (e.g. the 'Pharmaceutical discourse'). Once produced, such progressive discourses may then be recirculated and recontextualized in a *range* of genres and speech events, competing with non-progressive discourses, in 'long conversations'.

Another example of such non-confrontational but presumably *conscious* intervention in discourse (it is perceived in discourse intervention terms), comes from Bronwyn Davies' *Shards of Glass* (1993). Davies tells the story of a friend's young daughter:

> Claire had had her hair cut in a short, stylish, 'unisex' fashion. In the ensuing weeks she was somewhat taken aback when some people mistook her for a boy. At the same time, many people commented on how nice her hair looked. I told her about an article I had read in which the claim is made that in the world of art, the highest ideals of beauty have been closely linked with indeterminate sex. (1993: 21)

For Davies, this intervention was not just a conversational gambit, but presumably represented a hope that Claire would take up this subject positioning, and might herself then (re)produce this discourse.

In a well-known study, Davies also experimented with discourse intervention by reading feminist fairytales to pre-school children. The varying results are documented in *Frogs and Snails and Feminist Tales* (1989; see also Chapter 7). (Feminist fairytales themselves can be seen as interventions in gendered discourse, by providing new kinds of narrative, intertextually related to those children already know.) Davies' intention was to provide young children with other ways of seeing the world, and with alternative subject positions to those associated with heterosexual romance and a 'consistent male–female dualism'. She was thus producing counter-discourses to potentially 'damaging' discourses. Davies accepts that children feel a need to 'get their gender right', since 'within the discursive practices made available to children, the only comprehensible identity available to them is as "boy" or "girl", "male" or "female"', and that 'having a particular set of genitals is not enough to signify one's position as male or female' (1989: 141). At the same time, she claims, children need access to both

> a discourse which frees them from the burden of the liberal humanist obligations of coming to know a fixed reality in which they have a unified and rationally coherent identity separate and distinct from the social world

and, in particular,

> forms of discursive practice where their social practice is not defined in terms of the set of genitals they happen to have. (1989: 141)

The fourth form of intervention again involves principled deliberate and/or repeated use of discourses perceived as less or non-damaging, but in a way that constitutes not just explicit but also confrontational contestation of those discourses. Early interventional discursive practices of this sort included direct action in terms of painting out sexist words and slogans on advertising hoardings and replacing them with others. Shown below, the Fiat ad 'If it were a lady, it would get its bottom pinched' famously received a spray-painted addition of 'If this lady was a car she'd run you down.' This direct action achieved its effect by contesting Fiat's 'Woman as sex object discourse' with a critical 'Sexual harassment discourse' (and this was in 1979, when concepts like 'contestation' and 'feminist linguistic intervention' were not readily tossed around).

A second example of explicit discoursal intervention through counterdiscoursal contestation is the correspondence surrounding the workplace poster on which a woman's face superimposed on another woman's (possibly) naked body. The discourse contested was the traditional 'Woman as sex object' (or perhaps 'Objectification of the female body'). The protesting writer's sentence 'there is absolutely no excuse for objectifying, degrading and embarrassing women in this way' attempts to provide an alternative discourse – that such pictures constitute degradation of women, and, in effect, sexual harassment of all women. The response from the woman pictured, thanking her friends

Figure 9.1   Confrontational contestation of a sexist discourse

for this birthday surprise, can be seen as an attempt to reclaim the discoursal ground with a gendered discourse akin to 'sexual liberation' – a celebration of the woman concerned, at 40, as a still attractive and sexual being (in effect a contestation of traditional sexist discourses about older women – indeed, less fertile women – as past the first bloom of youth, asexual, and sexually uninteresting and uninterested). I would hazard a guess that this woman saw the feminist discourse in the first letter as humourless, puritanical, damaging and, above all, patronizing. The original intervention can certainly be seen as a 'traditionally feminist', 'modernist' one, drawing on second-wave feminist discourses. The response to this intervention consists of traces of what might be seen as a libertarian discourse, and certainly an individualistic one. Here, these two discourses are competing. We cannot predict from this exchange that the first woman does not share the second woman's views about sexual attractiveness. What she is contesting is the use of particular semiotic traces of an arguably anti-woman discourse to express this.

Relevant to this fourth type of discoursal intervention is Celia Kitzinger's interesting paper, 'How to Resist an Idiom' (2000b). This looks at ways women with breast cancer resist exhortations to 'think positive' in talk, ways that include strategic pauses, token agreements and competing idioms (e.g. 'take every day as it comes'). These forms of resistance could equally constitute discoursal intervention within conversations in which traces of an apparently damaging gendered discourse (rather than an idiom) are produced. This example is a useful reminder that confrontational contestation of discourses perceived as damaging can be done in private as well as public talk and academia, and is not the province only of those who perceive themselves as activists.

The fifth form of intervention is group discoursal deconstruction by people other than discourse analysts, facilitated by those with a professional interest in discourse. The following two examples come from education. In the first, Becky Francis, who investigated 'gender discourses' produced by primary school children, noted that what she called the 'Genders should have equal opportunity discourse' was largely 'contained by the hegemonic construction of gender dichotomy, and failed to challenge it' (1999: 312). She concluded that for this reason, even 'equity discourses can never effectively combat gender discriminatory discourse' (1999: 312). Francis' proposal for 'a practical contribution to the deconstruction of the discursive gender dichotomy among children' is

> to develop and extend the discussion of innate equality between genders in school. Teachers could focus on the lack of significant differences between men and women, and examine the constructions

of masculinity and femininity in the classroom, showing children how they are restrictive and nonsensical. [This]...might encourage children to question their gendered behaviour, and provide children with extra information, fantasies and discursive resources that they can adopt in their gender constructions. (1999: 314)

And indeed it might – though a pessimistic view would be that, given the dominant 'Gender differences discourse', such an intervention can only ever be better than no intervention at all. Such deconstruction is in any case already good practice in many classrooms (in Britain, in 'Personal, Social and Health Education' lessons). And though principled discussion of restrictive and nonsensical constructions and lack of significant differences between men and women indeed constitutes intervention into the 'common-sense' nature of more traditional gendered discourses, this might, ironically, simultaneously *contribute* to those traditional discourses through the focus on masculinity *and* femininity.

The second example of discoursal intervention through group deconstruction comes from teacher education. Cammack and Kalmbach Phillips (2002) (see Chapter 4) claim that 'we can teach pre-service teachers that multiple and competing [gendered] discourses can and do reside at the site of their own subjectivities' (2002: 131). They ask, self-critically, 'when discussing strategies for teaching students with diverse abilities and needs, do we imply the need for endless dedication as the underlying basis for teaching success?' The 'need' they refer to is the gendered 'Love and service discourse', which student teachers can learn to identify by being 'taught to read texts and in-service training critically' (2002: 131). More generally, Cammack and Kalmback Phillips suggest that student teachers can be taught

to deconstruct the discourses of teaching by placing them as historical studies in our classes. Students can become scholars of detecting discourses in such sources as letters to the editor, current news articles and in national and local debates about education. (2002: 131)

As I showed in the 'discourse spotting' activities in Chapter 2, such deconstructive 'discourse identification' can be taught to students in higher education – and perhaps earlier (see also Edley, 2001). It can be seen both as a form of intervention in discourse and as developing future teachers' awareness of ideology.

Cammack and Kalmbach Phillips, however, take this one stage further: 'when analysing classroom management pedagogy, students might identify how the teacher is constructed and then *reinvent her role without using a love and service lens'* (2002: 131; emphasis added). I have identified this as an example of the sixth way to intervene progressively in gendered discourses, which we might call 'rediscursivization'. (Retrospectively, 'rediscursivization' can also be seen in the earlier coinage and use of new words and phrases such as *sexism* and *sexual harassment*, and indeed in feminist fairytales.) Getting students to rethink and rearticulate a text using a different discourse from that in the original *is* intervention in discourse and a form of subject *re*positioning. Textually evidenced in those rewritten texts, these 'new' gendered discourses may be reproduced in the student teachers' subsequent talk and writing.

Concerned individuals are likely to adopt different discoursal strategies at different times, suiting sometimes their own and sometimes wider feminist ends. Women, for example, may 'uncritically accept pre-existing discursive practices … contest and seek to change them, or … shift strategically between these two positions' (Walsh, 2001: 1). Whatever, it has proved difficult to *effect* a relation between 'word and world' (see also Hollway, 1995). The production of a discourse *can* have political effects, but it may not, and a discourse approach to intervention must recognize this. It would be naïve to expect 'damaging discourses' simply to disappear (as Hollway notes, and as we have seen, 'Changes don't automatically eradicate what went before' (1984: 260)) nor to effect immediate improvements in women's lives. Cameron observes that attacks on particular representations (for which we can also read discourses) may 'help to undermine the legitimacy of the present order, the sense that the way things are is desirable, natural and immutable' (2003: 453), which is but a step in bringing about such improvements.

Lastly, 'newly produced' discourses as well as interventions in dominant discourses need to be considered in the light of the *diversity* of related discourses. A given feminist (or other) intervention may have an impact on subjectivities and future linguistic events, narrowly or widely, briefly or over a duration. However, it will do so as part of an order or network of discourses and discoursal interventions of all sorts, in which many 'always-historical' discourses articulate, being both 'at play' and 'at work' via their accumulated and current linguistic (and other) traces.

Theoretical approaches to and issues for discoursal intervention

We saw in Chapter 8 that although Bucholtz sees discourse analysis as 'highly compatible with the social-constructivist bent of much current feminist research' (1999: 4), Wilkinson and Kitzinger – citing the relativism often associated with discourse analysis – point out that 'there is considerable debate as to whether there is a necessary connection between discourse analysis (as theory or method) and a critical politics' (1995: 6). They then ask whether discourse analysis *is* necessarily of value to *feminist* political purposes. The answer depends on how discourse analysis is theorized, how it is carried out, how the findings are used, with and for whom it is done, and whether it is empowering (see also Cameron, 1992; Gill, 1995; Widdicombe, 1995), and, indeed, whether it makes sense to cite *any* approach as of special value for feminist political purposes. The value of a given discourse analysis for feminist purposes may depend, for example, on whether it is specially able to represent women's personal experience *and* to do so within a research paradigm in which personal experience has high epistemological value and status (see also Gill, 1995). It would certainly depend on the relationship between that analysis, analysis of the experience of some women *as a social group* and social transformation in feminist directions.

Social transformation is higher on some theoretical agendas of discourse analysis than others. Top of the list here would be CDA, which is committed to social and emancipatory change, Fairclough asking directly 'How can analyses ... contribute to democratic struggle?' (2001: 264). One focus of analysis in CDA is the possible ways past the obstacles to a given social problem, through identification of gaps and contradictions in the relevant network of practices (2001: 239). Fairclough analyses an extract from a consultation, pre-legislation document, the Green Paper on 'Welfare Reform' published by the Labour Government in March 1998. The 19-paragraph extract is on 'The importance of work'. He makes the point that the discourse of work drawn on is the *dominant* one of regular and stable work providing enough to live on, and notes that when the Green Paper refers to what parents do when they look after their children, 'it does not refer to that activity as "work"' (2001: 264). Occasionally referring to 'paid work', however, it implicitly signals other types of work (and there are indeed in the Green Paper occasional linguistic traces of *alternative* work discourses). Fairclough sees these different discourses of work (with their evident contradictions) as constituting a point of 'leverage' for change.

Fairclough, however, is not concerned only with deconstruction. For CDA, ensuring that critical analyses of texts contribute to struggle:

> [also] requires critical reflection on how we are working, on how we write, on the meta-language we use for analysing semiosis, on

where we publish, and so forth. For instance, as academics, when we identify and specify a problem, do we involve those whose problem it is? If we don't, are there ways that we could? (2000: 264)

Feminist standpoint theorists have also argued in this way (see Cameron et al., 1992). This means publishing in newspapers, magazines and on the Web as well as in academic genres (which poses a conflict for academics in today's Higher Education climate), and also working with activists and those being 'researched on' when designing research (see also O'Connor, 2003, on 'activist sociolinguistics').

In terms of more direct, *discursive* intervention in the gendered discourses of work, we could add that interactions might explicitly and regularly produce traces of (so far) alternative 'discourses of work', including what we might call 'Unpaid childcare as work' (a work discourse which has long been not just recognizable within but promoted by the Women's Movement). A trivial example is the avoidance of questions to new mothers like 'Do you plan to work again soon?' A less trivial one, might be the phrasing of institutional written guidelines around maternity and paternity leave in terms of childcare *as work* – non-confrontational but *conscious* intervention in discourse. This might go some way to raising the value and status of childcare for the (still mainly female) parents who do this work full-time.

Feminists using the notion of discourse from a post-structuralist perspective have had to struggle particularly to relate Foucault's work to feminist concerns, and to gender issues as they relate to women, and 'to make some of the political potential of the theorising of discourse more overt than Foucault did' (Mills, 1997: 77). Judith Baxter, whose (Feminist) post-structuralist discourse analysis is discussed in this chapter and in Chapter 4, has worked to achieve this and is concerned, in a theoretical as well as practical way, with social transformation:

> [(F)PDA] must...have a libertarian impulse to release the words of marginalised or minority speakers in order to express the richness and diversity of textual play that only emerges from the expression of different and competing points of view. (Baxter, 2002a: 9)

This is progressive social transformation of a particular kind: it is characterized by 'a loss of certainty about the existence of absolutes, or the benevolence of truth of any single paradigm or knowledge' (2002b: 830). Baxter continues:

> PDA cannot have an emancipatory agenda in the sense that it espouses a 'grand narrative' that becomes its own dominant

discourse.... For post-structuralists, social transformations are not other-driven, totalizing missions, but particular, contextualised localized and perspectival actions (e.g. the protest of a particular interest group, community or public campaign). PDA has an interest in the free play of multiple voices ...

The role of PDA theorists is to 'locat[e], observ[e], record[ ] and analys[e] discursive contexts where silenced or marginalised voices may be struggling to be heard' (2002b: 831). Important for Baxter is the notion of *competing* discourses – what shifting power relations are 'constantly negotiated through' – the existence of which negates any possibility of determinism. As we saw in Chapter 4, an individual may be positioned as powerful within one discourse and as powerless within another. Another example is male students 'doing power' over female teachers; those same male students are nevertheless ultimately controlled by the power of the teacher but in both cases have a measure of agency (2002b: 830). Baxter writes:

> The agency of individuals or oppressed groups to contest and resist their positions of powerlessness within prevailing or dominant discourses is the means by which spaces can be opened up for alternative voices, and diverse points of view. (2002b: 831)

This 'opening up for alternative voices' is what in principle allows for new and alternative discourses, and there are implications here for pedagogy.

One particular PDA intervention in discourse *in practice* takes the form of *resistance*. Practitioners are 'in a position to contest and resist [dominant discourses which disempower certain categories of school students] – in policy and practice', and 'girls can be taught to resist certain dominant classroom practices' (Baxter, 2002b: 827). Baxter develops this pedagogic theme in relation to FPDA as follows:

> teachers and educators do need to intervene to take some form of transformative action. Girls need to learn how to resist certain dominant classroom discourses, so that they can, for example, operate with multiple and competing conversations, or 'run the gauntlet' of male barracking in order to cope with the particular pressures of speaking in mixed-sex, public contexts. (2002a: 17)

Such 'resistance' would presumably include active contestation of these dominant discourses by drawing on alternative ones *in direct response*, rather than simply recognizing and 'rising above' them (having previously 'deconstructed' them) or 'quietly' producing alternative ones in situations when 'male barracking' is not going on. For example, in response to being called a 'slag', a girl's articulation of 'No, I'm not' does nothing to deconstruct or contest the 'Slags or drags' discourse (see Cowie and Lees, 1981), or even help her avoid or deal with such abuse in future. Responding by confronting abusive boys with their hypocrisy and double standards, however, just might help (see also Leap, 1999 on responses to homophobic insults).

Discursive psychologists who see their work as a form of (deconstructive) intervention include Nigel Edley (2001) and Ros Gill (1995). Drawing on post-structuralism, Edley notes that seeing masculinity as constantly being remade provides 'a positive sense of how change may be effected' (2001: 193), but warns that we should not exaggerate the ease of reconstructing identities. Gill critiques relativisms which do not allow for political interventions and argues for 'a relativism which is unashamedly political, in which we, as feminists, can make social transformation an explicit concern of our work' (1995: 171, 182). Wilkinson and Kitzinger claim that *all* the contributors to the discursive psychology collection *Feminism and Discourse* 'see language as a key site for feminist resistance' (1995: 3).

* * *

Finally in this chapter I revisit two further theoretical issues of relevance to discoursal intervention: *contradictions* (in competing/contesting/conflicting discourses) and the *extra-discursive*. In Chapter 3 I showed how Wetherell et al. (1987) saw contradictions as essential to the maintenance of an ideology: 'Egalitarian discourse' was not 'wiped out' by 'non-egalitarian discourse', and the latter in the form of 'practical considerations' talk 'serve[d] to naturalize and justify inequality' (1987: 69). Contradictions may indeed act as a conservative force. However, they are more frequently cited as potentially *emancipatory* (recall Fairclough's phrase 'leverage'), in part because they render discourses unsustainable.

Hollway, for example, who is as concerned with change in consciousness as with social structures, writes: 'The reproduction of gender differentiated practices depends on the circulation between subjectivities and discourses' and identifies as a way to interrupt this 'circle': 'a grasp of the contradictions between discourses and thus of contradictory subjectivities' (1984: 252). The contradictions she has in mind ('the weak points in the stronghold of gender difference') are 'gender-appropriate positions', i.e. men being expected to be rational, providing support, and women having and expressing feelings and *needing* support. These are contradictions since taking up these positions 'does not successfully express our multiple subjectivities'. It is possible to see how this might work in practice, if 'grasp of the contradictions' prompted the use of progressive, competing discourses and/or promoting awareness of contradictions in other discourses. Hollway sees plenty of opportunities for discoursal intervention: because 'every practice to some extent articulates such contradictions', it is 'a site of potential change as much as it is a site of reproduction' (1984: 260).

All the forms of intervention in discourse we have seen so far have been discursive – which seems logical. Earlier feminist campaigns can also be seen as, in part, discursive, given that all their objectives needed to be 'talked into' (as well as 'actioned into') acceptability. And improving the position of women in education and the professions – in terms of access, opportunities and institutional practices and structures – can also be seen as forms of successful intervention in discourse in that in these higher-status and more powerful spheres, women would use, and be subsequently empowered by, more powerful discourses.

Is *everything* discursively constituted though? This may be one theoretical position on *discourse*, i.e. that there is no *social* reality outside language (Cameron, 1998: 962). (There is of course an a-social reality, including such phenomena as volcanic eruptions.) But if some aspects of social reality are not discursively constituted, discursive intervention may not be *sufficient* to make a real and substantial contribution to progressive change. There is considerable debate here. CDA sees discourse as a form of social practice (Fairclough, 1992), but this does not mean discourse is all, for example, 'the question of power in social class, gender and race relations is *partly* a question of discourse' (Chouliaraki and Fairclough, 1999; emphasis added) and 'discourses ... [are] ... *tied into* projects to change the world in particular directions' (Fairclough, 2003: 124; emphasis added). Similarly, *material* practice cannot be seen as entirely discursive. Using the example of 'car theft', Edley shows how closely discourse and material practice are bound together. However, although *discourse* may shape cars and the desire for cars, 'the fact that a perpetrator's status of a "thief" is constructed via a set of texts or discourses (e.g. the magistrate's pronouncement and the resulting criminal "record") does little to diminish the damaging material effects of being so described' (2001: 192). The 'extra-discursive' may extend to the materiality of women's oppression – for example, sexual harassment – which feminists are likely to believe exists 'irrespective of whether and how it is talked about' (Cameron, 1998: 965; see also Gill, 1995; Kitzinger and Thomas, 1995).

From a post-structuralist (and (F)PDA) perspective, which accepts Foucault's dictum that discourses are 'practices that systematically form the objects of which they speak' (1972: 49), solely discursive intervention *is* sufficient. Not all discourse analysts assume this position – including many who do not locate themselves within CDA. Hollway (who gives considerable space to the extra-discursive; see Chapter 3 and also 1995), critiques the 'reductionist' premise 'that the world can be understood as discursive' (1995: 91) and observes that changing gender difference

> is not a problem to be addressed at the level of discourses alone.... It is through ... social changes [e.g. career and educational opportunities for girls, birth control] ... that alternative discourses – for example feminist ones – can be produced and used by women in the struggle to redefine our positions in gender-differentiated practices, thus challenging sexist discourses still further. (1984: 250, 262)

This view is broadly shared by many of the contributors to Wilkinson and Kitzinger's collection on discursive psychology, *Feminism and Discourse* (1995) (see e.g. Gill, 1995, for a related critique of relativism). However, despite its emphasis on the extra-discursive, Cameron (1998) documents the existence of little in the way of extra-discursive *strategy* in this collection, writes that 'there is more to be done than simply discourse analysis' (1998: 966) and challenges 'the idea that when the analyst has deconstructed something – taken it apart and understood how it works – she has thereby *changed* it'.

> Not so: at best she has only met one of the conditions on which it may be changed, through people using their new awareness that what counts as 'reality' is constructed, contingent, and (crucially) unjust and on that basis taking different actions in future (including discursive ones such as defining a particular experience as 'sexual harassment'). (1998: 966)

Cameron is rather charitably here extrapolating from the analyst's awareness to that of 'people' (presumably, readers of discourse analyses and those discourse analysts work with).

While I am inclined to agree that discursive intervention is unlikely to be sufficient in itself to bring about change, I hope that I have shown that discursive intervention can go *beyond* 'awareness-raising' to what Cameron describes as *use* of that new awareness with individuals not only experiencing new ways of seeing the world, but perhaps also acting on these in new, progressive ways.

Conclusion

In this book, I have explored gendered discourses through the findings of older and new, previously unpublished studies, and I have tried to do so in ways which will be of theoretical and practical ('operationalizable') interest to the experienced and novice discourse analyst alike. Is the identification of gendered discourses, an appropriate approach for feminist and 'gender studies' of language to take? Ros Gill expresses considerable reservations about the way much discourse analysis is 'underpinned at a theoretical level by a thoroughgoing relativism or epistemological scepticism' (1995: 169). In response to this, she argues for a relativism *with values*, and a reflexivity 'which requires analysts to make explicit the position from which they are theorizing, and to reflect critically upon their own role' (1995: 179) – a practice also associated with CDA, of course.

The interpretive identification of discourses as part of discourse analysis, as practised in particular by critical discourse analysts and analysts coming from a post-structuralist standpoint (including feminist post-structuralist discourse analysis – FPDA – and some discursive psychology), though subject to critique, would not seem to suffer from or promote a debilitating relativism. I hope I have shown this to be true in the gendered discourses I have provisionally identified – from a largely feminist position – in the classroom, children's literature, and different texts on fatherhood.

I have tried to clarify but not to over-simplify, and have suggested that the 'how' (and indeed the 'why') of much discourse analysis is related to the particular theoretical paradigm being drawn on. The use to which the analysis is (or can be) put, the nature of the claims that can be made, and the role and accountability of the discourse analyst in her analysis will vary here. More specifically, it seems that *each* theoretical paradigm has something to offer. While a form of critical discourse analysis (CDA), for example, may (at least for 'weak relativists' – again see Gill (1995)) at first sight seem *in principle* the 'natural' paradigm for a feminist linguistics concerned in some sense with the disadvantage *still* experienced by many women, worldwide, approaches such as feminist post-structuralist discourse analysis (FPDA), conversation analysis (CA), and a discursive psychology which draws either on CA or on post-structuralism, also have their own, *different*, perhaps supplementary, contributions to make (see Baxter, 2002a,b). This is *especially* true now that much of the field has moved away from seeking 'gender differences' in form of talk between X and Y in context Z to an acceptance of notions of multiple identities, subject positioning, performance, orientation and notions of power as diffuse and fluctuating. Just as teachers know that almost all teaching/learning activities have their place in the classroom (even if only as a focus for critique), it would seem foolish for the feminist or gender and language scholar working with discourse to reject any approach to provisional and interpretive gendered discourse identification outright. The challenge is partly theoretical. However, the challenge is also importantly to decide what, or what combination of approaches, works for a particular set of data in relation to a particular research question.

Notes

1 Discourse, Discourse Analysis and Gender

1. The programme of the 2000 International Gender and Language Association (IGALA 2) Conference (Lancaster University, UK, April 2002) included presentations of studies taking data from a wide range of sites, including proverbs, televised sports programmes, fantasy role-play games, dictionaries, women's prayer-hymns, courtrooms, business settings, *Fanny Hill* and the BBC Radio 4's *Today* programme.

2. The large 'family' of discourse terms and collocations includes *discursive resources*, *discursive contradictions*, *discursive resistance* and *new discursive possibilities* (e.g. Francis, 1999) and *discourse practices*, *strategies* and *space* (e.g. Thornborrow, 2002).

3. As early as 1967, Harold Garfinkel wrote that gender for women was socially accomplished in part *through the process of talking like a woman*. A post-structuralist approach would say that gender for both women *and* men is socially accomplished in the process not only of talking 'like' women/men (whatever that may mean), but also of talking *about* women and men.

4. It also undermined the idea that women were thus more status conscious than men – the explanation offered by both Labov and Trudgill when women *were* found to produce more standard speech, but a far from satisfactory one (Cameron, 1992).

5. *Identity* has taken the place of the theoretically outdated *role*, which came to sound not only institutional but also fixed. (Weatherall, 2002, discusses how *positioning* has also replaced *role*.)

6. It has been said (jocularly) that white Englishmen from a broadly Anglican background (WASPs) have *no* sense of identity because (in the UK as a whole) they are the 'norm' – they are not Irish or women or Jewish or black, for example – and 'normally' have no other group to compare themselves against. In most spaces, they will see others like themselves. However, when male WASPs *are* a minority group, their identity is likely to become newly paramount.

7. In semiotic theory, indexes (the resources) are referred to as *signifiers*. In *Reading Images: the Grammar of Visual Design*, Kress and van Leeuwen (1996: 7) identify a 'logic of inference' between signifier and signified.

8. In another sphere, I recall a Ruth Rendell novel in which one academic says to another, apparently non-ironically, 'Publish or perish', as an explanation of his efforts at output – presumably because this is the sort of spoken discourse the author thought her reading public would associate with academics. Similarly, a UK TV series 'The Women's Room', which focused on the social and sexual lives of sociologists, represented as their public (common room) talk academic discourse on the various forms of cohabitation.

2   Discourses, Discourse Identification and Discourse Naming

1. This was to check for recognizability. With one exception, and myself, the language education professionals were all American.
2. See *Discourse in Late Modernity* (Chouliaraki and Fairclough, 1999).
3. In the British National Corpus, there are no cases of *just first class*, but of the six cases of *just the best*, *just* is consistently intensifying. It is also worth noting that newspaper headlines are not normally written by the journalist who writes the text (Bell, 1999).
4. The BNC indicates a range of 'medical' collocates of *suffering* (*hypothermia, after-effects, pangs*), and 'extreme' collocates of *subjected* (e.g. *rigorous, brutal, unprecedented*).
5. I suggest that it is normally the most appropriate when invoking a new *phrase* for the first time to name a discourse (the indefinite article a 'Biggest day in a woman's life' discourse). This rightly suggests *several* such discourses can be co-constructed. The definite article may be more appropriate when the phrase is familiar (the 'Compulsory heterosexuality discourse'). I also suggest the use of scare quotes to distinguish between descriptive and interpretive discourse (for use with the latter), and a capitalized 'Discourse' for interpretive discourses of substance. I have used lower case for descriptive discourses, and for interpretive discourses which indicate relationships and function.
6. The '*Horse race*' discourse is something of an oddity. It *could* refer to literal horseracing, corresponding to the descriptive use of 'legal discourse', 'classroom discourse', and so on. Here, it is in italics since it is used *metaphorically*.
7. The discourses in the index of Litosseliti and Sunderland (2002) are organized into three different groups. The grouping here represents a development of that.

3   Some Gendered Discourses Identified to Date

1. See also Kitetu and Sunderland (2000) on 'Gender differences' discourses in relation to education: those they identify include '*Vive la différence!*', 'Gender fixedness' and 'What's all the fuss about?'
2. Genevieve Lloyd and Moira Gatens (and also Nancy Jay) all address the issue of hierarchization of such Cartesian dichotomies.
3. It has to be said, of course, that in *explicitly* distancing themselves ourselves from the 'Gender differences' discourse in research reports, it being 'a strict rule of academic discourse that one *must* refer to (and so recirculate) the discourse of one's predecessors in the same field of enquiry' (Cameron, 2003: 465), current gender and language scholars are also inadvertently recirculating this discourse. And, as Cameron also observes, 'every word we say on the subject of difference just underlines the salience and the importance of a division we are ultimately striving to end' (1992: 40).
4. As indicated, it is possible to see *ideology* as the cultural materialist antecedent of the post-structuralist term *discourse* (Judith Baxter, personal communication).

However, *discourse* does not carry the same negative connotations as ideology, and lends itself better to an *emancipatory* function (see also Mills, 1997).

5. The other topics were 'respondents' theories of individual nature, their analyses of how social change might occur, and their representations of past, present and future for women' (Wetherell et al., 1987: 61).

Introduction to Part II: The 'Fruitful Epistemological Site' for Gender and Discourse Study

1. However, a text which has been identified as of possible interest to the study of gendered discourses does not have to make frequent or explicit reference to social *actors* – a written text on prostitution, or caring, for example, could be written in such a way as to be (on the surface) gender-blind, though it must presumably make reference to *social* practices. If women and/or men are 'backgrounded' here, this is interesting in itself (van Leeuwen, 1995, 1996). It is also possible to use a text about animals, if it has relevance to human social practices. I have already referred to the anthropomorphically gendered behaviour of the dogs in Hollywood's *101 Dalmations*, and anthropomorphically gendered discourse has similarly been identified in the rhetoric of television wildlife programmes (Crowther and Leith, 1995).

2. It is not only the epistemological site but also the chosen data for which a rationale is needed. For each study, relating the chosen data to the topical epistemological site entails 'theorizing [ ] the relationship between the general topic, the definition of discourse, and the data to be analysed' (Taylor, 2001: 29; see also her examples).

3. See Taylor (2001: 27) for a discussion of 'naturally occurring' talk.

4. By 'post-feminism' I am not implying that we are beyond the need for feminism, rather that much interaction can now be seen as being constructed, or at least informed by, the experiences, insights and practices of feminism.

4 Gendered Discourses in the Classroom

1. This makes sense if lessons are seen as co-constructions by all classroom participants (e.g. Allwright, 1984, 2001).

2. Some might refer to it as a 'Sex difference' discourse, since here 'gender' was (as it sometimes still is) simply 'mapped onto' groups of biological males and biological females. However, I refer to *gender* here since the assumption was very much that differences were *socially constructed* rather than *biologically determined*.

3. 'Male dominance' cannot logically be applied to differential *teacher* treatment, since this is more about a gendered *asymmetry* in one classroom participant's (the teacher's) calling on of students (Sunderland, 1996). The '(cultural) difference' approach of the late 1980s and early 1990s (see Chapter 3) was never to my knowledge used as an explanation here, either of differential teacher treatment by gender or of gendered asymmetries in classroom talk.

4. Such policies are obviously politically and intertextually linked with governmental legislation: in the UK, for example, the Equal Pay and Sex Discrimination Acts came into being in 1975.

5. This double standard operates in classrooms elsewhere too. Sadker and Sadker (1985), for example, found that girls tended to be told off more often than boys for calling out.
6. This was saliently evidenced in the UK many years ago by the Jimmy Young Show on Radio 2, aired mid-morning and aimed at women who were at home during the day. The show featured the song lyrics 'Keep young and beautiful / If you want to be loved'. These traces of the 'Privileging of appearance – in women' discourse were contested and the song removed. However, the song has recently been featured in a UK TV ad for Kellogg's Special K breakfast cereal (targeted at slimmers) – using a simulated old gramophone record style.
7. See also Cammack and Kalmbach Phillips (2002) on gendered discourses about teachers.
8. Cameron suggests that the ideology of female superiority here has less to do with successful feminist intervention than with changing ideas about skilled use of language – a use associated with femininity rather than masculinity (2003: 458).
9. Baxter also raises Francis' (1998) criticism that writers often fail to explain how they categorize discourses. Baxter's own account can be found in her PhD thesis (2000; see also 2003).
10. We can add to this the possibility that dominant classroom behaviour on the part of some boys can also be 'read' through Baxter's *gender differentiation* discourse as disadvantageous to boys themselves (Swann, 1998: 158), through their own negative *self-positioning*.

5 Fatherhood Discourses in Parenting Magazines

1. See also Talbot (1998) on discourses of maternity in relation to antenatal care.
2. And In Britain, *M and M: the magazine for mothers-to-be and new mothers* is no longer in circulation.
3. Another American magazine ostensibly aimed at both parents is *Parents Expecting*, which focuses on the period before the birth. I found very little 'childcare advice' in this however, and therefore deselected this magazine from the sample. Other gender-neutrally named parenting magazines include the American *Child*, and, in the UK, *Junior*; this is apparently read mainly by women and is not widely available. A new magazine, *Dad* – edited by Jack O'Sullivan, a founder of Fathers Direct, the national information centre on fatherhood – was launched in April 2003. The parenting magazine most likely to include fathers may however be the more recent *And Baby – Refining Modern Parenting*, published in the US and targeted at gay families.
4. This excluded advice about children's names, care of house and garden, travel, exercise, shopping, education, fashion and beauty, managing the family finances and sex after a baby's birth (a favourite topic).
5. *He* and *she* are of interest too, as 'indirect interpellation'. Now that the genericity of *he* has been thoroughly contested (see e.g. Sunderland, 1991), thereby arguably making it even less generic than it ever was, we would not expect to find 'generic *he*' in parenting magazines as a referent for a parent. As potential pronominals of *parent*, 'generics' *he* and *she* pull in different ways. *He* has a distinctly masculine bias since *he* is also, and usually, used of an individual man. *She* has a distinctly feminine bias since *she* is much less familiar as a generic,

and, in the context of parenting when the dominant discourse is 'Mother as main parent/Part-time father' discourse, is likely to be read as specifically (non-generically) *she*. Neither thus works as a generic.

6. Such slippage is more widely true of English 'common' nouns like *neighbour* and *people* (Cameron, 1992), and a similar phenomenon has been observed in German (Hellinger, 2002).

7. With the references to breastfeeding, it would require a male reader to do so quite considerably – whether or not the reader is interpellated directly with *you*. And any occurrences of *you* which occur near such references, are, I suggest, likely also to be read (cataphorically or anaphorically) as female.

6 Celebrity Fatherhood: The 'Blair Baby'

1. Blair has been an epistemological site for linguists before, as the subject of Norman Fairclough's (2000) *New Labour, New Language?*, but in terms of his political speeches and written texts.

2. I am very grateful to Juliane Schwarz for her painstaking identification and scanning of the 'Blair baby' texts.

3. I say 'was considered a little left of centre' advisedly. As I write, the 2003 war with Iraq has recently ended, and Blair's political credentials have been considerably weakened in many quarters.

7 Gendered Discourses in Children's Literature

1. For a short bibliography of studies, see http://www.ling.lancs.ac.uk/groups/clsl/home.htm.

2. More widely, content analyses may show 'how sex categories can be made to matter in the most mundane descriptions of social doings' (West et al., 1997: 127).

3. Another example of a critical discourse analysis of a fictional text is Sara Mills' (1992) 'Marxist feminist stylistic' analysis of John Fuller's poem 'Valentine' (see Chapter 5).

4. Bakhtin (1981) refers to the importance of both *heteroglossia* ('differentiated speech' and in particular how this plays out in literary texts) and *polyphony*, i.e. *autonomous* characters' voices (see also Vice, 1997).

5. Of *Cinderella*, Stephens writes: 'the main character ... is always defined by her appearance and roles, deprived of individual subjectivity, and subjected to the wills and actions of others (step-family, godmother, prince). Ideologically, she represents a model of perfect wifehood – she is beautiful but abject, available but submissive, in that the slipper symbolizes her sexual aptness and her passivity, 'fitting' but waiting to be found' (1992: 140).

6. These books and their reception by pre-school children are the topic of Bronwyn Davies, *Frogs and Snails and Feminist Tales* (1989).

7. Gilbert and Gubar (1976) carry out this reinterpretation as a metaphor for the plight of the nineteenth-century woman writer. In relation to this, Cosslett continues: 'Her murderous hatred of her stepdaughter is excused by interpreting

Snow White as the ideal of the passive, good, angel-in-the-house woman, who would kill the Queen's chance of being an artist' (1996: 84).

8. See http://www.ala.org/alsc/newbery_terms.html, and http://www.ala.org/alsc/caldecott_terms.html. In the UK the two main awards are the Carnegie and the Greenaway. The US does not constitute a special epistemological site; I selected it since this chapter was written there and I had access to excellent public libraries.

9. Some would pounce on the fact that the majority of these authors (and illustrators) are male, and that this 'discursive practice' may be relevant in terms of authorial success. J.K. Rowling, author of the *Harry Potter* series, was apparently dissuaded by her publisher from using her first name, 'Joanna'. This is however a separate issue from gender representation and gendered discourses. Women writers will not necessarily create more positive and progressive representations of female characters, or of gender relations, than will male writers, nor will they necessarily draw on feminist or egalitarian discourses more, or even on different discourses.

10. This is also true of Crispin, in the 2003 Newbery winner *Crispin the Cross of Lead*.

11. See also Stephens (1992: Chapter 6) for an interesting discussion of historical fiction written for children.

12. This may not be true of these award-winners more widely. For example, in the previous year (1998) the Caldecott winner was Paul O. Zelinsky's *Rapunzel*, and the Newbury winner Karen Hesse's *Out of the Dust*, about a girl growing up in poverty in Oklahoma during the Depression. However, the 2003 Newbury winner, *Crispin the Cross of Lead*, is about a 13-year-old boy in fourteenth-century England, and in the 2003 Caldecott winner, Eric Rohmann's *My Friend Rabbit*, the rabbit is male.

8 The Discoursal Construction of Gender

1. A study investigating how claims are underpinned theoretically might study research papers for the various uses of such terms, or a corpus of academic English (e.g. Hyland, 2000). It would be necessary to distinguish between 'joint/co-construction' (e.g. of classroom talk), 'linguistic construction' (e.g. 'the construction *can I help who's next'*) and linguistic/discoursal construction (our concern here).

2. Butler claims that 'gender is an identity constituted in time ... through a stylized repetition of acts' and is created 'through sustained social performances' (1999: 179, 180).

3. This discourse was evident in the 'Mere Male' column of a UK women's magazine of a bygone era, in which readers sent in their favourite, and always affectionate, anecdotes of their husbands' little domestic incompetences.

4. Potter (1996: 121) refers to the 'rhetorical organisation of fact construction', which includes fact construction (*reification*), fact destruction (*ironization*) and *defensive* and *offensive* rhetoric.

5. Fairclough's own major contribution to the social sciences has been the role of actual *language* in discourse analysis, and, for the analyst, the importance of close reading of spoken and written texts as part of an analysis of wider social and discursive practices (see e.g. Fairclough, 1995).

9 'Damaging Discourses' and Intervention in Discourse

1. This theme has been taken up again recently by Hines (1999) in a paper entitled 'Rebaking the Pie: The *Woman as Dessert* Metaphor'.
2. The origin of the phrase for me may have come out of long-running discussions in the 'Gender and Language Research Group' at Lancaster University.
3. See also Candace West's (2002) 'Critical comment' on Baxter's paper, and Baxter's dignified reply (both also in *Discourse and Society* 13/6), in particular in relation to the category *gender* in Baxter's study, the use of CA and the value of PDA.
4. A recent survey of 5000 British women working full-time found that 36 per cent earned more than their husbands or boyfriends (*Sunday Times*, 11 May 2003).
5. Importantly, these questions are still of practical and theoretical interest, as Anne Pauwels' *Women Changing Language* (1998) and Marlis Hellinger and Hadumod Bußmann's *Gender across Languages: the Linguistic Representation of Women and Men* (2001) show; see also Livia (1999).

Bibliography

Acevedo, A. and Gower, M. (1996) *Highflyer Intermediate*. London: Longman.

Adamsky, Cathryn (1981) 'Changes in pronominal usage in a classroom situation'. *Psychology of Women Quarterly* 5: 773–9.

Adler, Sue (1993) 'Aprons and attitudes: a consideration of feminism in children's books'. In Claire, H., Maybin, J. and Swann, J. (eds) *Equality Matters: Case Studies from the Primary School*. Clevedon: Multilingual Matters.

Allwright, Dick (1984) 'The importance of interaction in classroom language learning'. *Applied Linguistics* 5/2: 156–71.

—— (2001) 'Learning (and teaching) as well as you know how: why is it so very difficult?' In Wagner, Johannes (ed.) *Paedagogik og laering I fremmed- og andetsprog*. Odense Working Papers in Language and Communications 22, January. Odense, Institute of Language and Communication, University of Southern Denmark. pp. 1–41.

Altani, Cleopatra (1995) 'Primary school teachers' explanations of boys' disruptiveness in the classroom: a gender-specific aspect of the hidden curriculum'. In Mills, Sara (ed.) *Language and Gender: Interdisciplinary Perspectives*. London: Longman. pp. 149–59.

Althusser, Louis (1984) *Essays on Intertextuality*. Verso: London.

Antaki, Charles, Condor, Susan and Levine, Mark (1996) 'Social identities in talk: speakers' own orientations'. *Journal of Social Psychology* 35: 473–92.

Arnot, Madeline, David, Miriam and Weiner, Gabi (1996) *Educational Reforms and Gender Equality in Schools*. Equal Opportunities Commission Research Discussion Series No. 17. Manchester: EOC.

Arnot, Madeline, Gray, J., James, M. Ruddock, J. with Duveen, G. (1998) *Recent Research on Gender and Educational Performance*. London: HMSO/Ofsted.

Austin, John (1962) *How To Do Things With Words*. Oxford: Oxford University Press.

Baker, Carolyn and Freebody, Peter (1989) *Children's First School Books*. Oxford: Basil Blackwell.

Baker, Paul (2002) 'Construction of gay identity via Polari in the Julian and Sandy radio sketches'. *Lesbian and Gay Review* 3/3: 75–84.

Bakhtin, Mikhail (1981) *The Dialogic Imagination: Four Essays*. Austin: University of Texas.

Bakhtin, Mikhail (1986) *Speech Genres and Other Late Essays*. Austin: Texas University Press.

Barrett, Rusty (1999) 'Indexing polyphonous identity in the speech of African American drag queens'. In Bucholtz, M., Liang, A.C. and Sutton, L.A (eds) *Reinventing Identities: The Gendered Self in Discourse*. New York: Oxford University Press. pp. 313–31.

Barthes, Roland (1986) *The Rustle of Language*. Oxford: Basil Blackwell.

Barton, Ellen (2002) 'Inductive discourse analysis: discovering rich features'. In Barton, Ellen and Stygall, G. (eds) *Discourse Studies in Composition*. Cresskill, NJ: Hampton Press.

Baxter, Judith (2000) 'Teaching girls to speak out: an investigation of the extent to which gender is a pertinent discourse for describing and assessing girls' and boys' speech in public contexts'. PhD thesis, University of Reading, UK.

—— (2002a) 'Competing discourses in the classroom: a post-structuralist discourse analysis of girls' and boys' speech in public contexts'. *Discourse and Society* 13/6: 827–42.

—— (2002b) 'A juggling act: a feminist post-structuralist analysis of girls' and boys' talk in the secondary classroom'. *Gender and Education* 14/1: 5–19.

—— (2003) *Positioning Gender in Discourse: A Feminist Methodology.* Basingstoke: Palgrave Macmillan.

Beach, Wayne (2000) 'Inviting collaborations in stories about a woman'. *Language in Society* 29: 379–407.

Bell, Allan (1999) 'News stories as narratives'. In Jaworski, Adam and Coupland, Nicholas (eds) (1999) *The Discourse Reader.* London: Routledge. pp. 236–51.

Bell, Jan and Gower, Roger (1992) *Upper Intermediate Matters.* Harlow: Longman.

Bem, Sandra and Bem, Daryl (1973) 'Does sex-biased job advertising "aid and abet" sex discrimination?' *Journal of Applied Social Psychology* 3: 6–18.

Benwell, Bethan (2002) 'Is there anything "new" about these lads?: the textual and visual construction of masculinity in men's magazines'. In Litosseliti, Lia and Sunderland, Jane (eds) *Gender Identity and Discourse Analysis.* Amsterdam: John Benjamins.

Bergvall, Victoria (1996) 'Constructing and enacting gender through discourse: negotiating multiple roles and female engineering students'. In Bergvall, V.L., Bing, J.M. and Freed, A.F. *Rethinking Language and Gender Research: Theory and Practice.* London: Longman. pp. 173–201.

Bergvall, Victoria (1999) 'Towards a comprehensive theory of language and gender'. *Language in Society* 28: 273–93.

Bergvall, Victoria and Remlinger, Kathryn (1996) 'Reproduction, resistance and gender in educational discourse: the role of Critical Discourse Analysis'. *Discourse and Society* 7/4: 453–79.

Bergvall, Victoria, Bing, Janet and Freed, Alice (eds) (1996) *Rethinking Language and Gender Research: Theory and Practice.* London: Longman.

Berman, R. (1998) 'No Joe Marches'. *Children's Literature in Education* 29/4: 237–47.

Billig, Mick, Condor, Susan, Edwards, Derek, Gane, Mike, Middleton, David and Radley, Allan (1988) *Ideological Dilemmas: A Social Psychology of Everyday Thinking.* London: Sage.

Bing, Janet and Bergvall, Victoria (1996) 'The question of questions: beyond binary thinking'. In Bergvall, V., Bing, J. and Freed, A. (eds) *Rethinking Language and Gender Research: Theory and Practice.* Harlow: Addison Wesley Longman. pp. 1–30.

Black, Maria and Coward, Rosalind (1981) 'Linguistic, social and sexual relations: a review of Dale Spender's *Man-made Language*'. *Screen Education* 39: 69–85.

Blaubergs, Maija 1980. 'An analysis of classic arguments against changing sexist language'. In Kramarae, Cheris (ed.) *The Voices and Words of Women and Men.* Oxford: Pergamon Press. pp. 135–47.

Boersma, P. Dee, Gay, Debora, Jones, Ruth, Morrison, Lynn and Remick, Helen (1981) 'Sex differences in college student-teacher interactions: fact or fantasy'. *Sex Roles* 7/8: 775–84.

Bourdieu, Pierre (1991) *Language and Symbolic Power*. Cambridge: Polity Press.

Brownmiller, Susan (1975) *Against Our Will*. Harmondsworth: Penguin.

Bucholtz, Mary (1999) 'Bad examples: transgression and progress in language and gender studies.' In Bucholtz, M., Liang, A.C. and Sutton, L.A (eds) *Reinventing Identities: The Gendered Self in Discourse*. New York: Oxford University Press. pp. 3–24.

—— (2000) *Reinventing Identities: the Gendered Self in Discourse*. Oxford: Oxford University Press.

—— (2002) 'Geek feminism'. In Benor, Sarah, Rose, Mary, Sharman, Devyani, Sweetland, Julie and Zhang, Qing (eds) *Gendered Practices in Language*. Stanford, Ca.: CSLI Publications. pp. 277–307.

Butler, Judith (1990, 1999) *Gender Trouble: Feminism and the Subversion of Identity*. New York: Routledge.

—— (1993) 'Extracts from Gender as Performance: an interview with Judith Butler' (by Peter Osborne and Lynne Segal). www.theory.org.uk Resources: Judith Butler interview. Originally and full version in *Radical Philosophy* 67 (Summer 1994).

Caldas-Coulthard, Carmen (1995) 'Men in the news: the misrepresentation of women speaking in news-as-narrative-discourse'. In S. Mills (ed.) *Language and Gender: Interdisciplinary Perspectives*. London: Longman.

—— (1996) ' "Women who pay for sex. And enjoy it." Transgression versus morality in women's magazines'. In Caldas-Coulthard, Carmen Rosa and Coulthard, Malcolm (eds) *Texts and Practices: Readings in Critical Discourse Analysis*. London: Routledge.

Cameron, Deborah (1992) *Feminism and Linguistic Theory*, 2nd edition. London: Macmillan.

—— (1994) 'Problems of sexist and non-sexist language'. In Sunderland, J. (ed.) *Exploring Gender: Questions and Implications for English Language Education*. Hemel Hempstead: Prentice Hall. pp. 26–33.

—— (1995) *Verbal Hygiene*. London: Routledge.

—— (1996) 'The language–gender interface: challenging co-optation'. In Bergvall, V., Bing, J. and Freed, A. (eds) *Rethinking Language and Gender Research*. Harlow, Essex: Addison-Wesley-Longman.

—— (1997a) 'Performing gender identity: young men's talk and the construction of heterosexual masculinity'. In Johnson, S. and Meinhof, U. (eds) *Language and Masculinity*. Oxford: Blackwell. pp. 47–64.

—— (1997b) 'Theoretical debates in feminist linguistics: questions of sex and gender'. In Wodak, R. (ed.) *Gender and Discourse*. London: Sage. pp. 21–36.

—— (1998a) 'Gender, language and discourse: a review essay'. *Signs* 1: 945–73.

—— (ed.) (1998b) *The Feminist Critique of Language*. 2nd edition. London: Routledge.

—— (2000) *Good to Talk? Living and Working in a Communication Culture*. London: Sage.

—— (2001) *Working with Spoken Discourse*. London: Sage.

—— (2003) 'Gender and language ideologies'. In Holmes, Janet and Meyerhoff, Miriam (eds) *Handbook of Gender and Language Research*. Oxford: Basil Blackwell. pp. 447–67.

Cameron, Deborah, McAlinden, Fiona and O'Leary, Kathy (1989) 'Lakoff in context: the social and linguistic functions of tag questions'. In Coates, J. and Cameron, D. (eds) *Women in Their Speech Communities*. Harlow: Longman. pp. 74–93.

Cameron, Deborah et al. (eds) (1992) *Researching Language: Issues of Power and Method*. London: Routledge.

Cammack, J. Camille and Kalmback Phillips, Donna (2002) 'Discourses and subjectivities of the gendered teacher'. *Gender and Education* 14/2: 123–33.

Cheng, Y., Payne, J. and Witherspoon, S. (1995) *Science and Mathematics in Full-time Education after 16*. Youth Cohort Report 36. London: DEE.

Chodorow, Nancy (1978) *The Reproduction of Mothering: Psychoanalysis and the Sociology of Gender*. Berkeley: University of California Press.

Chouliaraki, Lilie and Fairclough, Norman (1999) *Discourse in Late Modernity: Rethinking Critical Discourse Analysis*. Edinburgh: Edinburgh University Press.

Chris, Christie (1994) 'Theories of textual determination and audience agency: an empirical contribution to the debate'. In Mills, S. (ed.) *Gendering the Reader*. London: Harvester Wheatsheaf. pp. 47–66.

Christian-Smith, Linda (1989) 'Power, knowledge and curriculum: constructing femininity in adolescent romance novels'. In de Castell, S., Luke, A. and Luke, C. (eds) *Language, Authority and Criticism: Readings on the School Textbook*. London: Falmer Press. pp. 17–31.

—— (1991) 'Readers, texts and contexts: adolescent romance fiction in schools'. In Apple, Michael and Christian-Smith, Linda (eds) *The Politics of the Textbook*. New York: Routledge.

Clark, Kate (1998) 'The linguistics of blame: representations of blame in the *Sun's* reporting of crimes of sexual violence'. In Cameron, Deborah (ed.) *The Feminist Critique of Language*. London: Routledge. pp. 183–97.

Coates, Jennifer (1986, 1993) *Women, Men and Language*. London: Longman.

—— (1997) 'Competing discourses of femininity'. In Kotthof, H. and Wodak, R. (eds) *Communicating Gender in Context*. Amsterdam: John Benjamins. pp. 285–314.

—— (1999) 'Changing femininities: the talk of teenage girls'. In Bucholtz, M., Liang, A.C. and Sutton, L.A (eds) *Reinventing Identities: The Gendered Self in Discourse*. New York: Oxford University Press. pp. 13–144.

Cole, Babette (1987) *Prince Cinders*. London: Heinemann.

Cooper, Robert (1984) 'The avoidance of androcentric generics'. *International Journal of Social Language* 50: 5–20.

Cosslett, Tess (1996) 'Fairytales: revising the tradition', in Cosslett, T., Easton, A. and Summerfield, P. (eds) *Women, Power and Resistance*. Buckingham: Open University Press. pp. 81–90.

Coupland, Justine and Williams, Angie (2002) 'Conflicting discourses, shifting ideologies: pharmaceutical, "alternative" and feminist emancipatory texts on the menopause'. *Discourse and Society* 13/4: 419–45.

Cowie, C. and Lees, S. (1981) 'Slags or drags?' *Feminist Review* 9: 17–31.

Crawford, Mary (1995) *Talking Difference: On Gender and Language*. London: Sage.

Crowther, Barbara and Leith, Dick (1995) 'Feminism, language and the rhetoric of television wildlife programmes'. In Mills, S. (ed.) *Language and Gender: Interdisciplinary Perspectives*. London: Longman.

Dart, Barry and Clarke, John (1988) 'Sexism in schools: a new look'. *Educational Review* 40/1: 41–9.

Davies, Bronwyn (1989a) *Frogs and Snails and Feminist Tales: Pre-school Children and Gender*. Sydney: Allen and Unwin.

—— (1989b) 'Education for sexism: a theoretical analysis of the sex/gender bias in education'. *Educational Philosophy and Theory* 21/1: 1–19.

—— (1993). *Shards of Glass*. Sydney: Allen and Unwin.

—— and Banks, C. (1992) 'The gender trap: a feminist post-structuralist analysis analysis of primary school children's talk about gender'. *Curriculum Studies* 24: 1–25.

—— and Harré, Rom (1990) 'Positioning: the discursive production of selves'. *Journal for the Theory of Social Behaviour* 20/1: 43–63.

Delamont, Sara (1990) *Sex Roles and the School*. London: Routledge.

Derrida, Jacques (1987) *A Derrida Reader: Between the Blinds*. Brighton: Harvester Wheatsheaf.

Donald, Robyn (1990) *No Guarantees*. London: Mills and Boon.

Dunant, Sarah (eds) (1994)) *The War of the Words: the Political Correctness Debate*. London: Virago Press.

Dyer, Gillian (1982) *Advertising as Communication*. London: Methuen.

Eckert, Penelope (1989) *Jocks and Burnouts: Social Categories and Identity in the High School*. New York: Teachers College Press.

Eckert, Penelope and McConnell-Ginet, Sally (1992) 'Think practically and look locally: language and gender as community-based practice'. *Annual Review of Anthropology* 21: 46–490.

—— (1992b) 'Communities of practice: where language, gender, and power all live'. In Hall, K. et al. (eds) *Locating Power: Proceedings of the Second Berkeley Women and Language Conference*. Berkeley, CA: Women and Language Group. pp. 89–99.

—— (1992c) 'Think practically and look locally: language and gender as community-based practice'. *Annual Review of Anthropology* 21: 461–90.

—— (1995) 'Constructing meaning, constructing selves: snapshots of language, gender and class from Belten High'. In Hall, K. and Bucholtz, M. (eds) *Gender Articulated*. London: Routledge.

—— (1999) 'New generalisations and explanations in language and gender research'. *Language in Society* 28: 185–201.

—— (2003) *Language and Gender*. Cambridge: Cambridge University Press.

Edelsky, Carole (1977) 'Acquisition of an aspect of communicative competence: learning what it means to talk like a lady'. In Ervin-Tripp, S. and Mitchell-Kernan, C. (eds) *Child Discourse*. New York: Academic Press.

Edley, Nigel (2001) 'Analysing masculinity, interpretive repertoires, ideological dilemmas and subject positions'. In Wetherell, M., Taylor, S. and Yates, S. (eds) *Discourses as Data – A Guide for Analysis*. London: Sage/Open University.

Edwards, Derek (1997) *Discourse and Cognition*. London: Sage.

Edwards, Derek, Ashmore, M. and Potter, Jonathan (1995) 'Death and furniture: the rhetoric, politics and theology of bottom line arguments against relativism'. In *History of the Human Sciences*. 8: 25–49.

Edwards, Derek and Potter, Jonathan (1992) *Discursive Psychology*. London: Sage.

Eggins, Suzanne and Iedema, Rick (1997) 'Difference without diversity: semantic orientation and ideology in competing women's magazines'. In Wodak, R. (ed.) *Gender and Discourse*. London: Sage.

Eichler, Margaret (1991) *Non-sexist Research Methods: A Practical Guide*. New York: Allen and Unwin.

Ekstrand, Lars (1980) 'Sex differences in second language learning?: empirical studies and a discussion of related findings'. *International Review of Applied Psychology* 29: 205–59.

Epstein, Debbie (1998) 'Real boys don't work: "underachievement", masculinity and the harassment of "sissies" '. In Epstein, D., Elwood, J., Hey, V. and Maw, J.

(eds) *Failing Boys? Issue in Gender and Achievement*. Buckingham: Open University Press. pp. 96–108.

Epstein, Debbie, Elwood, J., Hey, V. and Maw, J. (1998) (eds) *Failing Boys: Issues in Gender and Achievement*. Buckingham: Open University Press.

Ervin-Tripp, Susan (2001) 'The place of gender in developmental pragmatics: cultural factors'. *Research on Language and Social Interaction* 34/1: 131–47.

Fairclough, Norman (1989) *Language and Power*. London: Longman.

—— (1992) *Discourse and Social Change*. Cambridge: Polity Press.

—— (1995) *Critical Discourse Analysis*. London: Longman.

—— (2000) *New Labour, New Language?* London: Routledge.

—— (2001) 'The discourse of New Labour: Critical Discourse Analysis'. In Wetherell, M., Taylor, S. and Yates, S.J. (eds) *Discourse as Data: A Guide for Analysis*. London: Sage/Open University. pp. 229–66.

—— and Wodak, Ruth (1997) 'Critical discourse analysis'. In van Dijk, T. (ed.) *Discourse Studies: A Multidisciplinary Introduction* Vol. 2. London: Sage. pp. 258–84.

Fetterley, Judith (1978) *The Resisting Reader: A Feminist Approach to American Fiction*. Bloomington: Indiana University Press.

Fishman, Pamela (1983) 'Interaction: the work women do'. In Thorne, B. et al. (eds) *Language, Gender and Society*. Rowley, Mass.: Newbury House. pp. 89–101.

Foucault, Michel (1978) *History of Sexuality: an Introduction*. Harmondsworth: Penguin.

Foucault, Michel (1981) 'The order of discourse'. In Young, R. (ed.) Untying the Text. Boston and London: Routledge and Kegan Paul. pp. 108–38.

—— (1972) *The Archaeology of Knowledge*. London: Tavistock Publications.

—— (1981) *The History of Sexuality: An Introduction* (Vol. 1). New York: Vintage/Random House.

—— (1984) 'What is enlightenment?' In Rabinov, P. (ed.) The Foucault Reader. London: Penguin.

—— (1989) *Foucault Live (Interviews, 1966–84)*. New York: Semiotext(e).

Francis, Becky (1999) 'An investigation of the discourses children draw on [in] their constructions of gender'. *Journal of Applied Social Psychology* 29/2: 300–16.

—— (2000) 'The gendered subject: students' subject preferences and discussion of gender and subject ability'. *Oxford Review of Education* 26/1: 35–48.

—— and Skelton, Christine (2001) 'Men teachers and the construction of heterosexual masculinity in the classroom'. *Sex Education* 1/1: 9–21.

Franckenstein, F. (1997) 'Making up Cher – a media analysis of the politics of the female body'. *European Journal of Women's Studies* 4/1: 7–23.

French, Jane and French, Peter. 1984. 'Gender imbalances in the primary classroom: an interactional account'. *Educational Research* 26/2: 127–36.

Fowler, Roger (1991) *Language in the News: Discourse and Ideology in the Press*. London: Routledge.

Gal, Susan (1978) 'Peasant men can't get wives: language change and sex roles in a bilingual community'. *Language in Society* 7: 1–17.

—— (1995) 'Language, gender and power: an anthropological review'. In Hall, K. and Bucholtz, M. (eds) *Gender Articulated: Language and the Socially Constructed Self*. London: Routledge. pp. 169–82.

Gannon, L.R. (1996) 'Perspectives on biological, social and psychological phenomena in middle- and old-age women: interference or intervention'.

In Clancy, S. and DiLalla, L. (eds) *Assessment and Intervention Issues Across the Lifespan*. New York: Erlbaum.

Garfinkel, Harold (1967) *Studies in Ethnomethodology*. Englewood Cliffs, NJ: Prentice Hall.

Gatens, Moira (1990) 'Modern rationalism'. In Jaggar, A. and Young, I.M. (eds) *A Companion to Feminist Philosophy*. Oxford: Basil Blackwell.

Gee, James (1992) *The Social Mind: Language, Ideology and Social Practice*. Series in Language and Ideology. New York: Bergin and Garvey.

—— (1999) *An Introduction to Discourse Analysis: Theory and Method*. London: Routledge.

Gertzman, Alice (2000) ' "Who will teach the children?" A critical ethnographic case study of teacher beliefs and practices in an all-male, African American third grade classroom'. PhD thesis, Lancaster University, UK.

Giddens, Anthony (1999) 'Modernity and self-identity: tribulations of the self'. In Jaworski, Adam and Coupland, Nicholas (eds) *The Discourse Reader*. London: Routledge. pp. 415–27.

Gilbert, Sandra and Gubar, Susan (1979) *The Madwoman in the Attic: the Woman Writer and the Nineteenth Century Literary Imagination*. New Haven: Yale University Press.

Gill, Ros (1995) 'Relativism, reflexivity and politics: interrogating discourse analysis from a feminist perspective'. In Wilkinson, Sue and Kitzinger, Celia (eds) *Feminism and Discourse: Psychological Perspectives*. London: Sage. pp. 165–86.

Glaser, Barry and Anselm Strauss (1967) *The Discovery of Grounded Theory: Strategies for Qualitative Research*. Chicago: Aldine.

Goldman, Robert (1992) *Reading Ads Socially*. London: Routledge.

Gough, Kathleen (1975) 'The origin of the family'. In [Rapp] Reiter, R. (ed.) *Toward an Anthropology of Women*. New York: Monthly Review Press. pp. 69–70.

Gray, John (1992) *Men are from Mars, Women are from Venus*. London: Element.

Greer, Germaine (1972) *The Female Eunuch*. London: Paladin.

Hall, Kira (1995) 'Lip service on the fantasy lines'. In Hall, K. and Bucholtz, M. (eds) *Gender Articulated: Language and the Socially Constructed Self*. New York: Routledge. pp. 183–216.

—— and Bucholz, Mary (eds) (1995) *Gender Articulated: Language and the Socially Constructed Self*. New York: Routledge.

Hall, Stuart (1997) *Representation: Cultural Representations and Signifying Practices*. Milton Keynes: Open University Press.

Halliday, Michael (1985) *An Introduction to Functional Grammar*. London: Edward Arnold.

Halliday, Michael (1994) *Introduction to Functional Grammar*, 2nd edition. London: Edward Arnold.

—— and Hasan, Ruquia (1989) *Language, Context and Text: Aspects of Language in a Social Semiotic Perspective*. Oxford: Oxford University Press.

Hanong Thetela, Puleng (2002) 'Sex discourses and gender construction in Southern Sotho: a case study of police interviews of rape/sexual assault victims'. *Southern African Linguistics and Applied Language Studies* 20: 177–89.

Hellinger, Marlis (2002) 'Gendered messages in covert style'. Plenary talk, International Gender and Language Conference (IGALA2), Lancaster University, UK.

Hellinger, Marlis and Bußmann, Hadumod (2001) *Gender across Languages: The Linguistic Representation of Women and Men*, Vol. 1. Amsterdam: John Benjamins.

Henley, Nancy (1987) 'This new species that seeks a new language: on sexism in language and language change'. In Penfield, J. (ed.) *Women and Language in Transition*. Albany, NY: SUNY Press.

Hennessy, Margaret (1994) 'Propagating half a species: gender in learners' dictionaries'. In Sunderland, J. (ed.) *Exploring Gender: Questions and Implications for English Language Education*. Hemel Hempstead: Prentice Hall. pp. 104–11.

Hines, Caitlin (1999) 'Rebaking the pie: the *woman as dessert* metaphor'. In Bucholtz, M., Liang, A.C. and Sutton, L.A (eds) *Reinventing Identities: The Gendered Self in Discourse*. New York: Oxford University Press. pp. 145–62.

Hirst, G. (1982) 'An evaluation of evidence for innate sex differences in linguistic ability'. *Journal of Psycholinguistic Research* 11/2: 95–113.

Hollway, Wendy (1984) 'Gender differences and the production of the subject'. In Henriques, J. et al. (eds) *Changing the Subject*. London: Methuen. pp. 227–63.

—— (1995) 'Feminist discourses and women's heterosexual desire'. In Wilkinson, Sue and Kitzinger, Celia (eds) *Feminism and Discourse: Psychological Perspectives*. London: Sage.

Holmes, Janet (1995) *Women, Men and Politeness*. London: Longman.

—— and Meyerhoff, Miriam (1999) 'The community of practice: Theories and methodologies in language and gender research'. *Language in Society* 28: 173–83.

Hopper, Robert and LeBaron, Curtis (1998) 'How gender creeps into talk'. *Research on Language and Social Interaction* 31/1: 59–74.

Humm, Maggie (1989) *The Dictionary of Feminist Theory*. London: Harvester Wheatsheaf.

Hyde, J. S. and Linn, M. C. (1988) 'Gender differences in verbal ability: a meta-analysis'. *Psychological Bulletin* 104/1: 53–69.

Hyland, Ken (2000) *Disciplinary Discourses: Social Interactions in Academic Writing*. Harlow: Pearson Education.

Ivanic, Roz (1998) *Writing and Identity*. Amsterdam: John Benjamins.

Jackson, Stevi and Scott, Sue (2001) 'Putting the body's feet on the ground: towards a sociological reconceptualisation of gendered and sexual embodiment'. In Backett-Milburn, Kathryn and McKie, Linda (eds) *Constructing Gendered Bodies*. Basingstoke: Palgrave. pp. 9–24.

Jaworski, Adam and Coupland, Nicholas (eds) (1999) *The Discourse Reader*. London: Routledge.

Jay, Nancy (1990) 'Gender and dichotomy'. In Gunew, S. (ed.) *A Reader in Feminist Knowledge*. London: Routledge.

Jeffreys, Sheila (1990) *Anticlimax: A Feminist Perspective on the Sexual Revolution*. London: The Women's Press.

Jenkins, Nancy and Cheshire, Jenny (1990) 'Gender issues in the GCSE oral English examination: Part 1'. *Language and Education* 4/4: 261–92.

Jespersen, Otto (1922) *Language: Its Nature, Development and Origin*. London: Allen and Unwin.

Johnson, Sally (1997) 'Theorising language and masculinity: a feminist perspective'. In Johnson, S. and Meinhof, U. (eds) (1997) *Language and Masculinity*. Oxford: Blackwell. pp. 8–26.

Johnson, Sally, Culpeper, Jonathan and Suhr, Stephanie (2003) 'From "politically correct councillors" to "Blairite nonsense": discourses of "political correctness" in three British newspapers'. *Discourse and Society* 14/1: 29–48.

—— and Suhr, Stephanie (2003) 'From "political correctness" to "politische Korrektheit": discourses of "PC" in the German newspaper, *Die Welt'*. *Discourse and Society* 14/1: 49–68.

Johnston, Rosemary (2000) 'The literacy of the imagination'. *Bookbird*, Spring 2000.

Jones, Alison (1993) 'Becoming a "girl": post-structuralist suggestions for educational research'. *Gender and Education* 5/2: 157–66.

Jones, Deborah (1980) 'Gossip: notes on women's oral culture'. In Cameron, D. (ed.) *The Feminist Critique of Language*. London: Routledge. pp. 242–50.

Jones, Martha, Kitetu, Catherine and Sunderland, Jane (1997) 'Discourse roles, gender and language textbook dialogues: who learns what from John and Sally?' *Gender and Education* 9/4: 469–90.

Jule, Allyson (2001) 'Speaking their sex: linguistic space and gender in a second language classroom'. Paper given at 34th BAAL Annual Meeting, Reading, September.

Kelly, Alison (1988) 'Gender differences in teacher-pupil interaction: a meta-analytic review'. *Research in Education* 39: 1–23.

Kiesling, Scott (1997) 'Power and the language of men'. In Johnson, S. and Meinhof, U. (eds) *Language and Masculinity*. Oxford: Basil Blackwell. pp. 65–85.

Kitetu, Catherine (1998) 'An examination of physics classroom discourse practices and the construction of gendered identities in a Kenyan secondary school'. PhD thesis, Lancaster University, UK.

—— and Sunderland, Jane (2000) 'Gendered discourses in the classroom: the importance of cultural diversity'. *Temple University of Japan Working Papers* 17. Tokyo: Temple University. pp. 26–40.

Kitzinger, Celia (2000a) 'How to resist an idiom'. *Research on Language and Social Interaction* 33/2: 121–54.

—— (2000b) 'Doing feminist comversation analysis'. *Feminism and Psychology* 10/2: 163–93.

—— and Thomas, Alison (1995) 'Sexual harassment: a discursive approach'. In Wilkinson, S. and Kitzinger, C. (eds) *Feminism and Discourse: Psychological Perspectives*. London: Sage.

Klann-Delius, Gisela (1981) 'Sex and language acquisition: is there any influence?' *Journal of Pragmatics* 5: 1–25.

Knowles, Murray and Malmkjaer, Kirsten (1996) *Language and Control in Children's Literature*. London: Routledge.

Kress, Gunther (1985) *Linguistic Processes in Sociocultural Practice*. Victoria: Deakin University. (Second edition, 1989: Oxford, Oxford University Press.)

—— and van Leewen, Theo (1996) *Reading Images: The Grammar of Visual Design*. London: Routledge.

Kristeva, Julia (1986) *The Kristeva Reader*, ed. Toril Moi. Oxford: Basil Blackwell.

Kumaravadivelu, B. (1999) 'Critical classroom discourse analysis'. *TESOL Quarterly* 33/3: 453–84.

Kyratsis, Amy (2001) 'Children's gender indexing in language: from the separate worlds hypothesis to considerations of culture, context and power'. *Research on Language and Social Interaction* 34/1: 1–13.

Labov, William (1966) *The Social Stratification of English in New York City.* Washington, DC: Center for Applied Linguistics.

—— (1991) 'The intersection of sex and class in the course of linguistic change'. *Language Variation and Linguistic Change* 2: 205–51.

Laclau, Ernesto and Mouffe, Chantal (1987) 'Post-Marxism without apologies'. *New Left Review* 166: 79–106.

Lakoff, Robin (1975) *Language and Woman's Place.* New York: Harper & Row.

Lave, Jean and Wenger, Etienne (1991) *Situated Learning: Legitimate Peripheral Participation.* Cambridge: Cambridge University Press.

Lazar, Michelle (1993) 'Equalising gender relations: a case of double talk. *Discourse and Society* 4/4: 443–65.

—— (2002) 'Consuming personal relationships: the achievement of feminine self-identity through other-centredness'. In Litosseliti, Lia and Sunderland, Jane (eds) *Gender Identity and Discourse Analysis.* John Benjamins. pp. 111–28.

Leap, William (1999) 'Language, socialization and silence in gay adolescence'. In Bucholtz, M. Liang, A.C. and Sutton, L. (eds) *Reinventing Identities: The Gendered Self in Discourse.* New York: Oxford University Press. pp. 259–72.

Lee, David (1992) *Competing Discourses: Perspective and Ideology in Language.* London: Longman.

Leontzakou, Christina (1997) 'How teachers deal with gendered EFL textbook material'. MA dissertation, Lancaster University, UK.

Levinson, Steven (1983) *Pragmatics.* Cambridge: Cambridge University Press.

Levorato, Alessandra (2003) *Language and Gender in the Fairy Tale Tradition* Basingstoke: Palgrave Macmillan.

Liang, A.C. (1999) 'Conversationally implicating lesbian and gay identities'. In Bucholtz, B., Liang, A.C. and Sutton, L. (eds) *Reinventing Identities: The Gendered Self in Discourse.* New York: Oxford University Press.

Litosseliti, Lia (2002) ' "Head to head": gendered repertoires in newspapaer articles'. In Litosseliti, Lia and Sunderland, Jane (eds) (2002) *Gender Identity and Discourse Analysis.* Amsterdam: John Benjamins. pp. 129–48.

—— and Sunderland, Jane (eds) (2002) *Gender Identity and Discourse Analysis.* Amsterdam: John Benjamins.

Livia, Anna (1999) ' "She sired six children": feminist experiments with linguistic gender'. In Bucholtz, M., Liang, A.C. and Sutton, L.A (eds) *Reinventing Identities: The Gendered Self in Discourse.* New York: Oxford University Press. pp. 332–47.

—— and Hall, Kira. (1997) *Queerly Phrased.* New York: Oxford University Press.

Lloyd, Genevive (1990) 'Reason as attainment'. In Gunew, S. (ed.) *A Reader in Feminist Knowledge.* London: Routledge.

Lotringer, Sylvere (ed.) (1989) *Foucault Live (Interviews 1966–84).* New York: Semiotext(e).

Luke, Allan (1988) *Literacy, Textbooks and Ideology: Postwar Literacy Instruction and the Mythology of Dick and Jane.* London: Falmer Press.

—— (1991) 'The secular word: Catholic reconstructions of Dick and Jane'. In Apple, Michael and Christian-Smith, Linda (eds) *The Politics of the Textbook.* New York: Routledge. pp. 166–90.

Maltz, Daniel and Borker, Ruth (1982) 'A cultural approach to male–female miscommunication'. In Gumperz, John (ed.) *Language and Social Identity.* Cambridge: Cambridge University Press. pp. 196–216.

Marshall, Harriette (1991) 'The social construction of motherhood: an analysis of childcare and parenting manuals'. In Phoenix, Ann, Woollett, Anne and Lloyd, Eva (eds) *Motherhood: Meanings, Practices and Ideologies*. London: Sage, pp. 66–85.

Martyna, Wendy (1983) 'Beyond the he/man approach: the case for non-sexist language'. In Thorne, B., Kramarae, C. and Henley, N. (eds) *Language, Gender and Society*. Rowley, Mass.: Newbury House, pp. 7–37.

Mason, Jennifer (2002) *Qualitative Researching*. London: Sage.

McIlhenny, Bonnie (1995) 'Challenging hegemonic masculinities: female and male police officers handling domestic violence'. In Hall, Kira and Bucholz, Mary (eds) (1995) *Gender Articulated: Language and the Socially Constructed Self*. New York: Routledge.

McIlvenny, Paul (2002) 'Introduction: researching talk, gender and sexuality'. In McIlvenny, Paul (ed.) *Talking Gender and Sexuality*. Amsterdam: John Benjamins. pp. 1–48.

Millard, Elaine (1997) *Differently Literate: Boys, Girls and the Schooling of Literacy*. London: Falmer Press.

Miller, Casey and Swift, Kate (1989) *Handbook of Non-sexist Writing*. London: Women's Press.

Mills, Sara (1992) 'Knowing your place: a Marxist feminist stylistics analysis'. In Toolan, Michael (ed.) *Language, Text and Context: Essays in Stylistics*. London: Routledge. pp. 182–205.

—— (ed.) (1994) *Gendering the Reader*. London: Harvester Wheatsheaf.

—— (1995) *Feminist Stylistics*. London: Routledge.

—— (1997) *Discourse*. London: Routledge.

—— (forthcoming) *Beyond Sexism*. Cambridge: Cambridge University Press.

Milroy, Lesley (1980) *Language and Social Networks*. Oxford: Basil Blackwell.

Mitchell, J. Clyde (1984) 'Typicality and the case study'. In Ellen, R.F. (ed.) *Ethnographic Research: A Guide to General Conduct*. London: Academic Press.

Morgan, Robin (1969) *Going Too Far*. New York: Random House.

Morrish, Elizabeth (2002) 'The case of the indefinite pronoun: discourse and the concealment of lesbian identity in class'. In Litosseliti, L. and Sunderland, J. (eds) *Gender Identity and Discourse Analysis*. Amsterdam: John Benjamins. pp. 177–92.

Moss, Gemma (1989) *Un/Popular Fictions*. London: Virago.

Munsch, R. and Marchenko, M. (1980) *The Paper Bag Princess*. Toronto: Annick Press.

Myers, Greg (2000) 'Becoming a group: face and sociability in moderated discussions'. In Sarangi, S. and Coulthard, M. (eds) *Discourse and Social Life*. Harlow: Longman. pp. 121–37.

Nelson, Cynthia (1999) 'Sexual identities in ESL: queer theory and classroom inquiry'. *TESOL Quarterly* 33/3: 371–91.

Nichols, Sue (2002) 'Parents' construction of their children as gendered, literate subjects – a critical discourse analysis'. *Journal of Early Childhood Literacy* 2/2: 23–44.

Nilsen, Alleen Pace (1977) 'Linguistic sexism as a social issue'. In Nilsen, Alleen Pace et al. (eds) *Sexism and Language*. Urbana, Ill.: NCTE.

O'Connor, Patricia (2003) 'Activist sociolinguistics in a critical discourse analysis perspective'. In Weiss, Gilbert and Wodak, Ruth (eds) *Critical Discourse*

Analysis: Theory and Interdisciplinarity. Basingstoke: Palgrave Macmillan. pp. 223–40.

Ochs, Elinor (1992) 'Indexing gender'. In Alessandro Duranti and Goodwin, Charles (eds) *Rethinking Context.* Cambridge: Cambridge University Press. pp. 335–58.

—— (1993) 'Indexing gender'. In Miller, B.D. (ed.) *Sex and Gender Hierarchies.* Cambridge: Cambridge University Press. pp. 146–69.

Ogbay, Sarah (1999) Gendered perceptions, silences and resistance in two Eritrean secondary schools: reasons for girls' lower performance than boys'. PhD thesis, Lancaster University, UK.

Pala, Achola (1989) 'Towards a new theory and method in the study of women in Africa'. In Mbeo, A. and Ooki-Ombaka, O. (eds) *Women and Law in Kenya.* Nairobi: Public Law Institute.

Pauwels, Anne (1989) 'Some thoughts on gender, inequality and language reform'. *Vox* 3: 78–84.

—— (1998) *Women Changing Language.* London: Longman.

Pavlenko, Aneta and Piller, Ingrid (2001) 'New directions in the study of multi-lingualism'. In Pavlenko, A., Blackledge, A. and Teutsch-Dwyer, M. (eds) *Multilingualism, Second Language Learning and Gender.* Berlin: Mouton de Gruyter.

Pease, Alan and Pease, Barbara (2001) *Why Men Don't Listen and Women Can't Read Maps.* London: Orion.

Pecheux, Michel (1982) *Language, Semantics and Ideology.* Basingstoke: Macmillan.

Petersen, Sharyl Bender and Lach, Mary Alyce (1990) 'Gender stereotypes in children's books: their prevalence and influence on cognitive and affective development'. *Gender and Education* 2/2: 185–97.

Peterson, Shelley (2002) 'Gender meanings in grade eight students' talk about classroom writing'. *Gender and Education* 14/4: 351–66.

Piller, Ingrid and Pavlenko, Aneta (2001) 'Introduction: Multilingualism, second language learning and gender'. In Pavlenko, Aneta, Blackledge, Adrian, Piller, Ingrid and Teutsch-Dwyer, Marya (eds) *Multilingualism, Second Language Learning and Gender.* Berlin: Mouton de Gruyter. pp. 1–52.

Popper, Karl (1966) *The Open Society and Its Enemies.* Vol. II, *The High Tide of Prophecy: Hegel, Marx, and the Aftermath.* London: Routledge & Kegan Paul.

Potter, Jonathan (1996) *Representing Reality: Discourse, Rhetoric and Social Construction.* London: Sage.

Register, Cheri (1975) 'American feminist literary criticism: a bibliographical introduction'. In Donovan, J. (ed.) *Feminist Literary Criticism.* Lexington: University Press of Kentucky. pp. 1–28.

Rich, Adrienne (1976) *Of Woman Born: Motherhood as Experience and Institution.* New York: W. W. Norton.

—— (1980) 'Compulsory heterosexuality and lesbian existence'. *Signs* 5/4: 631–60.

Robson, J. (1988) 'Ministry or profession: clergy doubletalk'. In M. Furlong (ed.) *Mirror to the Church: Reflections on Sexism.* London: SPCK. pp. 106–23.

Rowe, Clarissa (2000) ' "True Gay – hegemonic homosexuality?" – representations of gayness in conversations between gay men'. MA dissertation, Lancaster University, UK.

Sadker, Mary and Sadker, David (1985) 'Sexism in the schoolroom of the '80s'. *Psychology Today,* March: 54–7.

Santhakumaran, Dharshi (2002) 'Talking yourself out: why are there no "readers" of women's magazines?' Paper presented at 2nd International Gender and Language Association Conference (IGALA2), Lancaster, UK.

Schegloff, Emmanuel (1997) 'Whose text? whose context?' *Discourse and Society* 8: 165–87.

—— (1998) 'Reply to Wetherell'. *Discourse and Society* 9/3: 413–16.

Schneider, J. and Hacker, S. 1973. 'Sex role imagery and use of the generic "man" in introductory texts'. *American Sociologist* 8: 12–18.

Schultz, Muriel (1975) 'The semantic derogation of women'. In Thorne, B. et al. (eds) *Language and Sex: Difference and Dominance.* Rowley, Mass.: Newbury House. pp. 64–73.

Schwarz, Juliane (2003) 'Women's understandings of and reported practices in non-sexist language'. PhD thesis. Lancaster University, UK.

Scollon, Ron (2001) *Mediated Discourse: The Nexus of Practice.* London: Routledge.

Searle, John (1969) *Speech Acts: An Essay in the Philosophy of Language.* Cambridge: Cambridge University Press.

Semino, Elena, Short, Mick and Wynne, Martin (1999) 'Hypothetical words and thoughts in contemporary British narratives'. *Narrative* 7/3: 307–34.

—— and Culpepper, Jonathan (1997). 'Using a computer corpus to test a model of speech and thought presentation'. *Poetics* 25: 17–43.

Shattuck, Julie (1996) 'The interplay between EFL textbooks, teacher behaviour and gender'. MA dissertation, Lancaster University, UK.

Silveira, Jeanette (1980) 'Generic masculine words and thinking'. *Women's Studies International Quarterly* 3: 165–78.

Skelton, Christine (2001) *Schooling the Boys: Masculinity and Primary Education.* Buckingham: Open University Press.

Smith, Dorothy (1988) 'Femininity as discourse'. In Roman, Leslie G. and Christian-Smith, Linda with Ellsworth, Elizabeth (eds) *Becoming Feminine: The Politics of Popular Culture.* London: Falmer Press. pp. 37–58.

Speer, Susan (2002) 'Sexist talk: gender categories, participants' orientations and irony'. *Journal of Sociolinguistics* 6/3: 347–77.

Spender, Dale (1980) *Man Made Language.* London: Routledge.

—— (1982) *Invisible Women: The Schooling Scandal.* London: Women's Press.

Stacey, Jackie (1993) 'Untangling feminist theory'. In Richardson, D. and Robinson, V. (eds) *Introducing Women's Studies.* Basingstoke: Macmillan. pp. 49–73.

Stanworth, Michelle (1983) *Gender and Schooling.* London: Hutchinson.

Stapleton, Karyn (2001) 'Constructing a feminist identity: discourse and the community of practice'. *Feminism and Psychology* 11/4: 459–91.

Stephens, John (1992) *Language and Ideology in Children's Fiction.* London: Longman.

Stokoe, Elizabeth and Smithson, Janet (2001) 'Making gender relevant: conversation analysis and gender categories in interaction'. *Discourse and Society* 12/2: 217–44.

—— (2002) 'Gender and sexuality in talk-in-interaction: considering conversation analytic perspectives'. In McIlvenny, P. (ed.) *Talking Gender and Sexuality: Conversation, Performativity and Discourse in Interaction.* Amsterdam: John Benjamins.

Stubbs, Michael (1983) *Discourse Analysis.* London: Routledge.

Stubbs, Michael (2001) 'Texts, corpora, and problems of interpretation: a response to Widdowson'. *Applied Linguistics* 22/2: 149–72.

Suhr, Stephanie and Johnson, Sally (2003) 'Re-visiting "PC": introduction to special issue on "political correctness" '. *Discourse and Society* 14/1: 5–16.

Sunderland, Jane (1991) 'The decline of *man*'. *Journal of Pragmatics* 16: 505–22.

—— (ed.) (1994a) *Exploring Gender: Questions and Implications for English Language Education*. Hemel Hempstead: Prentice Hall.

—— (1994b) 'Pedagogical and other filters: the representation of non-sexist language change in British pedagogical grammars'. In Sunderland, J. (ed.) *Exploring Gender: Questions and Implications for English Language Education*. Hemel Hempstead: Prentice Hall. pp. 92–111.

—— (1995) ' "We're boys, miss!": Finding gendered identities and looking for gendering of identities in the foreign language classroom'. In Mills, S. (ed.) *Language and Gender: Interdisciplinary Perspectives*. Harlow: Longman.

—— (1996) 'Gendered discourse in the foreign language classroom: teacher–student and student–teacher talk, and the social construction of children's femininities and masculinities'. PhD dissertation, Lancaster University, UK.

—— (1998) 'Girls being quiet: a problem for the foreign language classroom?' *Language Teaching Research* 2/1: 48–82.

—— (2000) 'From bias "in the text" to "teacher talk around the text": an exploration of teacher discourse and gendered foreign language textbook texts'. *Linguistics and Education* 11/3: 251–86.

—— (2000a) 'Parenthood discourses: the construction of fatherhood and motherhood in parentcraft literature'. *Discourse and Society* 11/2: 249–74.

—— (2000b) 'New understandings of gender and language classroom research: texts, teacher talk and student talk'. *Language Teaching Research* 4/2: 149–73.

—— (2000c) 'Review article: issues of language and gender in second and foreign language education'. *Language Teaching* 33/4: 203–23.

—— (2002) 'From representation towards discursive practices: gender in the foreign language classroom revisited'. In Sunderland, J. and Litosseliti, L. (eds) *Gender Identity and Discourse Analysis*. Amsterdam: John Benjamins. pp. 223–55.

——, Abdul Rahim, Fauziah, Cowley, Maire, Leontzakou, Christina, Shuttuck, June and Shimanoff, Susan (1977) 'Man = human: empirical support for the Whorfian hypothesis'. *Bulletin: Women's Studies in Communication* 1/2: 21–7.

—— (2002) 'Baby entertainer, bumbling assistant and line manager: discourses of paternal identity in parentcraft texts'. In Sunderland, J. and Litosseliti, L. (eds) *Gender Identity and Discourse Analysis*. Amsterdam: John Benjamins. pp. 293–324.

—— and Litosseliti, Lia (2002) 'Gender identity and discourse analysis: theoretical and empirical considerations'. In Litosseliti, L. and Sunderland, J. (eds) *Gender Identity and Discourse Analysis*. Amsterdam: John Benjamins.

Sutton, Laurel (1999) 'All media are created equal: do-it-yourself identity in alternative publishing'. In Bucholtz, M., Liang, A.C. and Sutton, L.A (eds) *Reinventing Identities: The Gendered Self in Discourse*. New York: Oxford University Press. pp. 163–80.

Swales, John (2003) *Research Genres: Explorations and Applications*. Cambridge: Cambridge University Press.

Swan, Michael (1985) 'Where is the language going?' *English Today* 3: 7.

Swann, Joan (1992) *Girls, Boys and Language*. Oxford: Blackwell.
—— (2002) 'Yes, but is it gender?' In Litosseliti, L. and Sunderland, J. (eds) *Gender Identity and Discourse Analysis*. Amsterdam: John Benjamins. pp. 43–67.
—— and David Graddol (1988) 'Gender inequalities in classroom talk'. *English in Education* 22/1: 48–65.
Talbot, Mary (1995a) *Fictions at Work*. London: Longman
—— (1995b) 'A synthetic sisterhood: false friends in a teenage magazine'. In Hall, K. and Bucholtz, M. (eds) *Gender Articulated*. London: Routledge. pp. 143–65.
—— (1997) ' "Randy fish boss branded a stinker": coherence and construction of masculinities in a British national newspaper'. In Johnson, S. and Meinhof, U. (eds) *Language and Masculinity*. Oxford: Blackwell.
—— (1998) *Language and Gender*. Cambridge: Polity Press.
Tannen, Deborah (1990) *You Just Don't Understand*. London: Virago.
—— (1994) *Gender and Discourse*. Oxford: Oxford University Press.
—— (2002) 'Agonism in academic discourse'. *Journal of Pragmatics* 34: 1651–69.
Taylor, Stephanie (2001) 'Locating and conducting discourse analytic research'. In Wetherell, M., Taylor, S. and Yates, S. (eds) *Discourse as Data*. London: Sage. pp. 5–48.
Taylor, Yolande and Sunderland, Jane (2003) ' "I've always loved women": representation of the male sex worker in FHM'. In Benwell, B. (ed.) *Men's Lifestyle Magazines*. Edinburgh: Edinburgh University Press. pp. 69–187.
Thomas, Jenny (1995) *Meaning in Interaction*. London: Longman.
Thomas, Linda and Wareing, Sian (1999) *Language, Society and Power*. London: Routledge.
Thornborrow, Joanna (2002) *Power Talk: Language and Interaction in Institutional Discourse*. London: Longman.
Thorne, Barrie (1993) *Gender Play*. Milton Keynes: Open University Press.
Todd, Alexandra and Fisher, Sue (1988) 'Theories of gender, theories of discourse'. In Todd, A.D. and Fisher, S. (eds) *Gender and Discourse*. Norwood: Ablex. pp. 1–16.
Toolan, Michael J. (1996) *Total Speech: An Integrational Linguistic Approach to Language*. Durham, NC: Duke University Press.
Toth, Emily (1970) 'How can a woman "man" the barricades?' *Women: A Journal of Liberation* 2/1: 57.
Trudgill, Peter (1972) 'Sex, covert prestige and linguistic change in the urban British English of Norwich'. *Language in Society* 1: 179–95.
—— (1974) *The Social Differentiation of English in Norwich*. Cambridge: Cambridge University Press.
Urwin, Cathy (1985) 'Constructing motherhood: the persuasion of normal development'. In Steedman, Carolyn, Urwin, Cathy and Walkerdine, Valerie (eds) *Language, Gender and Childhood*. London: Routledge & Kegan Paul. pp. 164–202.
van Dijk, Teun (1988) 'Social cognition, social power and social discourse'. *Text* 8 (1–2): 129–57.
—— (1990) 'Social cognition and discourse'. In Giles, H. and Robinson, R.P. (eds) *Handbook of Social Psychology and Language*. Chichester: Wiley. pp. 163–83.
—— (1993) 'Principles of critical discourse analysis'. *Discourse and Society* 4/2: 249–83.

van Dijk, Teun (1998) *Ideology*. London: Sage.

van Leeuwen, Theo (1996) 'The representation of social actors'. In Caldas-Coulthard, C. and Coulthard, M. (eds) *Texts and Practices: Readings in Critical Discourse Analysis*. London: Routledge. pp. 32–70.

—— (1997) 'Representing social action'. *Discourse and Society* 6/1: 81–106.

Vandrick, Stephanie (1999) 'Who's afraid of critical feminist pedagogies?' *TESOL Matters* 9/1: 9.

Vavrus, Frances (2002) 'Uncoupling the articulation between girls' education and tradition in Tanzania'. *Gender and Education* 14/4: 367–89.

Vice, Sue (1997) *Introducing Bakhtin*. Manchester: Manchester Univesity Press.

Walker, E. and Elsworth, S. (1995) *Blueprint Intermediate*. London: Longman.

Walkerdine, Valerie (1990) *Schoolgirl Fictions*. London: Verso.

Walsh, Clare (2001) *Gender and Discourse: Language and Power in Politics, the Church and Organisations*. London: Longman.

Ward, Jean (1984) 'Check out your sexism'. *Women and Language* 7: 41–3.

Warrington, Molly and Younger, Michael (2000) 'The other side of the gender gap'. *Gender and Education* 12/4: 493–508.

Weatherall, Anne (2000) 'Gender relevance in talk-in-interaction and discourse'. *Discourse and Society* 11/2: 286–8.

—— (2002) *Gender, Language and Discourse*. New York: Routledge.

Weedon, Chris (1987) *Feminist Practice and Poststructuralist Theory*. Oxford: Basil Blackwell.

Weiss, Gilbert and Wodak, Ruth (2003) 'Introduction: theory, interdisciplinarity and critical discourse analysis'. In Weiss, Gilbert and Wodak, Ruth (eds) *Critical Discourse Analysis: Theory and Interdisciplinarity*. Basingstoke: Palgrave Macmillan. pp. 1–32.

West, Candace (2002) 'Peeling an onion: a critical comment on "Competing discourses"'. *Discourse and Society* 13/6: 843–51.

—— and Fenstermaker, Sarah (2002) 'Accountability in action: the accomplishment of gender, race and class in a meeting of the University of California Board of Regents'. *Discourse and Society* 13/4: 537–63.

—— and Zimmerman, Don (1983) 'Small insults: a study of interruptions in cross-sex conversations between unacquainted persons'. In Thorne, Barrie, Kramarae, Cheris and Henley, Nancy (eds) *Language, Gender and Society*. Rowley, Mass.: Newbury House.

——, Lazar, Michelle and Kramarae, Cheris (1997) 'Gender in discourse'. In van Djik, T. (ed.) *Discourse as Social Interaction. Discourse Studies: A Multidisciplinary Introduction*, Vol. 2. London: Sage. pp. 119–43.

Wetherell, Margaret (1998) 'Positioning and interpretative repertoires: conversation analysis and post-structuralism in dialogue'. *Discourse and Society* 9/3: 387–412.

——, Stiven, Hilda and Potter, Jonathan (1987) 'Unequal egalitarianism: a preliminary study of discourses concerning gender and employment opportunities'. *British Journal of Social Psychology* 26: 59–71.

——, Taylor, Stephanie and Yates, Simeon (eds) *Discourse as Data: A Guide for Analysis*. Milton Keynes: The Open University.

Wheeler, Kay (2002) 'How do we know gender is being constructed? A discussion of the warrants from which gender construction may be claimed'. MA dissertation, Lancaster University, UK.

White, Janet (1986) 'The writing on the wall: beginning or end of a girl's career?' *Women's Studies International Forum* 9/5: 561–74.

—— (1990) 'On literacy and gender'. In Carter, R. (ed.) *Knowledge about Language and Curriculum*. London: Hodder & Stoughton. pp. 181–96.

Widdicombe, Sue (1995) 'Identity, politics and talk: a case for the mundane and everyday'. In Wilkinson, Sue and Kitzinger, Celia (eds) *Feminism and Discourse: Psychological Perspectives*. London: Sage. pp. 106–27.

Widdowson, Henry (1995) 'Discourse analysis: a critical view'. *Language and Literature* 4/3: 157–72.

—— (2000) 'On the limitations of linguistics applied'. *Applied Linguistics* 21/1: 3–25.

Wilkinson, Sue and Kitzinger, Celia (eds) (1995) *Feminism and Discourse: Psychological Perspectives*. London: Sage.

Wodak, Ruth (1997) 'Introduction'. In Wodak, R. (ed.) *Gender and Discourse*. London: Sage. pp. 1–20.

Wolf, Naomi (1991) *The Beauty Myth*. London: Vintage.

Wolpe, Ann Marie (1988) *Within School Walls*. London: Routledge.

Zimmerman, Don and West, Candace (1975) 'Sex roles, interruptions and silences in conversations'. In Thorne, B. and Henley, N. (eds) *Language and Sex: Difference and Dominance*. Rowley, Mass.: Newbury House. pp. 105–29.

Zipes, J. (ed.) (1986) *Don't Bet on the Prince: Contemporary Feminist Fairy Tales in North America and England*. Aldershot: Gower.

Subject Index

absence, absent, 32, 44, 62, 103, 110
accumulation (of discoursal traces), 158, 160
'achronological intertextuality', 154
address, addressee(s), addressed, 108
advertisements, 31, 33–5, 53, 103, 104, 105, 207
advice, 105, 106, 107, 141
agency, agents, 7, 13, 22, 60
alternative voices, 212
analyst's intuition, 173
appropriation, 30
authorial choice, 32
award-winning books, 73, 147–9
awareness-raising, 215

binary opposition, 15
biological essentialism, 14
biological sex, 16, 17, 54–5
boundaries, 20
boys, 11, 80–1, 89, 94–5; see also 'boys will be boys discourse'; 'poor boys discourse'
breastfeeding, 105, 108, 114, 137

celebrity fatherhood, 77, 122ff
childcare, 107, 122, 127
children's literature, 77, 141ff; see also award-winning books; fairy tales
classroom talk, 16, 77, 79ff
co-construction, 3, 33, 63, 102
cognition, 28
collocations, 32, 37, 40
colonization, 30
'commodity feminism', 31, 91
community of practice (CofP), 14, 33, 74
competing discourses, 12
constitution, constitutiveness, 9
construction, social construction, 9, 17, 22, 23–4, 128–32, 169–73, 184–8

consumer capitalism, 105
consumer femininity, 105
consumer parenthood, 106
consumerism, 101, 105
'consumer maternity', 106, 121
consumption, 53, 119, 146
content analysis, 141
contestation, 159
contexts, 19, 25, 31, 33, 46
contradictions, 12–13, 46, 62, 63, 77
conversation analysis (CA), 5, 13, 97
Cosmopolitan, 53, 56, 60
critical discourse analysis (CDA), 3, 5, 10–13, 107, 141–2, 185–7, 210
cues, linguistic, 3, 7
'cultural difference', 86–7

damaging discourses, 190, 191ff
data, 73–4
deconstruction, 204, 207
description, 47
descriptive discourse, 6
dialectical relationship, 11
difference, '(cultural) difference', 14
direct analysis, 5
direct discourse, 127
discourse categorization, 33
discourse identification, 3, 32, 47
discourse naming, 26, 32, 34, 46–8
'discourse spotting', 32–6, 208
discourses (gendered)
    'Active man/Passive woman', 144
    'Alternative therapy', 65
    'Appearance as equally salient for women and for men', 91, 92
    'Battle of the sexes', 42–3, 48
    'Biggest/best day in a woman's life', 39–40, 46, 90
    'Blame the victim', 124
    'Blissful heterosexuality', 145
    'Bounded masculinity', 89
    'Boy as adventurer', 151

Name Index

Livia, Anna, 19
Lloyd, Genevive, 54

Marshall, Hariette, 102–3, 195
McConnell-Ginet, Sally, 6, 15,
   17, 20, 74
McIlhinney, Bonnie, 74
McIlvenny, Paul, 19
Millard, Elaine, 93, 163
Mills, Sara, 6, 20, 31, 108
Milroy, Lesley, 15
Morgan, Robin, 191

Ochs, Elinor, 25
Ogbay, Sarah, 87

Pauwels, Anne, 201
Pavlenko, Aneta, 16, 26, 74
Pease, Alan and Barbara, 52
Pecheux, Michel, 13, 16, 31
Peterson, Shelley, 11, 29, 54
Piller, Ingrid, 16, 26, 74
Popper, Karl, 6
Potter, Jonathan, 10, 14, 18, 29, 31,
   33, 62

Rich, Adrienne, 40, 50, 55–7,
   61, 122

Schegloff, Emanuel, 13, 14, 178
Smith, Dorothy, 105
Smithson, Janet, 13, 23
Speer, Susan, 75
Stapleton, Karyn, 19
Stephens, John, 24, 77

Stiven, Hilda, 62
Stokoe, Elizabeth, 13, 23
Sunderland, Jane, 12–13, 20, 31, 48,
   74, 89, 90, 93
Sutton, Laurel, 123
Swales, John, 13
Swann, Joan, 23, 172–3

Talbot, Mary, 6, 16, 28, 105, 142
Tannen, Deborah, 27, 52, 54
Taylor, Stephanie, 73
Thomas, Jenny, 23
Thornborrow, Joanna, 9
Todd, Alexandra, 15, 19
Toth, Emily, 191
Trudgill, Peter, 15

van Dijk, Teun, 6, 28
van Leeuwen, Theo, 31

Walsh, Clare, 8, 10, 32, 76
Weatherall, Anne, 9, 13, 17,
   18, 19, 22, 25, 29
Weedon, Chris, 7, 9
West, Candace, 17, 20, 21, 73
Wetherell, Margaret, 8, 14, 18,
   22, 29, 62–3
Wheeler, Kay, 76, 178–82
Widdowson, Sue, 14, 24
Wilkinson, Sue, 20
Williams, Angie, 64
Wodak, Ruth, 6, 11, 15
Wolpe, Ann Marie, 80

Zimmerman, Don, 21, 54

LIBRARY, UNIVERSITY OF CHESTER

Printed in the United States
142866LV00003B/13/A

9 781403 913456